Mastering Ceph
Second Edition

Infrastructure storage solutions with the latest Ceph release

Nick Fisk

BIRMINGHAM - MUMBAI

Mastering Ceph
Second Edition

Commissioning Editor: Pavan Ramchandani
Acquisition Editor: Meeta Rajani
Content Development Editor: Nithin George Varghese
Technical Editor: Rutuja Patade
Copy Editor: Safis Editing
Project Coordinator: Drashti Panchal
Proofreader: Safis Editing
Indexer: Tejal Daruwale Soni
Graphics: Tom Scaria
Production Coordinator: Aparna Bhagat

First published: May 2017
Second edition: February 2019

Production reference: 1010319

Published by Packt Publishing Ltd.
Livery Place
35 Livery Street
Birmingham
B3 2PB, UK.

ISBN 978-1-78961-070-3

www.packtpub.com

`mapt.io`

Mapt is an online digital library that gives you full access to over 5,000 books and videos, as well as industry leading tools to help you plan your personal development and advance your career. For more information, please visit our website.

Why subscribe?

- Spend less time learning and more time coding with practical eBooks and videos from over 4,000 industry professionals

- Improve your learning with Skill Plans built especially for you

- Get a free eBook or video every month

- Mapt is fully searchable

- Copy and paste, print, and bookmark content

Packt.com

Did you know that Packt offers eBook versions of every book published, with PDF and ePub files available? You can upgrade to the eBook version at `www.packt.com` and as a print book customer, you are entitled to a discount on the eBook copy. Get in touch with us at `customercare@packtpub.com` for more details.

At `www.packt.com`, you can also read a collection of free technical articles, sign up for a range of free newsletters, and receive exclusive discounts and offers on Packt books and eBooks.

Contributors

About the author

Nick Fisk is an IT specialist with a strong history in enterprise storage. Having worked in a variety of roles throughout his career, he has encountered a wide variety of technologies. In 2012, Nick was given the opportunity to focus more on open source technologies, and this is where he got his first exposure to Ceph. Having seen the potential of Ceph as a storage platform and the benefits of moving away from the traditional closed stack storage platforms, Nick pursued Ceph with keen interest.

Throughout the following years, his experience with Ceph increased with the deployment of several clusters and enabled him to spend time in the Ceph community, helping others and improving certain areas of Ceph.

I would like to thank my wife, Femi Fisk, for her support during the authoring of this book. I would also like to thank the team at Packt for giving me the opportunity again to write a further book on the subject of Ceph—their support during the whole process has been essential to the success of the process. I would also like to thank Sage Weil for the idea and development of the Ceph project.

About the reviewer

Michael Hackett is a storage and SAN expert in customer support. He has been working on Ceph and storage-related products for over 13 years. He co-authored the *Ceph Cookbook* and holds several storage and SAN-based certifications. Michael is currently working at Red Hat, based in Massachusetts, where he is a principal software maintenance engineer for Red Hat Ceph storage and the technical product lead for the global Ceph team.

Packt is searching for authors like you

If you're interested in becoming an author for Packt, please visit authors.packtpub.com and apply today. We have worked with thousands of developers and tech professionals, just like you, to help them share their insight with the global tech community. You can make a general application, apply for a specific hot topic that we are recruiting an author for, or submit your own idea.

Table of Contents

Preface

Ceph, a unified, highly resilient, distributed storage system that provides block, object, and file access, has enjoyed a surge in popularity over the last few years. Due to being open source, Ceph has enjoyed rapid adoption by both developers and end users alike, with several well-known corporations being involved in the project. With every new release, the scale of its performance and feature set continue to grow, further enhancing Ceph's status.

With the current demands for ever-increasing data storage, and the challenges faced by legacy RAID-based systems, Ceph is well placed to offer an answer to these problems. As the world moves toward adopting new cloud technologies and object-based storage, Ceph is ready and waiting to be the driving force behind the new era of storage technologies.

In this book, we will cover a wide variety of topics, from installing and managing a Ceph cluster, through to how to recover from disasters, should you ever find yourself in that situation. For those that have interest in getting their applications to talk directly to Ceph, this book will also show you how to develop applications that make use of Ceph's libraries, and even how to perform distributed computing by inserting your own code into Ceph. By the end of this book, you will be well on your way to mastering Ceph.

The second edition of *Mastering Ceph* now includes updates around the new BlueStore technology introduced in the Luminous release, with guides to help you understand BlueStore and upgrade your existing cluster to take advantage of it.

Who this book is for

If you are a storage professional, system administrator, or cloud engineer looking for solutions to build powerful storage systems for your cloud and on-premise infrastructure, then this book is for you.

What this book covers

Chapter 1, *Planning for Ceph*, covers the fundamentals of how Ceph works, its basic architecture, and examines some good use cases. It also discusses the planning steps that you should take before implementing Ceph, including setting design goals, developing proof of concepts and working on infrastructure design.

Chapter 2, *Deploying Ceph with Containers*, is a no-nonsense, step-by-step instructional chapter on how to set up a Ceph cluster. This chapter covers ceph-deploy for testing and goes onto cover Ansible. Finally, we take a look at the Rook project to deploy Ceph clusters running atop of a Kubernetes cluster. A section on change management is also included, and explains how this is essential for the stability of large Ceph clusters. This chapter also serves the purpose of providing the reader with a common platform on which you can build the examples that we use later in the book.

Chapter 3, *BlueStore*, explains that Ceph has to be able to provide atomic operations around data and metadata and how FileStore was built to provide these guarantees over the top of standard filesystems. We will also cover the problems around this approach.

The chapter then introduces BlueStore, and explains how it works and the problems that it solves. This will cover the components and how they interact with different types of storage devices. We'll explore an overview of key value stores, including RocksDB, which is used by BlueStore. Some of the BlueStore settings will be discussed, along with how they interact with different hardware configurations.

The chapter finishes by discussing the methods available to upgrade a cluster to BlueStore and walks the reader through an example upgrade.

Chapter 4, *Ceph and Non-Native Protocols*, discusses the storage abilities that Ceph provides to native Ceph clients and then highlights the issues in more legacy storage deployments where it currently doesn't enjoy widespread adoption. The chapter continues to explore the ways in which Ceph can be exported via NFS and iSCSI to clients that don't natively speak Ceph, and provides examples to demonstrate configuration.

Chapter 5, *RADOS Pools and Client Access*, explores how Ceph provides storage via the three main protocols of block, file, and object. This chapter discusses the use cases of each and the Ceph components used to provide each protocol. The chapter also covers the difference between replicated and erasure-coded pools, and takes a deeper look into the operation of erasure coded pools.

Chapter 6, *Developing with Librados*, explains how librados is used to build applications that can interact directly with a Ceph cluster. It then moves onto several different examples of using librados in different languages to give the reader an idea of how librados can be used, including in atomic transactions.

Chapter 7, *Distributed Computation with Ceph RADOS Classes*, discusses the benefits of moving processing directly into the OSD to effectively perform distributed computing. It then covers how to get started with RADOS classes by building simple ones with Lua. It then examines how to build your own C++ RADOS class into the Ceph source tree and conduct benchmarks against performing processing on the client versus the OSD.

Chapter 8, *Monitoring Ceph*, starts with a description of why monitoring is important, and discusses the difference between alerting and monitoring. The chapter then covers how to obtain performance counters from all the Ceph components, explains what some of the key counters mean, and how to convert them into usable values.

An example using graphite will show the value of being able to manipulate captured data to provide more meaningful output in graph form. A look at the new Ceph Dashboard, introduced in the Ceph Mimic release, is covered, along with a step-by-step example to enable it on a running Ceph cluster.

Chapter 9, *Tuning Ceph*, starts with a brief overview on how to tune Ceph and the operating system. It also covers basic concepts of avoiding trying to tune something that is not a bottleneck. It also covers the areas that you may wish to tune and establish how to gauge the success of tuning attempts. It then shows how to benchmark Ceph and take baseline measurements, so that any results achieved are meaningful. Finally, it discusses different tools and how benchmarks might relate to real-life performance.

Chapter 10, *Tiering with Ceph*, explains how RADOS tiering works in Ceph, where it should be used, and its pitfalls. The chapter goes on take the reader through a step-by-step guide on configuring tiering on a Ceph cluster, and finally covers the tuning options to be able to extract the best performance for tiering.

Chapter 11, *Troubleshooting*, outlines how, although Ceph is largely autonomous in taking care of itself and recovering from failure scenarios, in some cases, human intervention is required. This chapter will look at common errors and failure scenarios, and how to bring Ceph back to full health by troubleshooting them.

Chapter 12, *Disaster Recovery*, details how, when Ceph is such a state that a complete loss of service or data loss has occurred, less familiar recovery techniques are required to restore access to the cluster and hopefully recover data. This chapter arms you with the knowledge to attempt recovery in these scenarios.

To get the most out of this book

This book assumes a medium level of proficiency on the Linux operating system, and a basic knowledge of storage technologies and networking. Although the book will go through a simple multinode setup of a Ceph cluster, it would be advisable that the reader has some prior experience of using Ceph. Although the book uses Virtual Box, feel free to use any other lab environment, such as VMware Workstation or other tools.

This book requires that you have enough resources for the whole Ceph lab environment. The minimum hardware or virtual requirements are listed as follows:

- CPU: 2 cores
- Memory: 8 GB RAM (16 GB recommended)
- Disk space: 40 GB

To follow along with book, you'll need the following software:

- VirtualBox
- vagrant

Internet connectivity is required to install the necessary packages that are part of the examples in each chapter.

Download the example code files

You can download the example code files for this book from your account at www.packt.com. If you purchased this book elsewhere, you can visit www.packt.com/support and register to have the files emailed directly to you.

You can download the code files by following these steps:

1. Log in or register at www.packt.com.
2. Select the **SUPPORT** tab.
3. Click on **Code Downloads & Errata**.
4. Enter the name of the book in the **Search** box and follow the onscreen instructions.

Once the file is downloaded, please make sure that you unzip or extract the folder using the latest version of:

- WinRAR/7-Zip for Windows
- Zipeg/iZip/UnRarX for Mac
- 7-Zip/PeaZip for Linux

The code bundle for the book is also hosted on GitHub at `https://github.com/PacktPublishing/Mastering-Ceph-Second-Edition`. In case there's an update to the code, it will be updated on the existing GitHub repository.

We also have other code bundles from our rich catalog of books and videos available at `https://github.com/PacktPublishing/`. Check them out!

Download the color images

We also provide a PDF file that has color images of the screenshots/diagrams used in this book. You can download it here: `https://www.packtpub.com/sites/default/files/downloads/9781789610703_ColorImages.pdf`.

Conventions used

There are a number of text conventions used throughout this book.

`CodeInText`: Indicates code words in text, database table names, folder names, filenames, file extensions, pathnames, dummy URLs, user input, and Twitter handles. Here is an example: "Install the `corosync`, `pacemaker`, and `cmrsh` toolsets using the following code:"

A block of code is set as follows:

```
Vagrant.configure("2") do |config|
nodes.each do |node|
config.vm.define node[:hostname] do |nodeconfig|
nodeconfig.vm.box = "bento/ubuntu-16.04"
```

When we wish to draw your attention to a particular part of a code block, the relevant lines or items are set in bold:

```
Vagrant.configure("2") do |config|
nodes.each do |node|
config.vm.define node[:hostname] do |nodeconfig|
nodeconfig.vm.box = "bento/ubuntu-16.04"
```

Any command-line input or output is written as follows:

```
yum install *.rpm
```

Bold: Indicates a new term, an important word, or words that you see onscreen. For example, words in menus or dialog boxes appear in the text like this. Here is an example: "Click on the **Repo URL** link, which will take you to the repository directory tree."

Warnings or important notes appear like this.

Tips and tricks appear like this.

Get in touch

Feedback from our readers is always welcome.

General feedback: If you have questions about any aspect of this book, mention the book title in the subject of your message and email us at customercare@packtpub.com.

Errata: Although we have taken every care to ensure the accuracy of our content, mistakes do happen. If you have found a mistake in this book, we would be grateful if you would report this to us. Please visit www.packt.com/submit-errata, selecting your book, clicking on the Errata Submission Form link, and entering the details.

Piracy: If you come across any illegal copies of our works in any form on the Internet, we would be grateful if you would provide us with the location address or website name. Please contact us at copyright@packt.com with a link to the material.

If you are interested in becoming an author: If there is a topic that you have expertise in and you are interested in either writing or contributing to a book, please visit authors.packtpub.com.

Reviews

Please leave a review. Once you have read and used this book, why not leave a review on the site that you purchased it from? Potential readers can then see and use your unbiased opinion to make purchase decisions, we at Packt can understand what you think about our products, and our authors can see your feedback on their book. Thank you!

For more information about Packt, please visit `packt.com`.

Section 1: Planning And Deployment

In this section, the reader will be taken through the best practices involved when deploying Ceph in a production setting.

The following chapters are in this section:

- Chapter 1, *Planning for Ceph*
- Chapter 2, *Deploying Ceph with Containers*
- Chapter 3, *BlueStore*
- Chapter 4, *Ceph and Non-Native Protocols*

Planning for Ceph

1

The first chapter of this book covers all the areas you need to consider when deploying a Ceph cluster, from the initial planning stages through to hardware choices. The topics we will cover include the following:

- What Ceph is and how it works
- Good use cases for Ceph and important considerations
- Advice and best practices on infrastructure design
- Ideas about planning a Ceph project

What is Ceph?

Ceph is an open source, distributed, scaled-out, software-defined storage system that can provide block, object, and file storage. Through the use of the **Controlled Replication Under Scalable Hashing (CRUSH)** algorithm, Ceph eliminates the need for centralized metadata and can distribute the load across all the nodes in the cluster. Since CRUSH is an algorithm, data placement is calculated rather than based on table lookups, and can scale to hundreds of petabytes without the risk of bottlenecks and the associated single points of failure. Clients also form direct connections with the required OSDs, which also eliminates any single points becoming bottlenecks.

Ceph provides three main types of storage: block storage via the **RADOS Block Device (RBD)**, file storage via CephFS, and object storage via RADOS Gateway, which provides S3 and Swift-compatible storage.

Ceph is a pure SDS solution, and this means that you are free to run it on any hardware that matches Ceph's requirements. This is a major development in the storage industry, which has typically suffered from strict vendor lock-in.

 It should be noted that Ceph prefers consistency as per the CAP theorem, and will try at all costs to make protecting your data a higher priority than availability in the event of a partition.

How Ceph works

The core storage layer in Ceph is the **Reliable Autonomous Distributed Object Store (RADOS)**, which, as the name suggests, provides an object store on which the higher-level storage protocols are built. The RADOS layer in Ceph consists of a number of **object storage daemons (OSDs)**. Each OSD is completely independent and forms peer-to-peer relationships to form a cluster. Each OSD is typically mapped to a single disk, in contrast to the traditional approach of presenting a number of disks combined into a single device via a RAID controller to the OS.

The other key component in a Ceph cluster is the monitors. These are responsible for forming a cluster quorum via the use of Paxos. The monitors are not directly involved in the data path and do not have the same performance requirements of OSDs. They are mainly used to provide a known cluster state, including membership, via the use of various cluster maps. These cluster maps are used by both Ceph cluster components and clients to describe the cluster topology and enable data to be safely stored in the right location. There is one final core component—the manager—which is responsible for configuration and statistics. Because of the scale that Ceph is intended to be operated at, one can appreciate that tracking the state of every single object in the cluster would become very computationally expensive. Ceph solves this problem by hashing the underlying object names to place objects into a number of placement groups. An algorithm called CRUSH is then used to place the placement groups onto the OSDs. This reduces the task of tracking millions of objects to a matter of tracking a much more manageable number of placement groups, normally measured in thousands.

Librados is a Ceph library that can be used to build applications that interact directly with the RADOS cluster to store and retrieve objects.

For more information on how the internals of Ceph work, it is strongly recommended that you read the official Ceph documentation, as well as the thesis written by *Sage Weil*, the creator and primary architect of Ceph.

Ceph use cases

Before jumping into specific use cases, let's look at the following key points that should be understood and considered before thinking about deploying a Ceph cluster:

- **Ceph is not a storage array**: Ceph should not be compared to a traditional scale-up storage array; it is fundamentally different, and trying to shoe horn Ceph into that role using existing knowledge, infrastructure, and expectations will lead to disappointment. Ceph is software-defined storage with internal data movements that operate over TCP/IP networking, introducing several extra layers of technology and complexity compared to a simple SAS cable at the rear of a traditional storage array. Work is continuing within the Ceph project to expand its reach into areas currently dominated by legacy storage arrays with support for iSCSI and NFS, and with each release, Ceph gets nearer to achieving better interoperability.

- **Performance**: Because of Ceph's non-centralized approach, it can offer unrestrained performance compared to scale-up storage arrays, which typically have to funnel all I/O through a pair of controller heads. While technological development means that faster CPUs and faster network speeds are constantly being developed, there is still a limit to the performance that you can expect to achieve with just a pair of storage controllers. With recent advances in Flash technology, combined with new interfaces such as NVMe, which bring the promise of a level of performance not seen before, the scale-out nature of Ceph provides a linear increase in CPU and network resources with every added OSD node. However, we should also consider where Ceph is not a good fit for performance. This is mainly concerning use cases where extremely low latency is desired. The very reason that enables Ceph to become a scale-out solution also means that low latency performance will suffer. The overhead of performing a large proportion of the processing in software and additional network hops means that latency will tend to be about double that of a traditional storage array and at least ten times that of local storage. Thought should be given to selecting the best technology for given performance requirements. That said, a well-designed and tuned Ceph cluster should be able to meet performance requirements in all but the most extreme cases. It is important to remember that with any storage system that employs wide striping, where data is spread across all disks in the system, speed will often be limited to the slowest component in the cluster. It's therefore important that every node in the cluster should be of similar performance. With new developments of NVMe and NVDIMMS, the latency of storage access is continuing to be forced lower.

Work in Ceph is being done to remove bottlenecks to take advantage of these new technologies, but thought should be given to how to balance latency requirements against the benefits of a distributed storage system.

- **Reliability**: Ceph is designed to provide a highly fault-tolerant storage system by the scale-out nature of its components. While no individual component is highly available, when clustered together, any component should be able to fail without causing an inability to service client requests. In fact, as your Ceph cluster grows, failure of individual components should be expected and will become part of normal operating conditions. However, Ceph's ability to provide a resilient cluster should not be an invitation to compromise on hardware or design choice, and doing so will likely lead to failure. There are several factors that Ceph assumes your hardware will meet, which are covered later in this chapter. Unlike RAID, where disk rebuilds with larger disks can now stretch into time periods measured in weeks, Ceph will often recover from single disk failures in a matter of hours. With the increasing trend of larger capacity disks, Ceph offers numerous advantages to both the reliability and degraded performance when compared to a traditional storage array.

- **Use of commodity hardware**: Ceph is designed to be run on commodity hardware, which gives us the ability to design and build a cluster without the premium cost demanded by traditional tier 1 storage and server vendors. This can be both a blessing and a curse. Being able to choose your own hardware allows you to build your Ceph components to exactly match your requirements. However, one thing that branded hardware does offer is compatibility testing. It's not unknown for strange exotic firmware bugs to be discovered that can cause very confusing symptoms. Thought should be applied to whether your IT teams have the time and skills to cope with any obscure issues that may crop up with untested hardware solutions. The use of commodity hardware also protects against the traditional fork-lift upgrade model, where the upgrade of a single component often requires the complete replacement of the whole storage array. With Ceph, you can replace individual components in a very granular way, and with automatic data balancing, lengthy data migration periods are avoided.

Specific use cases

We will now cover some of the more common use cases for Ceph and discuss some of the concepts behind them.

OpenStack or KVM based virtualization

Ceph is the perfect match for providing storage to an OpenStack environment; in fact, Ceph is currently the most popular choice. The OpenStack survey in 2018 revealed that 61% of surveyed OpenStack users are utilizing Ceph to provide storage in OpenStack. The OpenStack Cinder block driver uses Ceph RBDs to provision block volumes for VMs, and OpenStack Manila, the **File as a Service (FaaS)** software, integrates well with CephFS. There are a number of reasons why Ceph is such a good solution for OpenStack, as shown in the following list:

- Both are open source projects with commercial offerings
- Both have a proven track record in large-scale deployments
- Ceph can provide block, CephFS, and object storage, all of which OpenStack can use
- With careful planning, it is possible to deploy a hyper-converged cluster

If you are not using OpenStack, or have no plans to, Ceph also integrates very well with KVM virtualization.

Large bulk block storage

Because of the ability to design and build cost-effective OSD nodes, Ceph enables you to build large, high-performance storage clusters that are very cost-effective compared to alternative options. The Luminous release brought support for Erasure coding for block and file workloads, which has increased the attractiveness of Ceph even more for this task.

Object storage

The very fact that the core RADOS layer is an object store means that Ceph excels at providing object storage either via the S3 or Swift protocols. Ceph currently has one of the best compatibility records for matching the S3 API. If cost, latency, or data security are a concern over using public cloud object storage solutions, running your own Ceph cluster to provide object storage can be an ideal use case.

Object storage with custom applications

Using librados, you can get your in-house application to talk directly to the underlying Ceph RADOS layer. This can greatly simplify the development of your application, and gives you direct access to high-performant reliable storage. Some of the more advanced features of librados that allow you to bundle a number of operations into a single atomic operation are also very hard to implement with existing storage solutions.

Distributed filesystem – web farm

A farm of web servers all need to access the same files so that they can all serve the same content no matter which one the client connects to. Traditionally, an HA NFS solution would be used to provide distributed file access, but can start to hit several limitations at scale. CephFS can provide a distributed filesystem to store the web content and allow it to be mounted across all the web servers in the farm.

Distributed filesystem – NAS or fileserver replacement

By using Samba in conjunction with CephFS, a highly available filesystem can be exported to Windows based clients. Because of the active and inactive nature of both Samba and CephFS, performance will grow with the expansion of the Ceph cluster.

Big data

Big data is the concept of analyzing large amounts of data that would not fit into traditional data analysis systems or for which the use of analysis methods would be too complex. Big data tends to require storage systems that are both capable of storing large amounts of data and also offering scale-out performance. Ceph can meet both of these requirements, and is therefore an ideal candidate for providing scale-out storage to big data systems.

Infrastructure design

While considering infrastructure design, we need to take care of certain components. We will now briefly look at these components.

SSDs

SSDs are great. Their price has been lowered enormously over the last 10 years, and all evidence suggests that it will continue to do so. They have the ability to offer access times several orders of magnitude lower than rotating disks and consume less power.

One important concept to understand about SSDs is that, although their read and write latencies are typically measured in tens of microseconds, to overwrite existing data in a flash block, requires the entire flash block to be erased before the write can happen. A typical flash block size in an SSD may be 128k, and even a 4 KB write I/O would require the entire block to be read, erased, and then the existing data and new I/O to be finally written. The erase operation can take several milliseconds, and without clever routines in the SSD firmware, this would make writes painfully slow. To get around this limitation, SSDs are equipped with a RAM buffer so they can acknowledge writes instantly while the firmware internally moves data around flash blocks to optimize the overwrite process and wear leveling. However, the RAM buffer is volatile memory, and would normally result in the possibility of data loss and corruption in the event of sudden power loss. To protect against this, SSDs can have power-loss protection, which is accomplished by having a large capacitor on board to store enough power to flush any outstanding writes to flash.

One of the biggest trends in recent years is the different tiers of SSDs that have become available. Broadly speaking, these can be broken down into the following categories:

- **Consumer**: These are the cheapest you can buy, and are pitched at the average PC user. They provide a lot of capacity very cheaply and offer fairly decent performance. They will likely offer no power-loss protection, and will either demonstrate extremely poor performance when asked to do synchronous writes or lie about stored data integrity. They will also likely have very poor write endurance, but still more than enough for standard use.
- **Prosumer**: These are a step up from the consumer models, and will typically provide better performance and have higher write endurance, although still far from what enterprise SSDs provide.

Before moving on to the enterprise models, it is worth just covering why you should not under any condition use the preceding models of SSDs for Ceph. These reasons are shown in the following list:

- Lack of proper power-loss protection will either result in extremely poor performance or not ensure proper data consistency
- Firmware is not as heavily tested, as enterprise SSDs often reveal data-corrupting bugs

- Low write endurance will mean that they will quickly wear out, often ending in sudden failure
- Because of high wear and failure rates, their initial cost benefits rapidly disappear
- The use of consumer SSDs with Ceph will result in poor performance and increase the chance of catastrophic data loss

Enterprise SSDs

The biggest difference between consumer and enterprise SSDs is that an enterprise SSD should provide the guarantee that, when it responds to the host system confirming that data has been safely stored, it actually has been permanently written to flash. That is to say that if power is suddenly removed from a system, all data that the operating system believes was committed to disk will be safely stored in flash. Furthermore, it should be expected that, in order to accelerate writes but maintain data safety, the SSDs will contain super capacitors to provide just enough power to flush the SSD's RAM buffer to flash in the event of a power-loss condition.

Enterprise SSDs are normally provided in a number of different flavors to provide a wide range of costs per GB options balanced against write endurance.

Enterprise – read-intensive

Read-intensive SSDs are a bit of a marketing term, as all SSDs will easily handle reads. The name refers to the lower write endurance. They will, however, provide the best cost per GB. These SSDs will often only have a write endurance of around 0.3-1 drive writes per day over a five-year period. That is to say that you should be able to write 400 GB a day to a 400 GB SSD and expect it to still be working in five years time. If you write 800 GB a day to it, it will only be guaranteed to last two and a half years. Generally, for most Ceph workloads, this range of SSDs is normally deemed not to have enough write endurance.

Enterprise – general usage

General usage SSDs will normally provide three to five DWPD, and are a good balance of cost and write endurance. For use in Ceph, they will normally be a good choice for an SSD based OSD assuming that the workload on the Ceph cluster is not planned to be overly write heavy. They also make excellent choices for storing the BlueStore DB partition in a hybrid HDD/SSD cluster.

Enterprise – write-intensive

Write-intensive SSDs are the most expensive type. They will often offer write endurances up to and over 10 DWPD. They should be used for pure SSD OSDs if very heavy write workloads are planned. If your cluster is still using the deprecated filestore object store, then high write endurance SSDs are also recommended for the journals.

For any new deployments of Ceph, BlueStore is the recommended default object store. The following information only relates to clusters that are still running filestore. Details of how filestore works and why it has been replaced is covered later in `Chapter 3`, *BlueStore*.

To understand the importance of choosing the right SSD when running filestore, we must understand that because of the limitations in normal POSIX filesystems, in order to provide atomic transactions that occur during a write, a journal is necessary to be able to roll back a transaction if it can't fully complete. If no separate SSD is used for the journal, a separate partition is created for it. Every write that the OSD handles will first be written to the journal and then flushed to the main storage area on the disk. This is the main reason why using an SSD for a journal for spinning disks is advised. The double write severely impacts spinning disk performance, mainly caused by the random nature of the disk heads moving between the journal and data areas.

Likewise, an SSD OSD using filestore still requires a journal, and so it will experience approximately double the number of writes and thus provide half the expected client performance.

As can now be seen, not all models of SSD are equal, and Ceph's requirements can make choosing the correct one a tough process. Fortunately, a quick test can be carried out to establish an SSD's potential for use as a Ceph journal.

Memory

Recommendations for BlueStore OSDs are 3 GB of memory for every HDD OSD and 5 GB for an SSD OSD. In truth, there are a number of variables that lead to this recommendation, but suffice to say that you never want to find yourself in the situation where your OSDs are running low on memory and any excess memory will be used to improve performance. Aside from the base-line memory usage of the OSD, the main variable affecting memory usage is the number of PGs running on the OSD. While total data size does have an impact on memory usage, it is dwarfed by the effect of the number of PGs. A healthy cluster running within the recommendation of 200 PGs per OSD will probably use less than 4 GB of RAM per OSD.

However, in a cluster where the number of PGs has been set higher than best practice, memory usage will be higher. It is also worth noting that when an OSD is removed from a cluster, extra PGs will be placed on remaining OSDs to re-balance the cluster. This will also increase memory usage as well as the recovery operation itself. This spike in memory usage can sometimes be the cause of cascading failures, if insufficient RAM has been provisioned. A large swap partition on an SSD should always be provisioned to reduce the risk of the Linux out-of-memory killer randomly killing OSD processes in the event of a low-memory situation.

As a minimum, the aim is to provision around 4 GB per OSD for HDDs and 5 GB per OSD for SSDs; this should be treated as the bare minimum, and 5 GB/6 GB (HDD/SSD respectively) per OSD would be the ideal amount. With both BlueStore and filestore, any additional memory installed on the server may be used to cache data, reducing read latency for client operations. Filestore uses Linux page cache, and so RAM is automatically utilized. With BlueStore, we need to manually tune the memory limit to assign extra memory to be used as a cache; this will be covered in more detail in `Chapter 3`, *BlueStore*.

If your cluster is still running filestore, depending on your workload and the size of the spinning disks that are used for the Ceph OSD's, extra memory may be required to ensure that the operating system can sufficiently cache the directory entries and file nodes from the filesystem that is used to store the Ceph objects. This may have a bearing on the RAM you wish to configure your nodes with, and is covered in more detail in the tuning section of this book.

Regardless of the configured memory size, ECC memory should be used at all times.

CPU

Ceph's official recommendation is for 1 GHz of CPU power per OSD. Unfortunately, in real life, it's not quite as simple as this. What the official recommendations don't point out is that a certain amount of CPU power is required per I/O; it's not just a static figure. Thinking about it, this makes sense: the CPU is only used when there is something to be done. If there's no I/O, then no CPU is needed. This, however, scales the other way: the more I/O, the more CPU is required. The official recommendation is a good safe bet for spinning-disk based OSDs. An OSD node equipped with fast SSDs can often find itself consuming several times this recommendation. To complicate things further, the CPU requirements vary depending on I/O size as well, with larger I/Os requiring more CPU.

If the OSD node starts to struggle for CPU resources, it can cause OSDs to start timing out and getting marked out from the cluster, often to rejoin several seconds later. This continuous loss and recovery tends to place more strain on the already limited CPU resource, causing cascading failures.

A good figure to aim for would be around 1-10 MHz per I/O, corresponding to 4 kb-4 MB I/Os respectively. As always, testing should be carried out before going live to confirm that CPU requirements are met both in normal and stressed I/O loads. Additionally, utilizing compression and checksums in BlueStore will use additional CPU per I/O, and should be factored into any calculations when upgrading from a Ceph cluster that had been previously running with filestore. Erasure-coded pools will also consume additional CPU over replicated pools. CPU usage will vary with the erasure coding type and profile, and so testing must be done to gain a better understanding of the requirements.

Another aspect of CPU selection that is key to determining performance in Ceph is the clock speed of the cores. A large proportion of the I/O path in Ceph is single threaded, and so a faster-clocked core will run through this code path faster, leading to lower latency. Because of the limited thermal design of most CPUs, there is often a trade-off of clock speed as the number of cores increases. High core count CPUs with high clock speeds also tend to be placed at the top of the pricing structure, and so it is beneficial to understand your I/O and latency requirements when choosing the best CPU.

A small experiment was done to find the effect of CPU clock speed on write latency. A Linux workstation running Ceph had its CPU clock manually adjusted using the user space governor. The following results clearly show the benefit of high-clocked CPUs:

CPU MHz	4 KB write I/O	Avg latency (us)
1600	797	1250
2000	815	1222
2400	1161	857
2800	1227	812
3300	1320	755
4300	1548	644

If low latency, and especially low write latency, is important, then go for the highest-clocked CPUs you can get, ideally at least above 3 GHz. This may require a compromise in SSD-only nodes on how many cores are available, and thus how many SSDs each node can support. For nodes with 12 spinning disks and SSD journals, single-socket quad core processors make an excellent choice, as they are often available with very high clock speeds, and are very aggressively priced.

Where extreme low latency is not as important—for example, in object workloads—look at entry-level processors with well-balanced core counts and clock speeds.

Another consideration concerning CPU and motherboard choice should be the number of sockets. In dual-socket designs, the memory, disk controllers, and NICs are shared between the sockets. When data required by one CPU is required from a resource located on another CPU, a socket is required that must cross the interlink bus between the two CPUs. Modern CPUs have high speed interconnections, but they do introduce a performance penalty, and thought should be given to whether a single socket design is achievable. There are some options given in the section on tuning as to how to work around some of these possible performance penalties.

Disks

When choosing the disks to build a Ceph cluster with, there is always the temptation to go with the biggest disks you can, as the total cost of ownership figures looks great on paper. Unfortunately, in reality this is often not a great choice. While disks have dramatically increased in capacity over the last 20 years, their performance hasn't. Firstly, you should ignore any sequential MB/s figures, as you will never see them in enterprise workloads; there is always something making the I/O pattern non-sequential enough that it might as well be completely random. Secondly, remember the following figures:

- 7.2k disks = 70–80 4k IOPS
- 10k disks = 120–150 4k IOPS
- 15k disks = You should be using SSDs

As a general rule, if you are designing a cluster that will offer active workloads rather than bulk inactive/archive storage, then you should design for the required IOPS and not capacity. If your cluster will largely contain spinning disks with the intention of providing storage for an active workload, then you should prefer an increased number of smaller capacity disks rather than the use of larger disks. With the decrease in cost of SSD capacity, serious thought should be given to using them in your cluster, either as a cache tier or even for a full SSD cluster. SSDs have already displaced 15k disks in all but very niche workloads; 10K disks will likely be going the same way by the end of the decade. It is likely that the storage scene will become a two-horse race, with slow, large-capacity disks filling the bulk storage role and flash-based devices filling the active I/O role.

Thought should also be given to the use of SSDs as either journals with Ceph's filestore or for storing the DB and WAL when using BlueStore. Filestore performance is dramatically improved when using SSD journals and it is not recommended that it should be used unless the cluster is designed to be used with very cold data.

When choosing SSDs for holding the BlueStore DB, it's important to correctly size the SSDs so that the majority, or ideally all, of the metadata will be stored on the SSD. Official recommendations are for the RocksDB database to be about 4% of the size of the HDD. In practice, you will rarely see this level of consumption in the real world, and the 4% figure is a conservative estimate. With 10 TB disks and larger becoming widely available, dedicating 400 GB of SSD to such a disk is not cost effective. If the RocksDB grows larger than the space allocated from the SSD, then metadata will overflow onto the HDD. So while the OSD will still operate, requests that require metadata to be read from the HDD will be slower than if all metadata was stored on an SSD. In real-world tests with clusters used for RBD workloads, DB usage is normally seen to lie in the 0.5% region. The Chapter 3, *BlueStore* of this book will contain more details on what data is stored in RocksDB and the space required for it.

As the SSDs used for storing the BlueStore DB are not used for storing data, their write endurance is not as critical as it has been in the past, when SSDs were used with filestore. You should also bear in mind that the default replication level of 3 will mean that each client write I/O will generate at least three times the I/O on the backend disks. When using filestore, because of the internal mechanisms in Ceph, in most instances, this number will likely be over six times write amplification.

Understand that even though, compared to a legacy RAID array, Ceph enables rapid recovery from a failed disk, this is because of the fact that Ceph involves a much larger number of disks in the recovery process. However, larger disks still pose a challenge, particularly when you want to recover from a node failure where several disks are affected. In a cluster comprised of ten 1TB disks, each 50% full, in the event of a disk failure, the remaining disks would have to recover 500 GB of data between them, around 55 GB each. At an average recovery speed of 20 MB/s, recovery would be expected in around 45 minutes. A cluster with a hundred 1TB disks would still have to recover 500 GB of data, but this time that task is shared between 99 disks, each having to recover about 5 GB; in theory, it would take around 4 minutes for the larger cluster to recover from a single disk failure. In reality, these recovery times will be higher as there are additional mechanisms at work that increase recovery time. In smaller clusters, recovery times should be a key factor when selecting disk capacity.

Networking

The network is a key and often overlooked component in a Ceph cluster. A poorly designed network can often lead to a number of problems that manifest themselves in peculiar ways and make for a confusing troubleshooting session.

10 G requirement

A 10 G network is strongly recommended for building a Ceph cluster; while 1 G networking will work, the amount of latency will almost be unacceptable, and will limit you as to the size of the nodes you can deploy. Thought should also be given to recovery; in the event of a disk or node failure, large amounts of data will need to be moved around the cluster. Not only will a 1 G network be table to provide sufficient performance for this, but normal I/O traffic will be impacted. In the very worst case, this may lead to OSDs timing out, causing cluster instabilities.

As mentioned, one of the main benefits of 10 G networking is the lower latency. Quite often, a cluster will never push enough traffic to make full use of the 10 G bandwidth; however, the latency improvement will be realized no matter the load on the cluster. The round trip time for a 4k packet over a 10 G network might take around 90 us, whereas the same 4k packet over 1 G networking will take over 1 ms. As you will learn in the tuning section of this book, latency has a direct affect on the performance of a storage system, particularly when performing direct or synchronous I/O.

Lately, the next generation of networking hardware has become available, supporting speeds starting at 25 G and climbing to 100 G. If you are implementing a new network when deploying your Ceph cluster, it is highly recommended that you look into deploying this next-generation hardware.

If your OSD node will come equipped with dual NICs, you should carefully work on for a network design that allows you to use them active for both transmit and receive. It is wasteful to leave a 10 G link in a passive state, and will help to lower latency under load.

Network design

A good network design is an important step to bringing a Ceph cluster online. If your networking is handled by another team, then make sure they are included in all stages of the design, as often an existing network will not be designed to handle Ceph's requirements, leading to poor Ceph performance and impacting existing systems.

It's recommended that each Ceph node be connected via redundant links to two separate switches so that, in the event of a switch failure, the Ceph node is still accessible. Stacking switches should be avoided if possible, as they can introduce single points of failure, and in some cases both will be required to be offline to carry out firmware upgrades.

If your Ceph cluster will be contained in only one set of switches, then feel free to skip this next section.

Traditional networks were mainly designed around a north–south access path, where clients at the north access data through the network to servers at the south. If a server is connected to an access switch that is needed to talk to another server connected to another access switch, then the traffic would be routed through the core switch. Because of this access pattern, the access and aggregation layers that feed into the core layer were not designed to handle a lot of intra-server traffic, which is fine for the environment they were designed to support. Server-to-server traffic is called east–west traffic, and is becoming more prevalent in the modern data center as applications become less isolated and require data from several other servers.

Ceph generates a lot of east–west traffic, both from internal cluster replication traffic, but also from other servers consuming Ceph storage. In large environments, the traditional core, aggregation, and access layer design may struggle to cope, as large amounts of traffic will be expected to be routed through the core switch. Faster switches can be obtained and faster or additional up-links can be added; however, the underlying problem is that you are trying to run a scale-out storage system on a scale-up network design. The layout of the layers is shown in the following diagram:

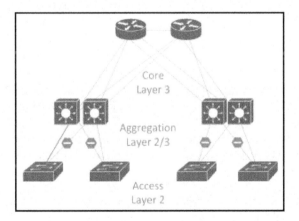

A traditional network topology

A design that is becoming very popular in data centers is the leaf spine design. This approach completely gets rid of the traditional model and replaces it with two layers of switches, the spine layer and the leaf layer. The core concept is that each leaf switch connects to each spine switch so that any leaf switch is only one hop anyway from any other leaf switch. This provides consistent hop latency and bandwidth. This is shown in the following diagram:

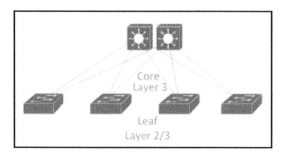

A leaf spine topology

The leaf layer is where the servers connect to, and is typically made up of a large number of 10 G ports and a handful of 40 G or faster up-link ports to connect into the spine layer. The spine layer won't normally connect directly into servers unless there are certain special requirements, and will just serve as an aggregation point for all the leaf switches. The spine layer will often have higher port speeds to reduce any possible contention of the traffic coming out of the leaf switches.

Leaf spine networks are typically moving away from pure layer 2 topologies, where the layer 2 domain is terminated on the leaf switches and layer 3 routing is done between the leaf and spine layer. It is advised that you do this using dynamic routing protocols, such as BGP or OSPF, to establish the routes across the fabric. This brings numerous advantages over large layer-2 networks. A spanning tree, which is typically used in layer-2 networks to stop switching loops, works by blocking an up-link. When using 40 G up-links, this is a lot of bandwidth to lose. When using dynamic routing protocols with a layer-3 design, ECMP (equal cost multipathing) can be used to fairly distribute data over all up-links to maximize the available bandwidth. In the example of a leaf switch connected to two spine switches via a 40 G up-link, there would be 80 G of bandwidth available to any other leaf switch in the topology, no matter where it resides.

Some network designs take this even further and push the layer-3 boundary down to the servers by actually running these routing protocols on servers as well, so that ECMP can be used to simplify the use of both NICs on the server in an active/active fashion. This is called routing on the host.

OSD node sizes

A common approach when designing nodes for use with Ceph is to pick a large-capacity server that contains large numbers of disk slots. In certain scenarios, this may be a good choice, but generally with Ceph, smaller nodes are preferable. To decide on the number of disks that each node in your Ceph cluster should contain, there are a number of things you should consider, as we will describe in the following sections.

Failure domains

If your cluster will have fewer than 10 nodes, then focusing on failure domains should be your main concern here.

With legacy scale-up storage, the hardware is expected to be 100% reliable; all components are redundant and the failure of a complete component, such as a system board or disk JBOD, would likely cause an outage. Therefore, there is no real knowledge of how such a failure might impact the operation of the system, just the hope that it doesn't happen! With Ceph, there is an underlying assumption that complete failure of a section of your infrastructure, be that a disk, node, or even rack, should be considered as normal and should not make your cluster unavailable.

Let's take two Ceph clusters, both comprised of 240 disks. Cluster A is comprised of 20 x 12 disk nodes and cluster B is comprised of 4 x 60 disk nodes. Now let's take a scenario where, for whatever reason, a Ceph OSD node goes offline. This could be because of planned maintenance or unexpected failure, but that node is now down and any data on it is unavailable. Ceph is designed to handle this situation, and will, if needed, even recover from it while maintaining full data access.

In the case of cluster A, we have now lost 5% of our disks and in the event of a permanent loss would have to reconstruct 72 TB of data. Cluster B has lost 25% of its disks and would have to reconstruct 360 TB. The latter would severely impact the performance of the cluster, and in the case of data reconstruction, this period of degraded performance could last for many days.

Even if a decision is made to override the automated healing and leave Ceph in a degraded state while you fix or perform maintenance on a node, in the 4 x 60 disk example, taking a node offline will also reduce the I/O performance of your cluster by 25%, which may mean that client applications suffer.

It's clear that on smaller-sized clusters, these very large, dense nodes are not a good idea. A 10 node Ceph cluster is probably the minimum size if you want to reduce the impact of node failure, and so in the case of 60-drive JBODs, you would need a cluster that at minimum is likely measured in petabytes.

Price

One often-cited reason for wanting to go with large, dense nodes is trying drive down the cost of the hardware purchase. This is often a false economy as dense nodes tend to require premium parts that often end up costing more per GB than less dense nodes.
For example, a 12-disk HDD node may only require a single quad processor to provide enough CPU resources for the OSDs. A 60-bay enclosure may require dual 10-core processors or greater, which are a lot more expensive per GHz provided. You may also need larger DIMMs, which demand a premium and perhaps even increased numbers of 10 G or faster NICs.

The bulk of the cost of the hardware will be made up of the CPUs, memory, networking, and disks. As we have seen, all of these hardware resource requirements scale linearly with the number and size of the disks. The only way in which larger nodes may have an advantage is the fact that they require fewer motherboards and power supplies, which is not a large part of the overall cost.

When looking at SSD only clusters, the higher performance of SSDs dictates the use of more powerful CPUs and greatly increased bandwidth requirements. It would certainly not be a good idea to deploy a single node with 60 SSDs, as the required CPU resource would either be impossible to provide or likely cost prohibitive. The use of 1-U and 2-U servers with either 10 or 24 bays will likely provide a sweet spot in terms of cost against either performance or capacity, depending on the use case of the cluster.

Power supplies

Servers can be configured with either single or dual redundant power supplies. Traditional workloads normally demand dual power supplies to protect against downtime in the case of a power supply or feed failure. If your Ceph cluster is large enough, then you may be able to look into the possibility of running single PSUs in your OSD nodes and allow Ceph to provide the availability in case of a power failure. Consideration should be given to the benefits of running a single power supply versus the worst-case situation where an entire power feed goes offline at a DC.

If your Ceph nodes are using RAID controllers with a write back cache, then they should be protected either via a battery or flash backup device. In the case of a complete power failure, the cache's contents will be kept safe until power is restored. If the raid controller's cache is running in write-through mode, then the cache backup is not required.

How to plan a successful Ceph implementation

The following are some general rules for deploying a successful Ceph cluster:

- Do use 10 G networking as a minimum
- Do research and test the correctly sized hardware you wish to use
- Don't use the no barrier mount option with filestore
- Don't configure pools with a size of two or a `min_size` of one
- Don't use consumer SSDs
- Don't use raid controllers in write back mode without battery protection
- Don't use configuration options you don't understand
- Do implement some form of change management
- Do carry out power-loss testing
- Do have an agreed backup and recovery plan

Understanding your requirements and how they relate to Ceph

As we have discussed, Ceph is not always the right choice for every storage requirement. Hopefully, this chapter has given you the knowledge to help you identify your requirements and match them to Ceph's capabilities, and hopefully, Ceph is a good fit for your use case and you can proceed with the project.

Care should be taken to understand the requirements of the project, including the following:

- Knowing who the key stakeholders of the project are. They will likely be the same people that will be able to detail how Ceph will be used.
- Collect the details of what systems Ceph will need to interact with. If it becomes apparent, for example, that unsupported operating systems are expected to be used with Ceph, then this needs to be flagged at an early stage.

Defining goals so that you can gauge whether the project is a success

Every project should have a series of goals that can help identify whether the project has been a success. Some of these goals may be the following:

- It should cost no more than X amount
- It should provide X IOPS or MB/s of performance
- It should survive certain failure scenarios
- It should reduce ownership costs of storage by X

These goals will need to be revisited throughout the life of the project to make sure that it is on track.

Joining the Ceph community

Whether it's by joining the Ceph mailing lists, the IRC channel, or attending community events, becoming part of the Ceph community is highly recommended. Not only will you be able to run proposed hardware and cluster configurations across a number of people who may have similar use cases, but the support and guidance provided by the community is excellent if you ever find yourself stuck.

By being part of the community, you will also gain insight into the development process of the Ceph project and see features being shaped prior to their introduction. For the more adventurous, thought should be given to actively contributing to the project. This could include helping others on the mailing lists, filing bugs, updating documentation, or even submitting code enhancements.

Choosing your hardware

The infrastructure section of this chapter will have given you a good idea of the hardware requirements of Ceph and the theory behind selecting the correct hardware for the project. The second biggest cause of outages in a Ceph cluster stems from poor hardware choices, making the right choices early on in the design stage crucial.

If possible, check with your hardware vendor to see whether they have any reference designs; these are often certified by Red Hat and will take a lot of the hard work off your shoulders in trying to determine whether your hardware choices are valid. You can also ask Red Hat or your chosen Ceph support vendor to validate your hardware; they will have had previous experience and will be able to answer any questions you may have.

Lastly, if you are planning on deploying and running your Ceph cluster entirely in house without any third-party involvement or support, consider reaching out to the Ceph community. The Ceph user's mailing list is contributed to by individuals from vastly different backgrounds stretching right across the globe. There is a high chance that someone somewhere will be doing something similar to you and will be able to advise you on your hardware choice.

Training yourself and your team to use Ceph

As with all technologies, it's essential that Ceph administrators receive some sort of training. Once the Ceph cluster goes live and becomes a business dependency, inexperienced administrators are a risk to stability. Depending on your reliance on third-party support, various levels of training may be required and may also determine whether you should look for a training course or self-teach.

Running a PoC to determine whether Ceph has met the requirements

A **proof of concept (PoC)** cluster should be deployed to test the design and identify any issues early on before proceeding with full-scale hardware procurement. This should be treated as a decision point in the project; don't be afraid to revisit goals or start the design again if any serious issues are uncovered. If you have existing hardware of similar specifications, then it should be fine to use it in the PoC, but the aim should be to try and test hardware that is as similar as possible to what you intend to build the production cluster with, so that you can fully test the design.

As well as testing for stability, the PoC cluster should also be used to forecast whether it looks likely that the goals you have set for the project will be met. Although it may be hard to directly replicate the workload requirements during a PoC, effort should be made to try and make the tests carried out match the intended production workload as best as possible. The PoC stage is also a good time to firm up your knowledge on Ceph, practice day-to-day operations, and test out features. This will be of benefit further down the line. You should also take this opportunity to be as abusive as possible to your PoC cluster. Randomly pull out disks, power off nodes, and disconnect network cables. If designed correctly, Ceph should be able to withstand all of these events. Carrying out this testing now will give you the confidence to operate Ceph at a larger scale, and will also help you understand how to troubleshoot them more easily if needed.

Following best practices to deploy your cluster

When deploying your cluster, you should focus on understanding the process rather than following guided examples. This will give you better knowledge of the various components that make up Ceph, and should you encounter any errors during deployment or operation, you will be much better placed to solve them. The next chapter of this book goes into more detail on deployment of Ceph, including the use of orchestration tools.

Initially, it is recommended that the default options for both the operating system and Ceph are used. It is better to start from a known state should any issues arise during deployment and initial testing.

RADOS pools using replication should have their replication level left at the default of three and the minimum replication level of two. This corresponds to the pool variables of size and min_size respectively. Unless there is both a good understanding and reason for the impact of lowering these values, it would be unwise to change them. The replication size determines how many copies of data will be stored in the cluster, and the effects of lowering it should be obvious in terms of protection against data loss. Less understood is the effect of min_size in relation to data loss, and is a common reason for it. Erasure-coded pools should be configured in a similar manner so that there is a minimum of two erasure-coded chunks for recovery. An example would be $k=4$ $m=2$; this would give the same durability as a size=3 replicated pool, but with double the usable capacity.

The min_size variable controls how many copies the cluster must write to acknowledge the write back to a client. A min_size of 2 means that the cluster must at least write two copies of data before acknowledging the write; this can mean that, in a severely degraded cluster scenario, write operations are blocked if the PG has only one remaining copy and will continue to be blocked until the PG has recovered enough to have two copies of the object. This is the reason you might want to decrease min_size to 1, so that, in this event, cluster operations can still continue, and if availability is more important than consistency, then this can be a valid decision. However, with a min_size of 1, data may be written to only one OSD, and there is no guarantee that the number of desired copies will be met anytime soon. During that period, any additional component failure will likely result in loss of data while written in the degraded state. In summary, downtime is bad, data loss is typically worse, and these two settings will probably have one of the biggest impacts on the probability of data loss.

The only scenario where a min_size setting of 1 should be used permanently is in extremely small clusters where there aren't really enough OSDs to have it set any higher, although at this scale, it is debatable whether Ceph is the correct storage platform choice.

Defining a change management process

The biggest cause of data loss and outages with a Ceph cluster are normally human error, whether it be by accidentally running the wrong command or changing configuration options, which may have unintended consequences. These incidents will likely become more common as the number of people in the team administering Ceph grows. A good way of reducing the risk of human error causing service interruptions or data loss is to implement some form of change control. This is covered in more detail in the next chapter.

Creating a backup and recovery plan

Ceph is highly redundant and, when properly designed, should have no single point of failure and be resilient to many types of hardware failures. However, one-in-a-million situations do occur, and as we have also discussed, human error can be very unpredictable. In both cases, there is a chance that the Ceph cluster may enter a state where it is unavailable, or where data loss occurs. In many cases, it may be possible to recover some or all of the data and return the cluster to full operation.

However, in all cases, a full backup and recovery plan should be discussed before putting any live data onto a Ceph cluster. Many a company has gone out of business or lost the faith of its customers when it's revealed that not only has there been an extended period of downtime, but critical data has also been lost. It may be that, as a result of discussion, it is agreed that a backup and recovery plan is not required, and this is fine. As long as risks and possible outcomes have been discussed and agreed, that is the most important thing.

Summary

In this chapter, you learned all of the necessary steps to allow you to successfully plan and implement a Ceph project. You also learned about the available hardware choices, how they relate to Ceph's requirements, and how they affect both Ceph's performance and reliability. Finally, you also learned of the importance of the processes and procedures that should be in place to ensure a healthy operating environment for your Ceph cluster.

The following chapters in this book will build on the knowledge you have learned in this chapter and help you put it to use to enable you to actually deploy, manage, and utilize Ceph storage.

Questions

1. What does RADOS stand for?
2. What does CRUSH stand for?
3. What is the difference between consumer and enterprise SSDs?
4. Does Ceph prefer the consistency or availability of your data?
5. Since the Luminous release, what is the default storage technology?
6. Who created Ceph?
7. What are block devices created on Ceph called?
8. What is the name of the component that actually stores data in Ceph?

2
Deploying Ceph with Containers

Once you have planned your Ceph project and are ready to deploy either a test or production cluster, you will need to consider the method you wish to use to both deploy and maintain it. This chapter will demonstrate how to quickly deploy test environments for testing and development by the use of Vagrant. It will also explain why you might want to consider using an orchestration tool to deploy Ceph rather than using the supplied Ceph tools. As a popular orchestration tool, Ansible will be used to show how quickly and reliably a Ceph cluster can be deployed and the advantages that using it can bring.

In this chapter, we will learn the following:

- How to prepare a testing environment with Vagrant and VirtualBox
- The differences between Ceph's deploy and orchestration tools
- The advantages over using orchestration tools
- How to install and use Ansible
- How to configure Ceph Ansible modules
- How to deploy a test cluster with Vagrant and Ansible
- Ideas concerning how to manage your Ceph configuration
- What the Rook project is and what it enables a Ceph operator to do
- How to deploy a basic Kubernetes cluster
- How to use Rook to deploy Ceph on Kubernetes

Technical requirements

In order to be able to run the Ceph environment described later in this chapter, it's important that your computer meets a number of requirements to ensure that the VM can be provided with sufficient resources. These requirements are as follows:

- Operating system compatible with Vagrant and VirtualBox, including Linux, macOS, and Windows
- 2-core CPU
- 8 GB ram
- Virtualization instructions enabled in the BIOS

Preparing your environment with Vagrant and VirtualBox

While a test cluster can be deployed on any hardware or virtual machine, for the purposes of this book a combination of Vagrant and VirtualBox will be used. This will allow rapid provision of the virtual machines and ensure a consistent environment.

VirtualBox is a free and open source hypervisor currently being developed by Oracle; while its performance and features may be lacking compared to high-end hypervisors, its lightweight approach and multi-OS support lend itself to its being a prime candidate for testing.

Vagrant assists in allowing an environment that may comprise many machines to be created quickly and efficiently. It works with the concepts of boxes, which are predefined templates for use with hypervisors and its Vagrantfile, which defines the environment to be built. It supports multiple hypervisors and allows a Vagrantfile to be portable across them.

How to install VirtualBox

Consult the VirtualBox website for the appropriate method to install VirtualBox on your operating system: `https://www.virtualbox.org/wiki/Downloads`:

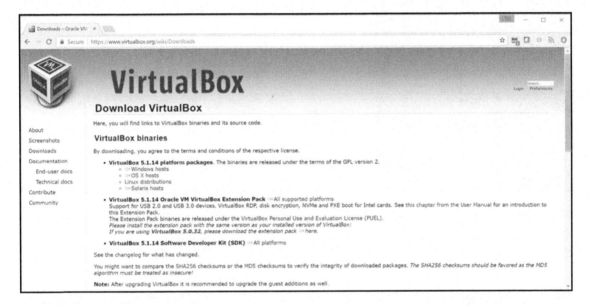

How to set up Vagrant

Follow the installation instructions on Vagrant's website to get Vagrant installed on your chosen OS: https://www.vagrantup.com/downloads.html:

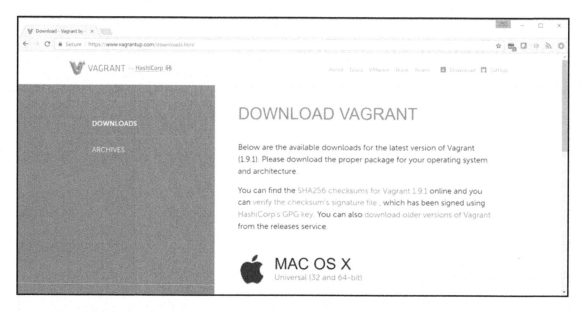

1. Create a new directory for your Vagrant project, for example `ceph-ansible`
2. Change to this directory and run the following commands:

```
vagrant plugin install vagrant-hostmanager
```

```
Installing the 'vagrant-hostmanager' plugin. This can take a few minutes...
Fetching: vagrant-hostmanager-1.8.5.gem (100%)
Installed the plugin 'vagrant-hostmanager (1.8.5)'!
```

```
vagrant box add bento/ubuntu-16.04
```

```
==> box: Loading metadata for box 'bento/ubuntu-16.04'
    box: URL: https://atlas.hashicorp.com/bento/ubuntu-16.04
This box can work with multiple providers! The providers that it
can work with are listed below. Please review the list and choose
the provider you will be working with.

1) parallels
2) virtualbox
3) vmware_desktop

Enter your choice: 2
==> box: Adding box 'bento/ubuntu-16.04' (v2.3.1) for provider: virtualbox
    box: Downloading: https://atlas.hashicorp.com/bento/boxes/ubuntu-16.04/versions/2.3.1/providers/virtualbox.box
    box: Progress: 100% (Rate: 5257k/s, Estimated time remaining: --:--:--)
==> box: Successfully added box 'bento/ubuntu-16.04' (v2.3.1) for 'virtualbox'!
```

Now create an empty file called `Vagrantfile` and place the following into it:

```
nodes = [
  { :hostname => 'ansible', :ip => '192.168.0.40', :box => 'xenial64' },
  { :hostname => 'mon1', :ip => '192.168.0.41', :box => 'xenial64' },
  { :hostname => 'mon2', :ip => '192.168.0.42', :box => 'xenial64' },
  { :hostname => 'mon3', :ip => '192.168.0.43', :box => 'xenial64' },
  { :hostname => 'osd1',  :ip => '192.168.0.51', :box => 'xenial64', :ram
=> 1024, :osd => 'yes' },
  { :hostname => 'osd2',  :ip => '192.168.0.52', :box => 'xenial64', :ram
=> 1024, :osd => 'yes' },
  { :hostname => 'osd3',  :ip => '192.168.0.53', :box => 'xenial64', :ram
=> 1024, :osd => 'yes' }
]

Vagrant.configure("2") do |config|
  nodes.each do |node|
    config.vm.define node[:hostname] do |nodeconfig|
      nodeconfig.vm.box = "bento/ubuntu-16.04"
      nodeconfig.vm.hostname = node[:hostname]
      nodeconfig.vm.network :private_network, ip: node[:ip]

      memory = node[:ram] ? node[:ram] : 512;
      nodeconfig.vm.provider :virtualbox do |vb|
        vb.customize [
          "modifyvm", :id,
          "--memory", memory.to_s,
        ]
        if node[:osd] == "yes"
          vb.customize [ "createhd", "--filename", "disk_osd-
#{node[:hostname]}", "--size", "10000" ]
          vb.customize [ "storageattach", :id, "--storagectl", "SATA
Controller", "--port", 3, "--device", 0, "--type", "hdd", "--medium",
"disk_osd-#{node[:hostname]}.vdi" ]
        end
```

```
        end
      end
    config.hostmanager.enabled = true
    config.hostmanager.manage_guest = true
  end
end
```

Run `vagrant up` to bring up the virtual machines defined in the `Vagrantfile`:

```
Bringing machine 'ansible' up with 'virtualbox' provider...
Bringing machine 'mon1' up with 'virtualbox' provider...
Bringing machine 'mon2' up with 'virtualbox' provider...
Bringing machine 'mon3' up with 'virtualbox' provider...
Bringing machine 'osd1' up with 'virtualbox' provider...
Bringing machine 'osd2' up with 'virtualbox' provider...
Bringing machine 'osd3' up with 'virtualbox' provider...
==> ansible: Importing base box 'bento/ubuntu-16.04'...
==> ansible: Matching MAC address for NAT networking...
==> ansible: Checking if box 'bento/ubuntu-16.04' is up to date...
==> ansible: Setting the name of the VM: ceph_ansible_1486503043550_56998
==> ansible: Clearing any previously set network interfaces...
==> ansible: Preparing network interfaces based on configuration...
    ansible: Adapter 1: nat
    ansible: Adapter 2: hostonly
==> ansible: Forwarding ports...
    ansible: 22 (guest) => 2222 (host) (adapter 1)
==> ansible: Running 'pre-boot' VM customizations...
==> ansible: Booting VM...
==> ansible: Waiting for machine to boot. This may take a few minutes...
```

Now, let's `ssh` into one of them:

```
vagrant ssh ansible
```

```
`ssh` executable not found in any directories in the %PATH% variable. Is an
SSH client installed? Try installing Cygwin, MinGW or Git, all of which
contain an SSH client. Or use your favorite SSH client with the following
authentication information shown below:

Host: 127.0.0.1
Port: 2200
Username: vagrant
```

If you are running `vagrant` on Windows, the `ssh` command will inform you that you need to use a SSH client of your choosing and provide the details to use with it. Putty would be a good suggestion for a SSH client. On Linux, the command will connect you straight onto the VM.

The username and password are both `vagrant`. After logging in, you should find yourself at the bash prompt for the `ansible vm`:

```
login as: vagrant
vagrant@127.0.0.1's password:
Welcome to Ubuntu 16.04.1 LTS (GNU/Linux 4.4.0-51-generic x86_64)

 * Documentation:  https://help.ubuntu.com
 * Management:      https://landscape.canonical.com
 * Support:         https://ubuntu.com/advantage

0 packages can be updated.
0 updates are security updates.


vagrant@ansible:~$
```

Simply type exit to return to your host machine.

Congratulations, you have just deployed three servers for use as Ceph monitors, three servers for use as Ceph OSDs, and an Ansible server. The `Vagrantfile` could have also contained extra steps to execute commands on the servers to configure them but for now let's shut down the servers; we can bring them back up when required by the examples later in this chapter:

```
vagrant destroy --force
```

Ceph-deploy

Ceph-deploy is the official tool for deploying Ceph clusters. It works on the principle of having an admin node with password-less SSH access to all machines in your Ceph cluster; it also holds a copy of the Ceph configuration file. Every time you carry out a deployment action, it uses SSH to connect to your Ceph nodes to carry out the necessary steps. While the Ceph-deploy tool is an entirely supported method that will leave you with a perfectly functioning Ceph cluster, ongoing management of Ceph will not be as easy as desired.

Larger-scale Ceph clusters will also cause a lot of management overhead if Ceph-deploy is used. For that reason, it is recommended that Ceph-deploy be limited to test or small-scale production clusters, although as you will see an orchestration tool allows for the rapid deployment of Ceph and is probably better suited for test environments where you might need to continually be building new Ceph clusters.

Orchestration

One solution to make installing and managing Ceph easier is to use an orchestration tool. There are several tools available, such as Puppet, Chef, Salt, and Ansible, all of which have Ceph modules available. If you are already using an orchestration tool in your environment, then it is recommended that you stick to using that tool. For the purposes of this book, Ansible will be used. This is due a number of reasons, as follows:

- It's the deployment method that is favored by Red Hat, who are the owners of both the Ceph and Ansible projects
- It has a well-developed, mature set of Ceph roles and playbooks
- Ansible tends to be easier to learn if you have never used an orchestration tool before
- It doesn't require a central server to be set up, which means demonstrations are more focused on using the tool than installing it

All tools follow the same principle, where you provide them with an inventory of hosts and a set of tasks to be carried out on the hosts. These tasks often reference variables that allow customization of the task at runtime. Orchestration tools are designed to be run on a schedule so that, if for any reason the state or configuration of a host changes, it will be correctly changed back to the intended state during the next run.

Another advantage of using orchestration tools is documentation. While they are not a replacement for good documentation, the fact that they clearly describe your environment, including roles and configuration options, means that your environment starts to become self-documenting. If you ensure that any installations or changes are carried out via your orchestration tool, then the configuration file of the orchestration tool will clearly describe the current state of your environment. If this is combined with something such as a Git repository to store the orchestration configuration, you have the makings of a change control system. This is covered in more detail later in this chapter. The only disadvantages center around the extra time it takes to carry out the initial setup and configuration of the tool.

So, by using an orchestration tool, not only do you get a faster and less error-prone deployment, you also get documentation and change management for free. If you haven't got the hint by now, this is something you should really be looking at.

Ansible

As mentioned earlier, Ansible will be the orchestration tool of choice for this book, so let's look at it in a bit more detail.

Ansible is an agent-less orchestration tool written in Python that uses SSH to carry out configuration tasks on remote nodes. It was first released in 2012, has gained widespread adoption, and is known for its ease of adoption and low learning curve. Red Hat purchased the commercial company Ansible Inc. in 2015 and so has a very well developed and close-knit integration for deploying Ceph.

Files called playbooks are used in Ansible to describe a list of commands, actions, and configurations to be carried out on specified hosts or groups of hosts and are stored in the `yaml` file format. Instead of having large unmanageable playbooks, Anisble roles can be created to allow a playbook to contain a single task, which may then carry out a number of tasks associated with the role.

The use of SSH to connect to remote nodes and execute playbooks means that it is very lightweight and does not require either an agent or a centralized server.

For testing Ansible also integrates well with Vagrant; an Ansible playbook can be specified as part of the Vagrant provisioning configuration and will automatically generate an inventory file from the VMs Vagrant that has been created and will run the playbook once the servers have booted. This allows a Ceph cluster, including its OS, to be deployed via just a single command.

Installing Ansible

You'll bring your Vagrant environment you created earlier back up that and ssh onto the Ansible server. For this example only `ansible`, `mon1`, and `osd1` will be needed:

> **Vagrant up ansible mon1 osd1**

- Add the Ansible PPA:

> **$ sudo apt-add-repository ppa:ansible/ansible-2.6**

```
 Ansible is a radically simple IT automation platform that makes your applications and systems easie
r to deploy. Avoid writing scripts or custom code to deploy and update your applications— automate i
n a language that approaches plain English, using SSH, with no agents to install on remote systems.

http://ansible.com/
 More info: https://launchpad.net/~ansible/+archive/ubuntu/ansible
Press [ENTER] to continue or ctrl-c to cancel adding it

gpg: keyring `/tmp/tmpt5a6qdao/secring.gpg' created
gpg: keyring `/tmp/tmpt5a6qdao/pubring.gpg' created
gpg: requesting key 7BB9C367 from hkp server keyserver.ubuntu.com
gpg: /tmp/tmpt5a6qdao/trustdb.gpg: trustdb created
gpg: key 7BB9C367: public key "Launchpad PPA for Ansible, Inc." imported
gpg: Total number processed: 1
gpg:               imported: 1  (RSA: 1)
OK
```

- Update `apt-get` sources and install Ansible:

> **$ sudo apt-get update && sudo apt-get install ansible -y**

```
Setting up libyaml-0-2:amd64 (0.1.6-3) ...
Setting up python-markupsafe (0.23-2build2) ...
Setting up python-jinja2 (2.8-1) ...
Setting up python-yaml (3.11-3build1) ...
Setting up python-crypto (2.6.1-6build1) ...
Setting up python-six (1.10.0-3) ...
Setting up python-ecdsa (0.13-2) ...
Setting up python-paramiko (1.16.0-1) ...
Setting up python-httplib2 (0.9.1+dfsg-1) ...
Setting up python-pkg-resources (20.7.0-1) ...
Setting up python-setuptools (20.7.0-1) ...
Setting up sshpass (1.05-1) ...
Setting up ansible (2.2.1.0-1ppa~xenial) ...
Processing triggers for libc-bin (2.23-0ubuntu4) ...
vagrant@ansible:~$
```

Creating your inventory file

The Ansible inventory file is used by Ansible to reference all known hosts and specify which group they belong to. A group is defined by placing its name in square brackets; groups can be nested inside other groups by the use of the children definition.

Before we add hosts to the inventory file, we first need to configure the remote nodes for password-less SSH, otherwise we will have to enter a password every time Ansible tries to connect to a remote machine as follows:

1. Generate a SSH key:

```
$ ssh-keygen
```

```
vagrant@ansible:~$ ssh-keygen
Generating public/private rsa key pair.
Enter file in which to save the key (/home/vagrant/.ssh/id_rsa):
Enter passphrase (empty for no passphrase):
Enter same passphrase again:
Your identification has been saved in /home/vagrant/.ssh/id_rsa.
Your public key has been saved in /home/vagrant/.ssh/id_rsa.pub.
The key fingerprint is:
SHA256:mdvKrx6ZG88AKQsPnaFpjKlPb8pmmnfqDiQPv4OQnpw vagrant@ansible
The key's randomart image is:
+---[RSA 2048]----+
|                 |
|                 |
|     .           |
| + + o . o       |
|=oB + o S        |
|*= + o . =       |
|*.* o    B .     |
|.E=oo    . O     |
|oBO*.   .*o+     |
+----[SHA256]-----+
```

2. Copy the key to the remote hosts:

```
$ ssh-copy-id mon1
```

```
vagrant@ansible:~$ ssh-copy-id mon1
/usr/bin/ssh-copy-id: INFO: Source of key(s) to be installed: "/home/vagrant/.ssh/id_rsa.pub"
The authenticity of host 'mon1 (192.168.0.41)' can't be established.
ECDSA key fingerprint is SHA256:RI5/3ep65qXeDkZSACi/rN0hBxiLrBxMvcyk9CfLkyg.
Are you sure you want to continue connecting (yes/no)? yes
/usr/bin/ssh-copy-id: INFO: attempting to log in with the new key(s), to filter out any that are alr
eady installed
/usr/bin/ssh-copy-id: INFO: 1 key(s) remain to be installed -- if you are prompted now it is to inst
all the new keys
vagrant@mon1's password:

Number of key(s) added: 1

Now try logging into the machine, with:   "ssh 'mon1'"
and check to make sure that only the key(s) you wanted were added.
```

This will need to be repeated for each host. Normally, you would include this step in your Vagrant provisioning stage, but it is useful to carry out these tasks manually the first couple of times, so that you understand the process.

Now try logging in to the machine with: `ssh mon1`:

```
vagrant@ansible:~$ ssh mon1
Welcome to Ubuntu 16.04.1 LTS (GNU/Linux 4.4.0-51-generic x86_64)

 * Documentation:  https://help.ubuntu.com
 * Management:     https://landscape.canonical.com
 * Support:        https://ubuntu.com/advantage

0 packages can be updated.
0 updates are security updates.


vagrant@mon1:~$ 
```

Type `exit` to return to the Ansible VM. Now let's create the `Ansible` inventory file. Edit the file called `hosts` in `/etc/ansible`:

```
$ sudo nano /etc/ansible/hosts
```

Create three groups called `osds`, `mgrs`, and `mons` and finally a fourth group called `ceph`. This fourth group will contain the `osds` and `mons` groups as children.

Enter a list of your hosts under the correct group:

```
[mons]
mon1
mon2
mon3

[mgrs]
mon1

[osds]
osd1
osd2
osd3

[ceph:children]
mons
osds
mgrs
```

Variables

Most playbooks and roles will make use of variables, which can be overridden in several ways. The simplest way is to create files in the host_vars and groups_vars folders; these allow you to override variables either based on the host or group membership, respectively.

Create a /etc/ansible/group_vars directory. Create a file in group_vars called mons and place the following inside it:

a_variable: "foo"

Create a file in group_vars called osds and place the following inside it:

a_variable: "bar"

Variables follow a precedence order; you can also create an all file which will apply to all groups. However, a variable of the same name that is in a more specific matching group will override it. Ceph Ansible modules make use of this to allow you to have a set of default variables and then specify different values for the specific roles.

Testing

To verify that Ansible is working correctly and that we can successfully connect and run commands remotely, let's use ping with Ansible to check one of our hosts. Note: this is not like a network ping; Ansible's ping confirms that it can communicate via SSH and execute commands remotely:

```
$ ansible mon1 -m ping
```

```
vagrant@ansible:~$ ansible mon1 -m ping
mon1 | SUCCESS => {
    "changed": false,
    "ping": "pong"
}
vagrant@ansible:~$
```

Excellent, that worked. Now let's run a simple command remotely to demonstrate Ansible's capabilities. The following command will retrieve the currently running kernel version on the specified remote node:

```
$ ansible mon1 -a 'uname -r'
```

```
vagrant@ansible:~$ ansible mon1 -a 'uname -r'
mon1 | SUCCESS | rc=0 >>
4.4.0-51-generic

vagrant@ansible:~$
```

A very simple playbook

To demonstrate how playbooks works, the following example will showcase a small playbook that also makes use of the variables we configured earlier:

```
- hosts: mon1 osd1
  tasks:
  - name: Echo Variables
    debug: msg="I am a {{ a_variable }}"
```

And now run the playbook. Notice that the command to run a playbook differs from running ad hoc Ansible commands:

```
$ ansible-playbook /etc/ansible/playbook.yml
```

```
vagrant@ansible:~$ ansible-playbook /etc/ansible/playbook.yml

PLAY [mon1 osd1] ***********************************************************

TASK [setup] **************************************************************
ok: [mon1]
ok: [osd1]

TASK [Echo Variables] *****************************************************
ok: [mon1] => {
    "msg": "I am a foo"
}
ok: [osd1] => {
    "msg": "I am a bar"
}

PLAY RECAP ****************************************************************
mon1                       : ok=2    changed=0    unreachable=0    failed=0
osd1                       : ok=2    changed=0    unreachable=0    failed=0

vagrant@ansible:~$
```

The output shows the playbook being executed on both mon1 and osd1 as they are in groups, which are children of the parent group, Ceph. Also note how the output of the two servers is different as they pick up the variables that you set earlier in the group_vars directory.

Finally, the last couple of lines show the overall run status of the playbook run. You can now destroy your Vagrant environment again, ready for the next section:

```
Vagrant destroy --force
```

This concludes the introduction to Ansible, but is no means meant to be a complete guide. It's recommended that you explore other resources to gain a more in-depth knowledge of Ansible before using it in a production environment.

Adding the Ceph Ansible modules

We can use Git to clone the Ceph Ansible repository, as follows:

```
git clone https://github.com/ceph/ceph-ansible.git
git checkout stable-3.2
sudo cp -a ceph-ansible/* /etc/ansible/
```

```
vagrant@ansible:~$ git clone https://github.com/ceph/ceph-ansible.git
Cloning into 'ceph-ansible'...
remote: Counting objects: 13875, done.
remote: Compressing objects: 100% (69/69), done.
remote: Total 13875 (delta 32), reused 0 (delta 0), pack-reused 13802
Receiving objects: 100% (13875/13875), 2.29 MiB | 1.94 MiB/s, done.
Resolving deltas: 100% (9234/9234), done.
Checking connectivity... done.
vagrant@ansible:~$ sudo cp -a ceph-ansible/* /etc/ansible/
vagrant@ansible:~$
```

We also need to install a few extra packages that `ceph-ansible` requires:

```
sudo apt-get install python-pip
```

```
vagrant@ansible:/etc/ansible$ sudo apt-get install python-pip
Reading package lists... Done
Building dependency tree
Reading state information... Done
The following additional packages will be installed:
  build-essential dpkg-dev g++ g++-5 libalgorithm-diff-perl libalgorithm-diff-xs-perl libalgorithm-merge-perl
  libexpat1-dev libpython-all-dev libpython-dev libpython2.7-dev libstdc++-5-dev python-all python-all-dev python-dev
  python-pip-whl python-wheel python2.7-dev
Suggested packages:
  debian-keyring g++-multilib g++-5-multilib gcc-5-doc libstdc++6-5-dbg libstdc++-5-doc
The following NEW packages will be installed:
  build-essential dpkg-dev g++ g++-5 libalgorithm-diff-perl libalgorithm-diff-xs-perl libalgorithm-merge-perl
  libexpat1-dev libpython-all-dev libpython-dev libpython2.7-dev libstdc++-5-dev python-all python-all-dev python-dev
  python-pip python-pip-whl python-wheel python2.7-dev
0 upgraded, 19 newly installed, 0 to remove and 42 not upgraded.
Need to get 39.9 MB of archives.
After this operation, 85.3 MB of additional disk space will be used.
Do you want to continue? [Y/n]
```

```
sudo pip install notario netaddr
```

```
vagrant@ansible:/etc/ansible$ sudo pip install notario
The directory '/home/vagrant/.cache/pip/http' or its parent directory is not owned by the current user and the cache has
 been disabled. Please check the permissions and owner of that directory. If executing pip with sudo, you may want sudo'
s -H flag.
The directory '/home/vagrant/.cache/pip' or its parent directory is not owned by the current user and caching wheels has
 been disabled. check the permissions and owner of that directory. If executing pip with sudo, you may want sudo's -H fl
ag.
Collecting notario
  Downloading https://files.pythonhosted.org/packages/95/19/9a01217482271ba85a9efd4caf42dc728850a516da2b7dd8a998fba681e9
/notario-0.0.14.tar.gz
Installing collected packages: notario
  Running setup.py install for notario ... done
Successfully installed notario-0.0.14
You are using pip version 8.1.1, however version 18.1 is available.
You should consider upgrading via the 'pip install --upgrade pip' command.
```

Let's also explore some key folders in the Git repository:

- group_vars: We've already covered what lives here and will explore possible configuration options in more detail later
- infrastructure-playbooks: This directory contains pre-written playbooks to carry out some standard tasks, such as deploying clusters or adding OSDs to an existing one. The comments at the top of the playbooks give a good idea of what they do.
- roles: This directory contains all the roles that make up the Ceph Ansible modules. You will see that there is a role for each Ceph component; these are called via playbooks to install, configure, and maintain Ceph.

In order to be able to deploy a Ceph cluster with Ansible, a number of key variables need to be set in the group_vars directory. The following variables are required to be set; alternatively, it's recommended you change them from their defaults. For the remaining variables, it suggested that you read the comments in the variable files. Key global variables include the following:

```
#mon_group_name: mons
#osd_group_name: osds
#rgw_group_name: rgws
#mds_group_name: mdss
#nfs_group_name: nfss
...
#iscsi_group_name: iscsigws
```

These control what group name modules use to identify the Ceph host types. If you will be using Ansible in a wider setting, it might be advisable to prepend `ceph-` to the start to make it clear that these groups are related to Ceph:

```
#ceph_origin: 'upstream' # or 'distro' or 'local'
```

Employ the `'upstream'` setting to use packages generated by the Ceph team, or `distro` for packages generated by your distribution maintainer. The former is recommended if you want to be able to upgrade Ceph independently of your distribution:

```
#fsid: "{{ cluster_uuid.stdout }}"
#generate_fsid: true
```

By default, a `fsid` will be generated for your cluster and stored in a file where it can be referenced again. You shouldn't need to touch this unless you want control over the `fsid` or you wish to hardcode the `fsid` in the group variable file:

```
#monitor_interface: interface
#monitor_address: 0.0.0.0
```

One of the preceding commands should be specified. If you are using a variable in `group_vars` then you probably want to use `monitor_interface`, which is the interface name in Linux, as they will probably be the same across all `mons`. Otherwise if you specify `monitor_address` in `host_vars`, you can specify the IP of the interface, which obviously will be different across your three or more `mons`:

```
#ceph_conf_overrides: {}
```

Not every Ceph variable is directly managed by Ansible, but the preceding variable is provided to allow you to pass any extra variables through to the `ceph.conf` file and its corresponding sections. An example of how this would look follows (notice the indentation):

```
ceph_conf_overrides:
  global:
    variable1: value
  mon:
    variable2: value
  osd:
    variable3: value
```

Key variables from the OSD variable file are as follows:

```
#copy_admin_key: false
```

If you want to be able to manage your cluster from your OSD nodes instead of just your monitors, set this to `true`, which will copy the admin key to your OSD nodes:

```
#devices: []
#osd_auto_discovery: false
#journal_collocation: false
#raw_multi_journal: false
#raw_journal_devices: []
```

These are probably the most crucial set of variables in the entire configuration of Ansible. They control what disks get used as OSDs and how journals are placed. You can either manually specify the devices that you wish to use as OSDs or you can use auto discovery. The examples in this book use static device configuration.

The `journal_collocation` variable sets whether you want to store the journal on the same disk as the OSD data; a separate partition will be created for it.

`raw_journal_devices` allows you to specify the devices you wish to use for journals. Quite often, a single SSD will be a journal for several OSDs; in this case, enable `raw_multi_journal` and simply specify the journal device multiple times; no partition numbers are needed if you want Ansible to instruct ceph-disk to create them for you.

These are the main variables that you should need to consider; it is recommended you read the comments in the variable files to see if there are any others you may need to modify for your environment.

Deploying a test cluster with Ansible

There are several examples on the internet that contain a fully configured `Vagrantfile` and associated Ansible playbooks; this allows you to bring up a fully functional Ceph environment with just one command. As handy as this may be, it doesn't help you learn how to correctly configure and use the Ceph Ansible modules as you would if you were deploying a Ceph cluster on real hardware in a production environment. As such, this book will guide you through configuring Ansible from the start, even though it's running on Vagrant provisioned servers. Its important to note that, like Ceph itself, Ansible playbooks are constantly changing and therefore it is recommended that you review the `ceph-ansible` documentation for any breaking changes.

At this point, your Vagrant environment should be up-and-running and Ansible should be able to connect to all six of your Ceph servers. You should also have a cloned copy of the Ceph Ansible module.

Create a file called `/etc/ansible/group_vars/ceph`:

```
ceph_origin: 'repository'
ceph_repository: 'community'
ceph_mirror: http://download.ceph.com
ceph_stable: true # use ceph stable branch
ceph_stable_key: https://download.ceph.com/keys/release.asc
ceph_stable_release: mimic # ceph stable release
ceph_stable_repo: "{{ ceph_mirror }}/debian-{{ ceph_stable_release }}"
monitor_interface: enp0s8 #Check ifconfig
public_network: 192.168.0.0/24
```

Create a file called `/etc/ansible/group_vars/osds`:

```
osd_scenario: lvm
lvm_volumes:
- data: /dev/sdb
```

Create a `fetch` folder and change the owner to the `vagrant` user:

```
sudo mkdir /etc/ansible/fetch
sudo chown vagrant /etc/ansible/fetch
```

Run the Ceph cluster deployment playbook:

```
cd /etc/ansible
sudo mv site.yml.sample site.yml
ansible-playbook -K site.yml
```

The `K` parameter tells Ansible that it should ask you for the `sudo` password. Now sit back and watch Ansible deploy your cluster:

```
PLAY RECAP ********************************************************************
mon1                       : ok=57    changed=15    unreachable=0    failed=0
mon2                       : ok=51    changed=12    unreachable=0    failed=0
mon3                       : ok=51    changed=12    unreachable=0    failed=0
osd1                       : ok=59    changed=11    unreachable=0    failed=0
osd2                       : ok=57    changed=11    unreachable=0    failed=0
osd3                       : ok=57    changed=11    unreachable=0    failed=0
```

Once this is completed, and assuming Ansible completed without errors, `ssh` into `mon1` and run:

```
vagrant@mon1:~$ sudo ceph -s
```

```
vagrant@mon1:~$ sudo ceph -s
  cluster:
    id:     66fd555c-7a6c-40e9-b775-9d712b4256e1
    health: HEALTH_WARN
            no active mgr

  services:
    mon: 3 daemons, quorum mon1,mon2,mon3
    mgr: no daemons active
    osd: 3 osds: 3 up, 3 in

  data:
    pools:   0 pools, 0 pgs
    objects: 0  objects, 0 B
    usage:   0 B used, 0 B / 0 B avail
    pgs:
```

And that concludes the deployment of a fully functional Ceph cluster via Ansible.

If you want to be able to stop the Vagrant Ceph cluster without losing your work so far, you can run the following command:

```
vagrant suspend
```

To pause all the VM's in their current state, run the following:

```
vagrant resume
```

This will power on the VMs; they'll resume running at the state you left them in.

Change and configuration management

If you deploy your infrastructure with an orchestration tool such as Ansible, managing Ansible playbooks becomes important. As we have seen, Ansible allows you to rapidly deploy both the initial Ceph cluster and also configuration updates further down the line. It must be appreciated that this power can also have devastating effects if incorrect configurations or operations are deployed. By implementing some form of configuration management, Ceph administrators will be able to see clearly what changes have been made to the Ansible playbooks before running them.

A recommended approach would be to store your Ceph Ansible configuration in a Git repository; this will allow you to track changes and implement some form of change control either by monitoring Git commits or by forcing people to submit merge requests into the master branch.

Ceph in containers

We have seen previously that by using orchestration tools such as Ansible we can reduce the work required to deploy, manage, and maintain a Ceph cluster. We have also seen how these tools can help you discover available hardware resources and deploy Ceph to them.

However, using Ansible to configure bare-metal servers still results in a very static deployment, possibly not best suited for today's more dynamic workloads. Designing Ansible playbooks also needs to take into account several different Linux distributions and also any changes that may occur between different releases; systemd is a great example of this. Furthermore, a lot of development in orchestration tools needs to be customized to handle discovering, deploying, and managing Ceph. This is a common theme that the Ceph developers have thought about; with the use of Linux containers and their associated orchestration platforms, they hope to improve Ceph's deployment experience.

One such approach, which has been selected as the preferred option, is to join forces with a project called Rook. Rook works with the container management platform Kubernetes to automate the deployment, configuration, and consumption of Ceph storage. If you were to draw up a list of requirements and features which a custom Ceph orchestration and management framework would need to implement, you would likely design something which functions in a similar fashion to Kubernetes. So it makes sense to build functionality on top of the well-established Kubernetes project, and Rook does exactly that.

One major benefit of running Ceph in containers is that is allows collocation of services on the same hardware. Traditionally in Ceph clusters it was expected that Ceph monitors would run on dedicated hardware; when utilizing containers this requirement is removed. For smaller clusters, this can amount to a large saving in the cost of running and purchasing servers. If resources permit, other container-based workloads could also be allowed to run across the Ceph hardware, further increasing the Return on Investment for the hardware purchase. The use of Docker containers reserves the required hardware resources so that workloads cannot impact each other.

To better understand how these two technologies work with Ceph, we first need to cover Kubernetes in more detail and actual containers themselves.

Containers

Although containers in their current form are a relatively new technology, the principle of isolating sets of processes from each other has been around for a long time. What the current set of technologies enhances is the completeness of the isolation. Previous technologies maybe only isolated parts of the filesystem, whereas the latest container technologies also isolate several areas of the operating system and can also provide quotas for hardware resources. One technology in particular, Docker, has risen to become the most popular technology when talking about containers, so much so that the two words are often used interchangeably. The word **container** describes a technology that performs operating system-level virtualization. Docker is a software product that controls primarily Linux features such as groups and namespaces to isolate sets of Linux processes.

It's important to note that, unlike full-blown virtualization solutions such as VMWare, Hyper-V, and KVM, which provides virtualized hardware and require a separate OS instance, containers utilize the operating system of the host. The full OS requirements of virtual machines may lead to several 10s of GB of storage being wasted on the operating system installation and potentially several GB of RAM as well. Containers typically consume overheads of storage and RAM measured in MB, meaning that a lot more containers can be squeezed onto the same hardware when compared to full virtualization technologies.

Containers are also much easier to orchestrate as they are completely configurable from the host system; this, when combined with their ability to be started in milliseconds, means that they are very well suited to dynamically changing environments. Particularly in DevOps environments, they are becoming extremely popular where the line between infrastructure and application is starting to become blurred. The management of infrastructure, which tends to operate at a slower pace than application development, means that in an Agile development environment the infrastructure team is often always playing catch-up. With DevOps and containers, the infrastructure team can concentrate on providing a solid base and the developers can ship their application combined with the OS and middleware required to run.

Kubernetes

The ability to quickly and efficiently spin up 10's of containers in seconds soon makes you realize that. if VM sprawl was bad enough, with containers the problem can easily get a whole lot worse. With the arrival of Docker in the modern IT infrastructure, a need to manage all these containers arose. Enter Kubernetes.

Although several container orchestration technologies are available, Kubernetes has enjoyed wide-ranging success and, as it is the product on which Rook is built, this book will focus on it.

Kubernetes is an open source container-orchestration system for automating the deployment, scaling, and management of containerized applications. It was originally developed at Google to run their internal systems but has since been open sourced and seen its popularity flourish.

Although this chapter will cover deploying an extremely simple Kubernetes cluster to deploy a Ceph cluster with Rook, it is not meant to be a full tutorial and readers are encouraged to seek other resources in order to learn more about Kubernetes.

Deploying a Ceph cluster with Rook

To deploy a Ceph cluster with Rook and Kubernetes, Vagrant will be used to create three VMs that will run the Kubernetes cluster.

The first task you'll complete is the deployment of three VMs via Vagrant. If you have followed the steps at that start of this chapter and used Vagrant to build an environment for Ansible, then you should have everything you require to deploy VMs for the Kubernetes cluster.

The following is the `Vagrantfile` to bring up three VMs; as before, place the contents into a file called `Vagrantfile` in a new directory and then run `vagrant up`:

```
nodes = [
  { :hostname => 'kube1',  :ip => '192.168.0.51', :box => 'xenial64', :ram
=> 2048, :osd => 'yes' },
  { :hostname => 'kube2',  :ip => '192.168.0.52', :box => 'xenial64', :ram
=> 2048, :osd => 'yes' },
  { :hostname => 'kube3',  :ip => '192.168.0.53', :box => 'xenial64', :ram
=> 2048, :osd => 'yes' }
]


Vagrant.configure("2") do |config|
  nodes.each do |node|
    config.vm.define node[:hostname] do |nodeconfig|
      nodeconfig.vm.box = "bento/ubuntu-16.04"
      nodeconfig.vm.hostname = node[:hostname]
      nodeconfig.vm.network :private_network, ip: node[:ip]


      memory = node[:ram] ? node[:ram] : 4096;
```

```
      nodeconfig.vm.provider :virtualbox do |vb|
        vb.customize [
          "modifyvm", :id,
          "--memory", memory.to_s,
        ]
        if node[:osd] == "yes"
          vb.customize [ "createhd", "--filename", "disk_osd-
#{node[:hostname]}", "--size", "10000" ]
          vb.customize [ "storageattach", :id, "--storagectl", "SATA
Controller", "--port", 3, "--device", 0, "--type", "hdd", "--medium",
"disk_osd-#{node[:hostname]}.vdi" ]
        end
      end
    end
    config.hostmanager.enabled = true
    config.hostmanager.manage_guest = true
  end
end
```

```
Bringing machine 'kube1' up with 'virtualbox' provider...
Bringing machine 'kube2' up with 'virtualbox' provider...
Bringing machine 'kube3' up with 'virtualbox' provider...
==> kube1: Importing base box 'bento/ubuntu-16.04'...
==> kube1: Matching MAC address for NAT networking...
==> kube1: Checking if box 'bento/ubuntu-16.04' is up to date...
==> kube1: Setting the name of the VM: ceph_kube_kube1_1539378707808_33813
==> kube1: Clearing any previously set network interfaces...
==> kube1: Preparing network interfaces based on configuration...
    kube1: Adapter 1: nat
    kube1: Adapter 2: hostonly
==> kube1: Forwarding ports...
    kube1: 22 (guest) => 2222 (host) (adapter 1)
==> kube1: Running 'pre-boot' VM customizations...
==> kube1: Booting VM...
==> kube1: Waiting for machine to boot. This may take a few minutes...
    kube1: SSH address: 127.0.0.1:2222
    kube1: SSH username: vagrant
    kube1: SSH auth method: private key
```

SSH in to the first VM, `Kube1`:

```
C:\Users\nick.fisk\Documents\ceph_kube>vagrant ssh kube1
Welcome to Ubuntu 16.04.5 LTS (GNU/Linux 4.4.0-116-generic x86_64)

 * Documentation:  https://help.ubuntu.com
 * Management:     https://landscape.canonical.com
 * Support:        https://ubuntu.com/advantage

0 packages can be updated.
0 updates are security updates.


vagrant@kube1:~$
```

Update the kernel to a newer version; this is required for certain Ceph features in Rook to function correctly:

```
vagrant@kube3:~$ sudo apt-get install linux-generic-hwe-16.04
Reading package lists... Done
Building dependency tree
Reading state information... Done
The following additional packages will be installed:
  amd64-microcode intel-microcode iucode-tool linux-headers-4.15.0-36 linux-headers-4.15.0-36-generic
  linux-headers-generic-hwe-16.04 linux-image-4.15.0-36-generic linux-image-generic-hwe-16.04
  linux-modules-4.15.0-36-generic linux-modules-extra-4.15.0-36-generic thermald
Suggested packages:
  fdutils linux-hwe-tools
The following NEW packages will be installed:
  amd64-microcode intel-microcode iucode-tool linux-generic-hwe-16.04 linux-headers-4.15.0-36
  linux-headers-4.15.0-36-generic linux-headers-generic-hwe-16.04 linux-image-4.15.0-36-generic
  linux-image-generic-hwe-16.04 linux-modules-4.15.0-36-generic linux-modules-extra-4.15.0-36-generic thermald
0 upgraded, 12 newly installed, 0 to remove and 38 not upgraded.
Need to get 67.1 MB of archives.
After this operation, 339 MB of additional disk space will be used.
Do you want to continue? [Y/n]
```

Install Docker, as follows:

```
sudo apt-get install docker.io
```

```
vagrant@kube1:~$ sudo apt-get install docker.io
Reading package lists... Done
Building dependency tree
Reading state information... Done
The following additional packages will be installed:
  bridge-utils cgroupfs-mount ubuntu-fan
Suggested packages:
  mountall aufs-tools debootstrap docker-doc rinse zfs-fuse | zfsutils
The following NEW packages will be installed:
  bridge-utils cgroupfs-mount docker.io ubuntu-fan
0 upgraded, 4 newly installed, 0 to remove and 0 not upgraded.
Need to get 17.1 MB of archives.
After this operation, 90.5 MB of additional disk space will be used.
Do you want to continue? [Y/n] y
```

Enable and start the Docker service, as follows:

```
sudo systemctl start docker
sudo systemctl enable docker
```

```
vagrant@kube1:~$ sudo systemctl enable docker
Synchronizing state of docker.service with SysV init with /lib/systemd/systemd-sysv-install...
Executing /lib/systemd/systemd-sysv-install enable docker
vagrant@kube1:~$ sudo systemctl start docker
vagrant@kube1:~$
```

Disable swap for future boots by editing /etc/fstab and commenting out the swap line:

```
  GNU nano 2.5.3                                    File: /etc/fstab

# /etc/fstab: static file system information.
#
# Use 'blkid' to print the universally unique identifier for a
# device; this may be used with UUID= as a more robust way to name devices
# that works even if disks are added and removed. See fstab(5).
#
# <file system> <mount point>   <type>  <options>       <dump>  <pass>
/dev/mapper/vagrant--vg-root /                ext4    errors=remount-ro 0       1
# /boot was on /dev/sda1 during installation
UUID=2a3d3902-d791-4890-b2ef-136541be4a1f /boot           ext2    defaults        0       2
#/dev/mapper/vagrant--vg-swap_1 none            swap    sw              0       0
```

And also disable swap now, as follows:

```
sudo swapoff -a
```

```
vagrant@kube1:~$ sudo swapoff -a
vagrant@kube1:~$
```

Add the Kubernetes repository, as follows:

```
sudo add-apt-repository "deb http://apt.kubernetes.io/ kubernetes-xenial
main"
```

```
vagrant@kube1:~$ sudo add-apt-repository "deb http://apt.kubernetes.io/ kubernetes-xenial main"
vagrant@kube1:~$
```

Add the Kubernetes GPG key, as follows:

```
sudo curl -s https://packages.cloud.google.com/apt/doc/apt-key.gpg | sudo
apt-key add
```

```
vagrant@kube1:~$ sudo curl -s https://packages.cloud.google.com/apt/doc/apt-key.gpg | sudo apt-key add
OK
vagrant@kube1:~$
```

Install Kubernetes, as follows:

```
sudo apt-get update && sudo apt-get install -y kubeadm kubelet kubectl
```

```
vagrant@kube1:~$ sudo apt-get update && sudo apt-get install -y kubeadm kubelet kubectl
Hit:1 http://security.ubuntu.com/ubuntu xenial-security InRelease
Hit:2 http://archive.ubuntu.com/ubuntu xenial InRelease
Hit:3 http://archive.ubuntu.com/ubuntu xenial-updates InRelease
Hit:4 http://archive.ubuntu.com/ubuntu xenial-backports InRelease
Get:5 https://packages.cloud.google.com/apt kubernetes-xenial InRelease [8,993 B]
Get:6 https://packages.cloud.google.com/apt kubernetes-xenial/main amd64 Packages [20.2 kB]
Fetched 29.2 kB in 1s (24.0 kB/s)
Reading package lists... Done
Reading package lists... Done
Building dependency tree
Reading state information... Done
The following additional packages will be installed:
  cri-tools ebtables kubernetes-cni socat
The following NEW packages will be installed:
  cri-tools ebtables kubeadm kubectl kubelet kubernetes-cni socat
0 upgraded, 7 newly installed, 0 to remove and 38 not upgraded.
Need to get 54.9 MB of archives.
After this operation, 364 MB of additional disk space will be used.
```

Repeat the installation steps for Docker and Kubernetes on both the `kube2` and `kube3` VMs.

Once all the VMs have a working copy of Docker and Kubernetes, we can now initialize the Kubernetes cluster:

```
sudo kubeadm init --apiserver-advertise-address=192.168.0.51 --pod-network-cidr=10.1.0.0/16 --ignore-preflight-errors=NumCPU
```

```
vagrant@kube1:~$ sudo kubeadm init --apiserver-advertise-address=192.168.0.51 --pod-network-cidr=10.1.0.0/16
[init] using Kubernetes version: v1.12.1
[preflight] running pre-flight checks
[preflight/images] Pulling images required for setting up a Kubernetes cluster
[preflight/images] This might take a minute or two, depending on the speed of your internet connection
[preflight/images] You can also perform this action in beforehand using 'kubeadm config images pull'
```

At the end of the process, a command string is output; make a note of this as it is needed to join our additional nodes to the cluster. An example of this is as follows:

```
You can now join any number of machines by running the following on each node
as root:

  kubeadm join 192.168.0.51:6443 --token c68o8u.92pvgestk26za6md --discovery-token-ca-cert-hash sha256:3954fad0089dcf72d0d828b440888b6e97465f783bde403868f098af67e8f073
```

Now that we have installed Docker and Kubernetes on all our nodes and have initialized the master, let's add the remaining two nodes into the cluster. Remember that string of text you were asked to note down? Now we can run it on the two remaining nodes:

```
sudo kubeadm join 192.168.0.51:6443 --token c68o8u.92pvgestk26za6md --discovery-token-ca-cert-hash sha256:3954fad0089dcf72d0d828b440888b6e97465f783bde403868f098af67e8f073
```

```
vagrant@kube2:~$ sudo kubeadm join 192.168.0.51:6443 --token c68o8u.92pvgestk26za6md --discovery-token-ca-cert-hash sha256:3954fad0089dcf72d0d828b44
0888b6e97465f783bde403868f098af67e8f073
[preflight] running pre-flight checks
        [WARNING RequiredIPVSKernelModulesAvailable]: the IPVS proxier will not be used, because the following required kernel modules are not loade
d: [ip_vs_rr ip_vs_wrr ip_vs_sh ip_vs] or no builtin kernel ipvs support: map[ip_vs:{} ip_vs_rr:{} ip_vs_wrr:{} ip_vs_sh:{} nf_conntrack_ipv4:{}]
you can solve this problem with following methods:
1. Run 'modprobe -- ' to load missing kernel modules;
2. Provide the missing builtin kernel ipvs support

[discovery] Trying to connect to API Server "192.168.0.51:6443"
[discovery] Created cluster-info discovery client, requesting info from "https://192.168.0.51:6443"
[discovery] Requesting info from "https://192.168.0.51:6443" again to validate TLS against the pinned public key
[discovery] Cluster info signature and contents are valid and TLS certificate validates against pinned roots, will use API Server "192.168.0.51:6443
[discovery] Successfully established connection with API Server "192.168.0.51:6443"
[kubelet] Downloading configuration for the kubelet from the "kubelet-config-1.12" ConfigMap in the kube-system namespace
[kubelet] Writing kubelet configuration to file "/var/lib/kubelet/config.yaml"
[kubelet] Writing kubelet environment file with flags to file "/var/lib/kubelet/kubeadm-flags.env"
[preflight] Activating the kubelet service
[tlsbootstrap] Waiting for the kubelet to perform the TLS Bootstrap...
[patchnode] Uploading the CRI Socket information "/var/run/dockershim.sock" to the Node API object "kube2" as an annotation

This node has joined the cluster:
* Certificate signing request was sent to apiserver and a response was received.
* The Kubelet was informed of the new secure connection details.

Run 'kubectl get nodes' on the master to see this node join the cluster.
```

```
mkdir -p $HOME/.kube
sudo cp -i /etc/kubernetes/admin.conf $HOME/.kube/config
sudo chown $(id -u):$(id -g) $HOME/.kube/config
```

```
vagrant@kube1:~$ kubectl get nodes
NAME     STATUS   ROLES    AGE      VERSION
kube1    Ready    master   32m      v1.12.1
kube2    Ready    <none>   9m34s    v1.12.1
kube3    Ready    <none>   6m25s    v1.12.1
```

We can now install some additional container networking support. Flannel, a simple networking add-on for Kubernetes, uses VXLAN as an overlay to enable container-to-container networking. First download the `yaml` file from GitHub:

```
wget
https://raw.githubusercontent.com/coreos/flannel/master/Documentation/kube-
flannel.yml
```

```
vagrant@kube1:~ $ wget https://raw.githubusercontent.com/coreos/flannel/master/Documentation/kube-flannel.yml
--2018-10-13 21:19:35--  https://raw.githubusercontent.com/coreos/flannel/master/Documentation/kube-flannel.yml
Resolving raw.githubusercontent.com (raw.githubusercontent.com)... 151.101.0.133, 151.101.64.133, 151.101.128.133, ...
Connecting to raw.githubusercontent.com (raw.githubusercontent.com)|151.101.0.133|:443... connected.
HTTP request sent, awaiting response... 200 OK
Length: 10599 (10K) [text/plain]
Saving to: 'kube-flannel.yml'

kube-flannel.yml           100%[===================================================================>]  10.35K  --.-KB/s    in 0s

2018-10-13 21:19:35 (138 MB/s) - 'kube-flannel.yml' saved [10599/10599]
```

Before we install the Flannel networking component, we need to make a few changes to the YAML spec file:

```
nano kube-flannel.yml
```

Don't indent with tabs, use spaces.

We need to find the following lines and make the required changes, as follows:

- Line 76: `"Network": "10.1.0.0/16":`

```
            ]
        }
    net-conf.json: |
        {
            "Network": "10.1.0.0/16",
            "Backend": {
                "Type": "vxlan"
            }
        }
    ---
```

- Line 126: `- --iface=eth1:`

```
        containers:
        - name: kube-flannel
          image: quay.io/coreos/flannel:v0.10.0-amd64
          command:
          - /opt/bin/flanneld
          args:
          - --ip-masq
          - --kube-subnet-mgr
          - --iface=eth1
          resources:
            requests:
              cpu: "100m"
```

Now we can issue the relevant Kubernetes command to apply the specification file and install Flannel networking:

```
kubectl apply -f kube-flannel.yml
```

```
vagrant@kube1:~$ kubectl apply -f kube-flannel.yml
clusterrole.rbac.authorization.k8s.io/flannel unchanged
clusterrolebinding.rbac.authorization.k8s.io/flannel unchanged
serviceaccount/flannel unchanged
configmap/kube-flannel-cfg unchanged
daemonset.extensions/kube-flannel-ds-amd64 created
daemonset.extensions/kube-flannel-ds-arm64 created
daemonset.extensions/kube-flannel-ds-arm created
daemonset.extensions/kube-flannel-ds-ppc64le created
daemonset.extensions/kube-flannel-ds-s390x created
```

After networking has been installed, we can confirm everything is working and that our Kubernetes worker nodes are ready to run workloads:

```
$ kubectl get nodes
```

```
vagrant@kube1:~$ kubectl get nodes
NAME     STATUS   ROLES      AGE      VERSION
kube1    Ready    master     32m      v1.12.1
kube2    Ready    <none>     9m34s    v1.12.1
kube3    Ready    <none>     6m25s    v1.12.1
```

Now let's also check that all containers that support internal Kubernetes services are running:

```
$ kubectl get pods --all-namespaces -o wide
```

```
vagrant@kube1:~$ kubectl get pods --all-namespaces -o wide
NAMESPACE     NAME                             READY   STATUS    RESTARTS   AGE   IP             NODE    NOMINATED NODE
kube-system   coredns-576cbf47c7-jqdvs         1/1     Running   0          23h   10.1.1.2       kube2   <none>
kube-system   coredns-576cbf47c7-xhcvr         1/1     Running   0          23h   10.1.1.3       kube2   <none>
kube-system   etcd-kube1                       1/1     Running   0          23h   192.168.0.51   kube1   <none>
kube-system   kube-apiserver-kube1             1/1     Running   0          23h   192.168.0.51   kube1   <none>
kube-system   kube-controller-manager-kube1    1/1     Running   0          23h   192.168.0.51   kube1   <none>
kube-system   kube-flannel-ds-amd64-5vrft      1/1     Running   0          22h   192.168.0.52   kube2   <none>
kube-system   kube-flannel-ds-amd64-88zkl      1/1     Running   0          22h   192.168.0.53   kube3   <none>
kube-system   kube-flannel-ds-amd64-xsqw6      1/1     Running   0          22h   192.168.0.51   kube1   <none>
kube-system   kube-proxy-ctf59                 1/1     Running   0          22h   192.168.0.53   kube3   <none>
kube-system   kube-proxy-fjxfl                 1/1     Running   0          22h   192.168.0.52   kube2   <none>
kube-system   kube-proxy-jzxgv                 1/1     Running   0          23h   192.168.0.51   kube1   <none>
kube-system   kube-scheduler-kube1             1/1     Running   0          23h   192.168.0.51   kube1   <none>
```

Note that the container networking service (Flannel) that we installed in the previous step has automatically been deployed across all three nodes. At this point, we have a fully functioning Kubernetes cluster that is ready to run whatever containers we wish to run on it.

We can now deploy Rook into the Kubernetes cluster. First, let's clone the Rook project from GitHub:

```
$ git clone https://github.com/rook/rook.git
```

```
vagrant@kube1:~$ git clone https://github.com/rook/rook.git
Cloning into 'rook'...
remote: Enumerating objects: 42, done.
remote: Counting objects: 100% (42/42), done.
remote: Compressing objects: 100% (34/34), done.
remote: Total 19118 (delta 9), reused 30 (delta 8), pack-reused 19076
Receiving objects: 100% (19118/19118), 6.39 MiB | 1.67 MiB/s, done.
Resolving deltas: 100% (12291/12291), done.
Checking connectivity... done.
```

Change to the `examples` directory, as follows:

```
$ cd rook/cluster/examples/kubernetes/ceph/
```

```
vagrant@kube1:~$ cd rook/cluster/examples/kubernetes/ceph/
vagrant@kube1:~/rook/cluster/examples/kubernetes/ceph$
```

And now finally create the Rook-powered Ceph cluster by running the following two commands:

```
$ kubectl create -f operator.yaml
```

```
vagrant@kube1:~/rook/cluster/examples/kubernetes/ceph$ kubectl create -f operator.yaml
namespace/rook-ceph-system created
customresourcedefinition.apiextensions.k8s.io/clusters.ceph.rook.io created
customresourcedefinition.apiextensions.k8s.io/filesystems.ceph.rook.io created
customresourcedefinition.apiextensions.k8s.io/objectstores.ceph.rook.io created
customresourcedefinition.apiextensions.k8s.io/pools.ceph.rook.io created
customresourcedefinition.apiextensions.k8s.io/volumes.rook.io created
clusterrole.rbac.authorization.k8s.io/rook-ceph-cluster-mgmt created
role.rbac.authorization.k8s.io/rook-ceph-system created
clusterrole.rbac.authorization.k8s.io/rook-ceph-global created
serviceaccount/rook-ceph-system created
rolebinding.rbac.authorization.k8s.io/rook-ceph-system created
clusterrolebinding.rbac.authorization.k8s.io/rook-ceph-global created
deployment.apps/rook-ceph-operator created
```

```
$ kubectl create -f cluster.yaml
```

```
vagrant@kube1:~/rook/cluster/examples/kubernetes/ceph$ kubectl create -f cluster.yaml
namespace/rook-ceph created
serviceaccount/rook-ceph-cluster created
role.rbac.authorization.k8s.io/rook-ceph-cluster created
rolebinding.rbac.authorization.k8s.io/rook-ceph-cluster-mgmt created
rolebinding.rbac.authorization.k8s.io/rook-ceph-cluster created
cluster.ceph.rook.io/rook-ceph created
```

To confirm our Rook cluster is now working, let's check the running containers under the Rook namespace:

```
$ kubectl get pods --all-namespaces -o wide
```

```
rook-ceph-system   rook-ceph-agent-bd8jb              1/1   Running   0   9m16s   192.168.0.52   kube2   <none>
rook-ceph-system   rook-ceph-agent-rtsz6              1/1   Running   0   9m16s   192.168.0.53   kube3   <none>
rook-ceph-system   rook-ceph-operator-7dd46f4549-68tnk 1/1  Running   0   11m     10.1.1.4       kube2   <none>
rook-ceph-system   rook-discover-cj7f5                1/1   Running   0   9m16s   10.1.2.2       kube3   <none>
rook-ceph-system   rook-discover-nmp58                1/1   Running   0   9m16s   10.1.1.5       kube2   <none>
rook-ceph          rook-ceph-mon-a-77f669c4d6-fmmqk   1/1   Running   0   9m      10.1.1.6       kube2   <none>
rook-ceph          rook-ceph-mon-b-75779984c9-vb9zg   1/1   Running   0   8m40s   10.1.2.3       kube3   <none>
```

You will see that Rook has deployed a couple of `mons` and has also started some discover containers. These discover containers run a discovery script to locate storage devices attached to the Kubernetes physical host. Once the discovery process has completed for the first time, Kubernetes will then run a one-shot container to prepare the OSD by formatting the disk and adding the OSD into the cluster. If you wait a few minutes and re-run the `get pods` command, you should hopefully see that Rook has detected the two disks connected to `kube2` and `kube3` and created `osd` containers for them:

```
rook-ceph-system   rook-ceph-agent-bd8jb                    1/1   Running     0   21m     192.168.0.52   kube2   <none>
rook-ceph-system   rook-ceph-agent-rtsz6                    1/1   Running     0   21m     192.168.0.53   kube3   <none>
rook-ceph-system   rook-ceph-operator-7dd46f4549-68tnk      1/1   Running     0   23m     10.1.1.4       kube2   <none>
rook-ceph-system   rook-discover-cj7f5                      1/1   Running     0   21m     10.1.2.2       kube3   <none>
rook-ceph-system   rook-discover-nmp58                      1/1   Running     0   21m     10.1.1.5       kube2   <none>
rook-ceph          rook-ceph-mgr-a-bd7857c5d-prkvj          1/1   Running     0   7m14s   10.1.2.4       kube3   <none>
rook-ceph          rook-ceph-mon-a-77f669c4d6-fmmqk         1/1   Running     0   21m     10.1.1.6       kube2   <none>
rook-ceph          rook-ceph-mon-b-75779984c9-vb9zg         1/1   Running     0   21m     10.1.2.3       kube3   <none>
rook-ceph          rook-ceph-mon-d-78775579cf-kcg95         1/1   Running     0   7m38s   10.1.1.7       kube2   <none>
rook-ceph          rook-ceph-osd-0-964d6456c-f6tk6          1/1   Running     0   6m57s   10.1.1.9       kube2   <none>
rook-ceph          rook-ceph-osd-1-5d746f779c-4cnrw         1/1   Running     0   6m57s   10.1.2.6       kube3   <none>
rook-ceph          rook-ceph-osd-prepare-kube2-68hvg        0/1   Completed   0   7m10s   10.1.1.8       kube2   <none>
rook-ceph          rook-ceph-osd-prepare-kube3-dbqrk        0/1   Completed   0   7m10s   10.1.2.5       kube3   <none>
```

To interact with the cluster, let's deploy the toolbox container; this is a simple container containing the Ceph installation and the necessary cluster keys:

```
$ kubectl create -f toolbox.yaml
```

```
vagrant@kube1:~/rook/cluster/examples/kubernetes/ceph$ kubectl create -f toolbox.yaml
deployment.apps/rook-ceph-tools created
```

Now execute `bash` in the toolbox container:

```
kubectl -n rook-ceph exec -it $(kubectl -n rook-ceph get pod -l "app=rook-ceph-tools" -o jsonpath='{.items[0].metadata.name}') bash
```

This will present you with a root shell running inside the Ceph toolbox container, where we can check the status of the Ceph cluster by running `ceph -s` and see the current OSDs with `ceph osd tree`:

```
[root@kube3 /]# ceph -s
  cluster:
    id:     a636514f-2cf9-461f-a4f1-c402f3f0470e
    health: HEALTH_OK

  services:
    mon: 3 daemons, quorum a,d,b
    mgr: a(active)
    osd: 2 osds: 2 up, 2 in

  data:
    pools:   0 pools, 0 pgs
    objects: 0 objects, 0 bytes
    usage:   14575 MB used, 108 GB / 122 GB avail
    pgs:

[root@kube3 /]# ceph osd tree
ID CLASS WEIGHT  TYPE NAME       STATUS REWEIGHT PRI-AFF
-1       0.12000 root default
-3       0.06000     host kube2
 0   hdd 0.06000         osd.0      up  1.00000 1.00000
-2       0.06000     host kube3
 1   hdd 0.06000         osd.1      up  1.00000 1.00000
[root@kube3 /]# exit
```

You will notice that, although we built three VMs, Rook has only deployed OSDs on `kube2` and `kube3`. This is because by default Kubernetes will not schedule containers to run on the master node; in a production cluster this is the desired behavior, but for testing we can remove this limitation.

Exit back to the master Kubernetes node and run the following:

```
kubectl taint nodes $(hostname) node-role.kubernetes.io/master:NoSchedule-
```

```
vagrant@kube1:~/rook/cluster/examples/kubernetes/ceph$ kubectl taint nodes $(hostname) node-role.kubernetes.io/master:NoSchedule-
node/kube1 untainted
```

You will notice that Kubernetes will deploy a couple of new containers onto `kube1`, but it won't deploy any new OSDs; this is due to a current limitation to the effect that the `rook-ceph-operator` component only deploys new OSDs on first startup. In order to detect newly available disks and prepare them as OSDs, the `rook-ceph-operator` container needs to be deleted.

Run the following command, but replace the container name with the one that is listed from the `get pods` command:

```
kubectl -n rook-ceph-system delete pods rook-ceph-operator-7dd46f4549-68tnk
```

```
vagrant@kube1:~/rook/cluster/examples/kubernetes/ceph$ kubectl -n rook-ceph-system delete pods,services rook-ceph-operator-7dd46f4549-68tnk
pod "rook-ceph-operator-7dd46f4549-68tnk" deleted
```

Kubernetes will now automatically spin up a new `rook-ceph-operator` container and in doing so will kick-start the deployment of the new `osd`; this can be confirmed by looking at the list of running containers again:

```
rook-ceph-system    rook-ceph-agent-bd8jb                   1/1    Running     0    25h     192.168.0.52    kube2    <none>
rook-ceph-system    rook-ceph-agent-nvszl                   1/1    Running     2    58m     192.168.0.51    kube1    <none>
rook-ceph-system    rook-ceph-agent-rtsz6                   1/1    Running     0    25h     192.168.0.53    kube3    <none>
rook-ceph-system    rook-ceph-operator-7dd46f4549-8tpkx     1/1    Running     0    5m26s   10.1.1.11       kube2    <none>
rook-ceph-system    rook-discover-6grvv                     1/1    Running     1    58m     10.1.0.4        kube1    <none>
rook-ceph-system    rook-discover-cj7f5                     1/1    Running     0    25h     10.1.2.2        kube3    <none>
rook-ceph-system    rook-discover-nmp58                     1/1    Running     0    25h     10.1.1.5        kube2    <none>
rook-ceph           rook-ceph-mgr-a-bd7857c5d-prkvj         1/1    Running     0    24h     10.1.2.4        kube3    <none>
rook-ceph           rook-ceph-mon-a-77f669c4d6-fmmqk        1/1    Running     0    25h     10.1.1.6        kube2    <none>
rook-ceph           rook-ceph-mon-b-75779984c9-vb9zg        1/1    Running     0    25h     10.1.2.3        kube3    <none>
rook-ceph           rook-ceph-mon-d-78775579cf-kcg95        1/1    Running     0    24h     10.1.1.7        kube2    <none>
rook-ceph           rook-ceph-mon-e-6584984554-r4886        1/1    Running     0    56s     10.1.0.6        kube1    <none>
rook-ceph           rook-ceph-osd-0-964d6456c-f6tk6         1/1    Running     0    24h     10.1.1.9        kube2    <none>
rook-ceph           rook-ceph-osd-1-5d746f779c-4cnrw        1/1    Running     0    24h     10.1.2.6        kube3    <none>
rook-ceph           rook-ceph-osd-2-6765c4f9c6-74rcr        1/1    Running     0    16s     10.1.0.8        kube1    <none>
rook-ceph           rook-ceph-osd-prepare-kube1-pq5mc       0/1    Completed   0    34s     10.1.0.7        kube1    <none>
rook-ceph           rook-ceph-osd-prepare-kube2-spsfb       0/1    Completed   0    32s     10.1.1.12       kube2    <none>
rook-ceph           rook-ceph-osd-prepare-kube3-vwrcw       0/1    Completed   0    30s     10.1.2.7        kube3    <none>
rook-ceph           rook-ceph-tools-5bc8b8f97-fqx5g         1/1    Running     0    68m     192.168.0.53    kube3    <none>
```

You can see `kube1` has run a `rook-discover` container, a `rook-ceph-osd-prepare`, and finally a `rook-ceph-osd` container, which in this case is `osd` number 2.

We can also check, by using our toolbox container as well, that the new `osd` has joined the cluster successfully:

```
[root@kube3 /]# ceph -s
  cluster:
    id:     a636514f-2cf9-461f-a4f1-c402f3f0470e
    health: HEALTH_WARN
            clock skew detected on mon.e

  services:
    mon: 4 daemons, quorum a,d,e,b
    mgr: a(active)
    osd: 3 osds: 3 up, 3 in

  data:
    pools:   0 pools, 0 pgs
    objects: 0 objects, 0 bytes
    usage:   22737 MB used, 162 GB / 184 GB avail
    pgs:
```

Now that Rook has deployed our full test Ceph cluster, we need to make use of it and create some RADOS pools and also consume some storage with a client container. To demonstrate this process, we will deploy a CephFS filesystem.

Before we jump straight into deploying the filesystem, let's first have a look at the example yaml file we will be deploying. Make sure you are still in the `~/rook/cluster/examples/kubernetes/ceph` directory and use a text editor to view the `filesystem.yaml` file:

```yaml
apiVersion: ceph.rook.io/v1beta1
kind: Filesystem
metadata:
  name: myfs
  namespace: rook-ceph
spec:
  # The metadata pool spec
  metadataPool:
    replicated:
      # Increase the replication size if you have more than one osd
      size: 1
  # The list of data pool specs
  dataPools:
    - failureDomain: osd
      replicated:
        size: 1
  # The metadata service (mds) configuration
  metadataServer:
    # The number of active MDS instances
    activeCount: 1
```

You can see that the file contents describe the RADOS pools that will be created and the MDS instances that are required for the filesystem. In this example, three pools will be deployed, two replicated and one erasure-coded for the actual data. Two MDS servers will be deployed, one running as active and the other running as a standby-replay.

Exit the text editor and now deploy the CephFS configuration in the yaml file:

```
$ kubectl create -f filesystem.yaml
```

```
vagrant@kube1:~/rook/cluster/examples/kubernetes/ceph$ kubectl create -f filesystem.yaml
filesystem.ceph.rook.io/myfs created
```

Now let's jump back into our toolbox container, check the status, and see what's been created:

```
[root@kube3 /]# ceph -s
  cluster:
    id:     a636514f-2cf9-461f-a4f1-c402f3f0470e
    health: HEALTH_WARN
            1/4 mons down, quorum a,d,b

  services:
    mon: 4 daemons, quorum a,d,b, out of quorum: e
    mgr: a(active)
    mds: myfs-0/0/1 up
    osd: 3 osds: 3 up, 3 in

  data:
    pools:   2 pools, 200 pgs
    objects: 0 objects, 0 bytes
    usage:   22892 MB used, 162 GB / 184 GB avail
    pgs:     200 active+clean
```

```
[root@kube3 /]# ceph osd lspools
3 myfs-metadata,4 myfs-data0,
```

We can see that two pools have been created, one for the CephFS metadata and one for the actual data stored on the CephFS filesystem.

To give an example of how Rook can then be consumed by application containers, we will now deploy a small NGINX web server container that stores its HTML content on the CephFS filesystem.

Place the following inside a file called `nginx.yaml`:

```
apiVersion: v1
kind: Pod
metadata:
 name: nginx
spec:
 containers:
 - name: nginx
 image: nginx:1.7.9
 ports:
 - containerPort: 80
 volumeMounts:
 - name: www
 mountPath: /usr/share/nginx/html
 volumes:
 - name: www
```

```
flexVolume:
driver: ceph.rook.io/rook
fsType: ceph
options:
fsName: myfs
clusterNamespace: rook-ceph
```

And now use the `kubectl` command to create the `pod/nginx`:

```
vagrant@kube1:~$ kubectl create -f nginx.yaml
pod/nginx created
```

After a while, the container will be started and will enter a running state; use the `get pods` command to verify this:

```
vagrant@kube1:~$ kubectl get pods --all-namespaces -o wide
NAMESPACE       NAME        READY   STATUS    RESTARTS   AGE   IP           NODE    NOMINATED NODE
default         nginx       1/1     Running   0          18s   10.1.0.34    kube1   <none>
```

We can now start a quick Bash shell on this container to confirm the CephFS mount has worked:

```
$ kubectl exec -it nginx bash
```

```
vagrant@kube1:~$ kubectl exec -it nginx bash
root@nginx:/# df -h
Filesystem                                                Size  Used Avail Use% Mounted on
none                                                      62G   5.6G   53G  10% /
tmpfs                                                     1001M    0 1001M   0% /dev
tmpfs                                                     1001M    0 1001M   0% /sys/fs/cgroup
/dev/mapper/vagrant--vg-root                              62G   5.6G   53G  10% /dev/termination-log
shm                                                       64M     0   64M   0% /dev/shm
/dev/mapper/vagrant--vg-root                              62G   5.6G   53G  10% /etc/resolv.conf
/dev/mapper/vagrant--vg-root                              62G   5.6G   53G  10% /etc/hostname
/dev/mapper/vagrant--vg-root                              62G   5.6G   53G  10% /etc/hosts
/dev/mapper/vagrant--vg-root                              62G   5.6G   53G  10% /var/cache/nginx
10.104.57.91:6790,10.98.94.164:6790,10.110.120.205:6790:/ 185G  24G  161G  13% /usr/share/nginx/html
tmpfs                                                     1001M  12K 1001M   1% /run/secrets/kubernetes.io/serviceaccount
tmpfs                                                     1001M    0 1001M   0% /proc/kcore
tmpfs                                                     1001M    0 1001M   0% /proc/timer_list
tmpfs                                                     1001M    0 1001M   0% /proc/timer_stats
tmpfs                                                     1001M    0 1001M   0% /proc/sched_debug
tmpfs                                                     1001M    0 1001M   0% /sys/firmware
```

We can see that the CephFS filesystem has been mounted into `/usr/share/nginx/html`. This has been done without having to install any Ceph components in the container and without any configuration or copying of key rings. Rook has taken care of all of this behind the scenes; once this is understood and appreciated, the real power of Rook can be seen. If the simple NGINX pod example is expanded to become an auto-scaling service that spins up multiple containers based on load, the flexibility given by Rook and Ceph to automatically present the same shared storage across the web farm with no additional configuration is very useful.

Summary

In this chapter, you learned about Ceph's various deployment methods and the differences between them. You will now also have a basic understanding of how Ansible works and how to deploy a Ceph cluster with it. It would be advisable at this point to continue investigating and practicing the deployment and configuration of Ceph with Ansible, so that you are confident enough to use it in production environments. The remainder of this book will also assume that you have fully understood the contents of this chapter in order to manipulate the configuration of Ceph.

You have also learned about the exciting new developments in deploying Ceph in containers running on the Kubernetes platform. Although the Rook project is still in the early stages of development, it is clear it is already a very powerful tool that will enable Ceph to function to the best of its ability while at the same time simplifying the deployment and administration required. With the continued success enjoyed by Kubernetes in becoming the recommended container management platform, integrating Ceph with the use of Rook will result in a perfect match of technologies.

It is highly recommended that the reader should continue to learn further about Kubernetes as this chapter has only scratched the surface of the functionality it offers. There are strong signs across the industry that containerization is going to be the technology for deploying and managing applications and having an understanding of both Kubernetes and how Ceph integrates with Rook is highly recommended.

Questions

1. What piece of software can be used to rapidly deploy test environments?
2. Should vagrant be used to deploy production environments?
3. What project enables the deployment of Ceph on top of Kubernetes?
4. What is Docker?
5. What is the Ansible file called which is used to run a series of commands?

3
BlueStore

In this chapter, you'll learn about BlueStore, the new object store in Ceph designed to replace the existing filestore. Its increased performance and enhanced feature set are designed to allow Ceph to continue to grow and provide a resilient high-performance distributed storage system for the future. Since the Luminous release, BlueStore is now the recommended and default object store that's used when creating new OSDs. This chapter will cover how BlueStore works and why it is much better suited than Filestore for Ceph's requirements. Then by following a step by step tutorial you will be guided through how to upgrade a Ceph cluster to BlueStore.

In this chapter, you'll learn the following topics:

- What is BlueStore?
- The limitations of filestore
- What problems BlueStore overcome
- The components of BlueStore and how it works
- Introduction to `ceph-volume`
- How to deploy BlueStore OSDs
- Approaches to upgrading live clusters from filestore to BlueStore

What is BlueStore?

BlueStore is a Ceph object store that's primarily designed to address the limitations of filestore, which, prior to the Luminous release, was the default object store. Initially, a new object store named NewStore was being developed to replace filestore. NewStore was a combination of RocksDB, a key–value store that stored metadata and a standard **Portable Operating System Interface (POSIX)** filesystem for the actual objects. However, it quickly became apparent that using a POSIX filesystem introduced high overheads and restrictions, which was one of the key reasons for trying to move away from using filestore in the first place.

Hence, BlueStore was born. Using raw block devices in combination with RocksDB, a number of problems that had stunted NewStore were solved. The name BlueStore was a reflection of the combination of the words Block and NewStore:

> *Block + NewStore = BlewStore = BlueStore*

BlueStore is designed to remove the double write penalty associated with filestore and improve performance that can be obtained from the same hardware. Also, with the new ability to have more control over the way objects are stored on disk, additional features, such as checksums and compression, can be implemented.

Why was it needed?

The previous object store in Ceph, filestore, has a number of limitations that have started to limit the scale at which Ceph can operate, as well as the features that it can offer. The following are some of the main reasons why BlueStore was needed.

Ceph's requirements

An object in Ceph along with its data also has certain metadata associated with it, and it's crucial that both the data and metadata are updated atomically. If either of this metadata or data is updated without the other, the whole consistency model of Ceph is at risk. To ensure that these updates occur atomically, they need to be carried out in a single transaction.

Filestore limitations

Filestore was originally designed as an object store to enable developers to test Ceph on their local machines. Because of its stability, it quickly became the standard object store and found itself in use in production clusters throughout the world.

Initially, the thought behind filestore was that the upcoming **B-tree file system (btrfs)**, which offered transaction support, would allow Ceph to offload the atomic requirements to btrfs. Transactions would allow an application to send a series of requests to btrfs and only receive acknowledgement once all were committed to stable storage. Without a transaction support, if there was an interruption halfway through a Ceph write operation, either the data or metadata could have been missing or one could be out of sync with the other.

Unfortunately, the reliance on btrfs to solve these problems turned out to be a false hope, and several limitations were discovered. Btrfs can still be used with filestore, but there are numerous known issues that can affect the stability of Ceph.

In the end, it turned out that XFS was the best choice to use with filestore, but XFS had the major limitation that it didn't support transactions, meaning that there was no way for Ceph to guarantee atomicity of its writes. The solution to this was the write-ahead journal. All writes, including data and metadata, would first be written into a journal, located on a raw block device. Once the filesystem containing the data and metadata confirmed that all data had been safely flushed to disk, the journal entries could be flushed. A beneficial side effect of this is that, when using an SSD to hold the journal for a spinning disk, it acts like a write back cache, lowering the latency of writes to the speed of the SSD; however, if the filestore journal resides on the same storage device as the data partition, then throughput will be at least halved.

In the case of spinning-disk OSDs, this can lead to very poor performance, as the disk heads will constantly be moving between two areas of the disks, even for sequential operations. Although filestore on SSD-based OSDs doesn't suffer nearly the same performance penalty, their throughput is still effectively halved because double the amount of data needs to be written due to the filestore journal. In either case, this loss of performance is very undesirable, and in the case of flash drives, this wears the device faster, requiring the more expensive version of flash, called write endurance flash. The following diagram shows how filestore and its journal interacts with a block device. You can see that all data operations have to go through the filestore journal and the filesystems journal:

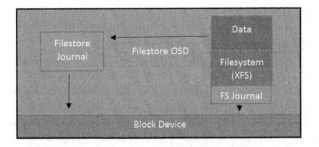

Additional challenges with filestore arose from developers trying to control the actions of the underlying POSIX filesystem to perform and behave in a way that Ceph required. A large amount of work has been done over the years by filesystem developers to try and make filesystems intelligent and to predict how an application might submit I/O. In the case of Ceph, a lot of these optimizations interfere with what it's trying to instruct the filesystem to do, requiring more workarounds and complexity.

Object metadata is stored in combinations of filesystem attributes, called **extended attributes (XATTRs)**, and in a **LevelDB** key–value store, which also resides on the OSD disk. LevelDB was chosen at the time of filestore's creation rather than RocksDB, as RocksDB wasn't available and LevelDB suited a lot of Ceph's requirements.

Ceph is designed to scale to petabytes of data and store billions of objects. However, because of limitations around the number of files you can reasonably store in a directory, further workarounds to help limit this were introduced. Objects are stored in a hierarchy of hashed directory names; when the number of files in one of these folders reaches the set limit, the directory is split into another level and the objects are moved.

However, there's a trade-off to improving the speed of object enumeration: when these directory splits occur, they impact performance as the objects are moved into the correct directories. On larger disks, the increased number of directories puts additional pressure on the VFS cache and can lead to additional performance penalties for infrequently accessed objects.

As this book will cover in the chapter on performance tuning, a major performance bottleneck in filestore is when XFS has to start looking up inodes and directory entries that aren't currently cached in RAM. For scenarios where there are a large number of objects stored per OSD, there is currently no real solution to this problem, and it's quite common to for a Ceph cluster to gradually slow down as it fills up.

Moving away from storing objects on a POSIX filesystem is really the only way to solve most of these problems.

Why is BlueStore the solution?

BlueStore was designed to address these limitations. Following the development of NewStore, it was obvious that trying to use a POSIX filesystem as the underlying storage layer in any approach would introduce a number of issues that were also present in filestore. In order for Ceph to be able to achieve a guaranteed level of performance, that was expected from the underlying storage, it also needed to have direct block-level access to the storage devices without the additional overheads of a separate Linux filesystem. By storing metadata in RocksDB and the actual object data directly on block devices, Ceph can leverage much better control over the underlying storage and at the same time provide better performance.

How BlueStore works

The following diagram shows how BlueStore interacts with a block device. Unlike filestore, data is directly written to the block device and metadata operations are handled by RocksDB:

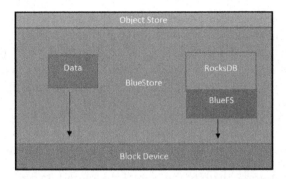

The block device is divided between RocksDB data storage and the actual user data stored in Ceph. Each object is stored as a number of blobs allocated from the block device. RocksDB contains metadata for each object and tracks the utilization and allocation information for the data blobs.

RocksDB

RocksDB is a high-performance key–value store that was originally forked from LevelDB, but, after development, Facebook went on to offer significant performance improvements suited for multiprocessor servers with low-latency storage devices. It has also had numerous feature enhancements, some of which are used in BlueStore.

RocksDB is used to store metadata about the stored objects, which was previously handled using a combination of LevelDB and XATTRs in filestore.

A key characteristic of RocksDB is the way in which data is written down in the levels of the database. It owes this characteristic to its origins in LevelDB. New data is written into a memory-based table with an optional transaction log on persistent storage, the WAL; as this memory-based table fills up, data is moved down to the next level of the database by a process called compaction. When that level fills up, data is migrated down again, and so on. All of these levels are stored in what RocksDB calls SST files. In Ceph, each of these levels are configured to be 10 times the size of the previous level, which brings some interesting factors into play if you're trying to store the whole of the RocksDB on SSD in a hybrid HDD–SSD layout.

All new data is written into the memory-based table and WAL, the memory based table is known as level 0. BlueStore configures level 0 as 256 MB. The default size multiplier between levels is a factor of ten, this means that level 1 is also 256 MB, level 2 is 2.56 GB, level 3 is 25.6 GB, and level 4 would be 256 GB. For most Ceph use cases the average total metadata size per OSD should be around 20-30GB, with the hot data set typically being less than this. It would be hoped that levels 0, 1, and 2 would contain most of the hot data for writes, and so sizing an SSD partition to at least 3 GB should mean that these levels are stored on SSD. Write performance should be good as the metadata for writes will be hitting the SSDs; however, when reading metadata—say, during client read requests—there is a chance that the metadata may live in level 3 or 4, and so will have to be read off of a spinning disk, which would have a negative impact on latency and increase disk load.

Therefore, the obvious solution would be to somehow calculate how big you believe the BlueStore metadata may grow for your dataset and size the RocksDB storage to ensure that it can all be stored on SSD. There are two difficulties in accomplishing this.

Firstly, it's very difficult to precalculate the size of the metadata based on the size of the actual data. Depending on the client model—RBD, CephFS, or RGW—differing amounts of metadata will be stored. Additionally, things such as snapshots and whether you are using replicated- or erasure-coded pools will also lead to differing sizes of metadata.

The next challenge is sizing your flash device correctly to ensure that all of the metadata fits. As mentioned previously, RocksDB compacts data down through the various levels of the database. When BlueStore creates the files for the RocksDB, it will only place a certain level on your flash device if the whole of that level would fit in it. Therefore, there are minimum sizes required for each level to ensure that the level is actually located on flash. For example, to ensure that the 2.56 GB level 2 part of the DB fits on flash, you need to have at least a 4-5 GB SSD partition. This is because level 0 and level 1 and level 2 all need to fit, as well as a small amount of overhead. For level 3 to fit in its entirety, you would need just over 30 G; any smaller and the extra space over level 2 would not be used. To ensure that level 4 would fit, you would likely need over 300 GB of flash space.

Storing the WAL on a faster storage device—which can help to lower the latency of RocksDB operations—is recommended if you are using flash storage for the actual data and you need further increases in performance. If you are using spinning disks, moving the WAL to a dedicated device will likely show minimal improvement. There are a number of possible storage layout configurations, where the WAL, DB, and data can be placed on different storage devices. The following list shows three examples of such configurations:

- WAL, DB, and data all on spinning disk or flash
- WAL and DB on SSD, data on spinning disk
- WAL on NVMe, DB on SSD, and data on spinning disk

Compression

Another handy feature introduced with BlueStore is that it enables compression of data at the sub-object level, blobs inside BlueStore. This means that any data written into Ceph, no matter the client access model, can benefit from this feature. Compression is enabled on a per-pool basis but is disabled by default.

As well as the ability to enable compression per-pool, there are also a number of extra options to control the behavior of the compression, as shown in the following list:

- `compression_algorithm`: This controls which compression library is used to compress data. The default is snappy, a compression library written by Google. Although its compression ratio isn't the best, it has very high performance, and unless you have specific capacity requirements, you should probably stick with snappy. Other options are `zlib` and `zstd`.
- `compression_mode`: This controls the operating status of compression on a per-pool basis. It can be set to either `none`, `passive`, `aggressive`, or `force`. The `passive` setting enables the use of compression, but will only compress objects that are marked to be compressed from higher levels. The `aggressive` setting will try and compress all objects unless explicitly told not to. The `force` setting will always try and compress data.
- `compress_required_ratio`: By default, this is set at 87.5%. An object that has been compressed must have been compressed to at least below this value to be considered worth compressing; otherwise, the object will be stored in an uncompressed format.

Although compression does require additional CPU, snappy is very efficient, and the distributed nature of Ceph lends itself well to this task as the compression duties are spread over a large number of CPUs across the cluster. In comparison, a legacy storage array would have to use more of its precious, finite dual controller CPU's resource.

An additional advantage of using compression over the reduction in space consumed is also I/O performance when reading or writing large blocks of data. Because of the data being compressed, the disks or flash devices will have less data to read or write, meaning faster response times. Additionally, flash devices will possibly see less write wear because of the reduced amount of total data written.

Checksums

For increased protection of stored data, BlueStore calculates and stores the checksums of any data written. On each read request, BlueStore reads the checksum and compares with the data read from the device. If a mismatch is discovered, BlueStore will report a read error and repair the damage. Ceph will then retry the read from another OSD holding that object. Although modern hardware has sophisticated checksums and error detection of its own, introducing another level in BlueStore goes a long way to eliminating the risk of silent data corruption. By default, BlueStore creates checksums using crc32, which is highly likely to catch any silent data corruption; however, alternative algorithms are available, if required.

BlueStore cache tuning

Unlike in filestore, where any free RAM in the OSD node is used by the page cache, in BlueStore, RAM has to be statically assigned to the OSD on startup. For spinning disk OSDs, this amount is 1 GB; flash-based SSDs have 3 GB assigned to them. This RAM is used for a number of different caches internally: the RocksDB cache, the BlueStore metadata cache, and the BlueStore data cache. The first two are responsible for ensuring the smooth operating of the BlueStore internals when looking up essential metadata; the defaults have been set to offer good performance and increasing them further will show diminishing returns. The final BlueStore data cache will actually cache user data stored in the Ceph cluster. It's set relatively low by default compared to what some filestore OSDs may have stored in the page cache; this is to prevent BlueStore having high memory consumption by default.

If your OSD nodes have plenty of free memory after all your OSDs are running and storing data, then it's possible to increase the amount of memory assigned to each OSD and decide how it's split between the different caches.

Recent versions of Ceph contain a feature in BlueStore that auto-tunes the assignment of memory between the different caches in BlueStore. By default, the OSD will aim to consume around 4 GB of memory, and by continually analyzing the memory usage will adjust the allocation to each cache. The major improvement that auto-tuning brings is that different workloads utilize the different caches in BlueStore differently, and trying to pre-allocate memory with static variables is an extremely difficult task. Aside from potentially tweaking the target memory threshold, the rest of the auto-tuning is largely automatic and hidden from the Ceph administrator.

If auto-tuning is disabled, then BlueStore will fall back to its manual cache assignment behavior. The following section describes the various BlueStore caches in detail that can be controlled via the manual mode. In this mode, there are two OSD-based settings that control the amount of memory assigned to each OSD, `bluestore_cache_size_hdd` and `bluestore_cache_size_ssd`. As per the name, you can adjust either one to control the assigned memory for either HDDs or SSDs. However, we can do more than just change the overall amount of memory assigned to an OSD; there are a number of further settings to control the split between the three caches, as shown in the following list:

- The `bluestore_cache_kv_ratio` setting, set by default to 0.5, will allocate 50% of the allocated memory to the RocksDB cache. This cache is used internally by RocksDB and is not directly managed by Ceph. It's currently believed to offer the best return in performance when deciding where to allocate memory.
- The `bluestore_cache_meta_ratio` setting, set by default to 0.5, will allocate 50% of the available allocated memory to caching BlueStore metadata. Note that, depending on the available memory and the value of `bluestore_cache_kv_min`, less than 50% may end up being allocated to caching metadata. The BlueStore metadata cache contains the raw metadata before it's stored in RocksDB.
- The `bluestore_cache_kv_min` setting, set by default to 512 MB, ensures that at least 512 MB of memory is used for the RocksDB cache. Anything over this value will be shared 50:50 with the BlueStore metadata cache.

Finally, any memory left over from the preceding two ratios will be used for caching actual data. By default, because of `kv` and `meta_ratios`, this will be 0%. Most Ceph clients will have their own local read cache, which will hopefully keep extremely hot data cached; however, in the case where clients are used that don't have their own local cache, it might be worth investigating whether adjusting the caching ratios to reserve a small amount of cache for data use brings improvements.

By default, the auto-tuning of BlueStore should provide the best balance of memory usage and provide the best performance, and it isn't recommended that you change to the manual method.

Deferred writes

Unlike in filestore, where every write is written in its entirety to both the journal and then finally to disk, in BlueStore, the data part of the write in most cases is written directly to the block device. This removes the double-write penalty and, on pure spinning-disk OSDs, dramatically improves performance and lowers SSD wear. However, as mentioned previously, this double write has a positive side effect of decreasing write latency when the spinning disks are combined with SSD journals. BlueStore can also use flash-based storage devices to lower write latency by deferring writes, first writing data into the RocksDB WAL and then later flushing these entries to disk. Unlike filestore, not every write is written into the WAL; configuration parameters determine the I/O size cut-off as to what writes are deferred. The configuration parameter is shown in the following code:

```
bluestore_prefer_deferred_size
```

This controls the size of I/Os that will be written to the WAL first. For spinning disks, this defaults to 32 KB, and SSDs by default don't defer writes. If write latency is important and your SSD is sufficiently fast, then by increasing this value, you can increase the size of I/Os that you wish to defer to WAL.

BlueFS

Although the main motivation for BlueStore's development was to not use an underlying filesystem, BlueStore still needs a method to store RocksDB and the data on the OSD disk. BlueFS was developed to meet this requirement, which is an extremely minimal filesystem that provides just the minimal set of features that BlueStore requires. It also means that it has been designed to operate in a dependable manner for the slim set of operations that Ceph submits. It also removes the overhead of the double filesystem journal write that would be present when using a standard POSIX filesystem.

Unlike with filestore, you can't simply browse the folder structure and manually look at the objects as BlueFS is not a native Linux filesystem; however, it's possible to mount a BlueFS filesystem with the ceph-objectstore-tool to enable exploration or to be able to manually correct errors. This will be covered further in the section on disaster recovery.

ceph-volume

Although not strictly part of BlueStore, the ceph-volume tool was released around the same time as BlueStore and is the recommended tool for provisioning Bluestore OSDs. It's a direct replacement for the ceph-disk tool, which had a number of issues surrounding race conditions and the predictability of OSDs being correctly enumerated and starting up. The ceph-disk tool used udev to identify OSDs that were then mounted and activated. The ceph-disk tool has now been deprecated, and all new OSDs should be created using ceph-volume.

Although ceph-volume can function in a simple mode, the recommended approach is to use the lvm mode. As the name suggests, this utilizes the Linux logical volume manager to store information regarding the OSDs and to manage the block devices. Additionally, the dm-cache, which is a part of lvm, can be used to provide block-level caching underneath the OSDs.

The ceph-volume tool also has a batch mode, which aims to intelligently provision OSDs given a list of block devices. Care should be taken to use the --report mode to ensure that its intended action matches your expectations. Otherwise, it's recommended that you manually partition and create OSDs.

How to use BlueStore

To create a BlueStore OSD using ceph-volume, you run the following command, specifying the devices for the data and RocksDB storage. As previously mentioned, you can separate the DB and WAL parts of RocksDB if you so wish:

```
ceph-volume create --bluestore /dev/sda --block.wal /dev/sdb --block.db
/dev/sdc (--dmcrypt)
```

Shown in brackets is the encryption option. It's recommended that you encrypt all new OSDs unless you have a specific reason not to. Encryption with modern CPUs generates very little overhead, and makes the often-forgotten security measures around disk replacements much simpler. With the recent introduction of various new data-protection laws, such as GDPR in Europe, having data encrypted at rest is highly recommended.

The preceding code assumes that your data disk is /dev/sda. For this example, assume that you are using a spinning disk, and that you have a faster device, such as an SSD (/dev/sdb) and a very fast NVMe device (/dev/sdc). The ceph-volume tool would create two partitions on the data disk: one for storing the actual Ceph objects and another small XFS partition for storing details about the OSD. It would then place a link to the SSD to store the RocksDB on it and a link to the NVMe device to store the WAL. You can create multiple OSDs sharing the same SSD for DB and WAL by partitioning the devices, or by using lvm to carve logical volumes out of them.

However, as we discovered in Chapter 2, *Deploying Ceph with Containers*, using a proper deployment tool for your Ceph cluster helps to reduce deployment time and ensures consistent configuration across the cluster. Although the Ceph Ansible modules also support deploying BlueStore OSDs, at the time of writing, it doesn't currently support automatically creating multiple DB and WAL partitions on a single device.

Now that you understand how to create BlueStore OSD's the next topic that is required to be discussed is the upgrading of an existing cluster.

Strategies for upgrading an existing cluster to BlueStore

It's likely that some readers of this book are running existing Ceph clusters that are utilizing filestore. These readers might be wondering if they should upgrade to BlueStore, and if so, what the best method is for doing this.

It should be understood that while filestore is still supported, it's very much at the end of its life, with no further development work planned aside from any critical bug fixes that may be required. Therefore, it's highly recommended that you make plans to upgrade your cluster to BlueStore to take advantage of any current and future enhancements and continue to run a supported Ceph release. The support path for filestore in future releases hasn't been announced, but it would be wise to aim to be running BlueStore OSDs by the Ceph release after Nautilus.

There is no special migration path for upgrading an OSD to BlueStore; the process is to simply destroy the OSD, rebuild it as BlueStore, and then let Ceph recover the data on the newly created OSD. It's more than likely that, because of the differing size requirements between filestore journals and BlueStore's RocksDB, altering partition sizes will require multiple OSDs to be destroyed at once. Therefore, it may be worth considering whether operating system rebuilds should be carried out at this point.

There are two main approaches to the upgrade process that are largely determined by the Ceph operator's appetite for risk and the availability of spare capacity, listed as follows:

- **Degraded upgrade**: A degraded upgrade destroys the current OSDs without redistributing their contents across the remaining OSDs. Once the OSDs come back online as BlueStore OSDs, then the missing copies of data are rebuilt. Until the cluster returns to full health, a portion of the data on the Ceph cluster will be in a degraded state, and although multiple copies will still exist, they'll be at a higher risk should the cluster experience a failure of some sort. Recovery times will depend on the number of OSDs that need to be recovered and the size of data stored on each OSD. As it's highly likely that several OSDs will be upgraded at once, expect the recovery time to be higher than it would be for a single OSD. Please also note that, with the default pool settings of `size=3` and `min_size=2`, should an additional disk fail, some PGs will only have one copy, and now that they're less than `min_size`, the I/O will be suspended to these PGs until the recovery recreates a second copy. The benefits of performing a degraded upgrade is that you only have to wait for the cluster to re-balance once during recovery and you don't require any additional space, which may mean that this is the only option for clusters that are more or less full.

- **Out-and-in upgrade**: If you want to guard against any possibility of data loss or unavailability and have sufficient space to redistribute the contents of the OSDs that are to be upgraded across the cluster, then an out-and-in upgrade is the recommended approach. By marking the OSDs to be upgraded as out, Ceph will re-balance the PGs across other OSDs. Once this process has finished, the OSDs can be stopped and destroyed without impacting data durability or availability. When the BlueStore OSDs are reintroduced, the PGs will flow back and, throughout this period, there will be no reduction in the number of copies of data. Either method will result in exactly the same configuration and so will ultimately come down to personal preference. If your cluster has a large number of OSDs, then some form of automation may be required to lessen the burden on the operator; however, if you want to automate the process, then care should be taken around the destruction of the filestore OSD step, as one mistake could easily wipe more than the intended OSDs. A halfway measure may be to create a small script that automates the zapping, partitioning, and creation steps. This can then be run manually on each OSD node.

Upgrading an OSD in your test cluster

For the basis of demonstrating BlueStore, we will use `ceph-volume` to non-disruptively manually upgrade a live Ceph cluster's OSDs from filestore to BlueStore. If you wish to carry out this procedure for real, you could work through the *Ansible* section in `Chapter 2`, *Deploying Ceph with Containers*, to deploy a cluster with filestore OSDs and then go through the following instructions to upgrade them. The OSDs will be upgraded following the degraded method where OSDs are removed while still containing data.

Make sure that your Ceph cluster is in full health by checking with the `ceph -s` command, as shown in the following code. We'll be upgrading OSD by first removing it from the cluster and then letting Ceph recover the data onto the new BlueStore OSD, so we need to be sure that Ceph has enough valid copies of your data before we start. By taking advantage of the hot maintenance capability in Ceph, you can repeat this procedure across all of the OSDs in your cluster without downtime:

```
cluster:
    id:     c1703b54-b4cd-41ab-a3ba
    health: HEALTH_OK

services:
    mon: 3 daemons, quorum mc-ceph-mon1,mc-ceph-mon2,mc-ceph-mon3
    mgr: mc-ceph-mon1(active), standbys: mc-ceph-mon2
    mds: cephfs-1/1/1 up  {0=mc-ceph-mds1=up:active}, 1 up:standby-replay
    osd: 192 osds: 191 up, 191 in

data:
    pools:   6 pools, 10688 pgs
    objects: 81.71M objects, 311TiB
    usage:   934TiB used, 392TiB / 1.29PiB avail
    pgs:     10657 active+clean
             17    active+clean+scrubbing+deep
             14    active+clean+scrubbing
```

Now we need to stop all of the OSDs from running, unmount the disks, and then wipe them by going through the following steps:

1. Use the following command to stop the OSD services:

   ```
   sudo systemctl stop ceph-osd@*
   ```

   The preceding command gives the following output:

   ```
   root@mc-8c-osd02:~# systemctl stop ceph-osd@*
   root@mc-8c-osd02:~#
   ```

We can confirm that the OSDs have been stopped and that Ceph is still functioning using the `ceph -s` command again, as shown in the following screenshot:

```
cluster:
    id:     c1703b54-b4cd-41ab-a3
    health: HEALTH_WARN
            12 osds down
            1 host (12 osds) down
            Degraded data redundancy: 16169431/245143173 objects degraded (6.596%), 2120 pgs degraded, 2120 pgs
dersized

services:
    mon: 3 daemons, quorum mc-ceph-mon1,mc-ceph-mon2,mc-ceph-mon3
    mgr: mc-ceph-mon1(active), standbys: mc-ceph-mon2
    mds: cephfs-1/1/1 up  {0=mc-ceph-mds1=up:active}, 1 up:standby-replay
    osd: 192 osds: 179 up, 191 in

data:
    pools:   6 pools, 10688 pgs
    objects: 81.71M objects, 311TiB
    usage:   934TiB used, 392TiB / 1.29PiB avail
    pgs:     16169431/245143173 objects degraded (6.596%)
             8543 active+clean
             2120 active+undersized+degraded
             18   active+clean+scrubbing+deep
             7    active+clean+scrubbing
```

2. Now, unmount the XFS partitions; the errors can be ignored:

```
sudo umount /dev/sd*
```

```
root@mc-8c-osd02:~# umount /dev/sd*
umount: /dev/sda: not mounted
umount: /dev/sdb: not mounted
umount: /dev/sdc: not mounted
umount: /dev/sdd: not mounted
umount: /dev/sde: not mounted
umount: /dev/sdf: not mounted
umount: /dev/sdg: not mounted
umount: /dev/sdh: not mounted
umount: /dev/sdi: not mounted
umount: /dev/sdj: not mounted
umount: /dev/sdk: not mounted
umount: /dev/sdl: not mounted
root@mc-8c-osd02:~#
```

3. Unmounting the filesystems will mean that the disks are no longer locked and we can wipe the disks using the following code:

```
sudo ceph-volume lvm zap /dev/sd<x>
```

```
root@mc-8c-osd02:~# sudo ceph-volume lvm zap /dev/sdl
--> Zapping: /dev/sdl
Running command: /sbin/cryptsetup status /dev/mapper/
 stdout: /dev/mapper/ is inactive.
Running command: wipefs --all /dev/sdl
 stdout: /dev/sdl: 8 bytes were erased at offset 0x00000200 (gpt): 45 46 49 20 50 41 52 54
/dev/sdl: 8 bytes were erased at offset 0x74702555e00 (gpt): 45 46 49 20 50 41 52 54
/dev/sdl: 2 bytes were erased at offset 0x000001fe (PMBR): 55 aa
/dev/sdl: calling ioctl to re-read partition table: Success
Running command: dd if=/dev/zero of=/dev/sdl bs=1M count=10
 stderr: 10+0 records in
10+0 records out
 stderr: 10485760 bytes (10 MB, 10 MiB) copied, 0.00293342 s, 3.6 GB/s
--> Zapping successful for: /dev/sdl
root@mc-8c-osd02:~#
```

4. Now we can also edit the partition table on the flash device to remove the filestore journals and recreate them as a suitable size for BlueStore's RocksDB using the following code. In this example, the flash device is an NVMe:

```
sudo fdisk /dev/sd<x>
```

```
root@mc-8c-osd02:~# fdisk /dev/nvme0n1

Welcome to fdisk (util-linux 2.27.1).
Changes will remain in memory only, until you decide to write them.
Be careful before using the write command.


Command (m for help): p
Disk /dev/nvme0n1: 372.6 GiB, 400088457216 bytes, 781422768 sectors
Units: sectors of 1 * 512 = 512 bytes
Sector size (logical/physical): 512 bytes / 512 bytes
I/O size (minimum/optimal): 512 bytes / 512 bytes
Disklabel type: gpt
Disk identifier: 90D14639-8774-4724-A53A-D0011CA3A41A

Device             Start        End   Sectors   Size Type
/dev/nvme0n1p1      2048     976895    974848   476M EFI System
/dev/nvme0n1p2    976896   26781695  25804800  12.3G Linux filesystem
/dev/nvme0n1p4  98633728  109119487  10485760    5G Ceph Journal
/dev/nvme0n1p5 109119488  119605247  10485760    5G Ceph Journal
/dev/nvme0n1p6 119605248  130091007  10485760    5G Ceph Journal
/dev/nvme0n1p7 130091008  140576767  10485760    5G Ceph Journal
/dev/nvme0n1p8 140576768  151062527  10485760    5G Ceph Journal
/dev/nvme0n1p9 151062528  161548287  10485760    5G Ceph Journal
/dev/nvme0n1p10 161548288 172034047  10485760    5G Ceph Journal
/dev/nvme0n1p11 172034048 182519807  10485760    5G Ceph Journal
/dev/nvme0n1p12 182519808 193005567  10485760    5G Ceph Journal
/dev/nvme0n1p13 193005568 203491327  10485760    5G Ceph Journal
/dev/nvme0n1p14 203491328 213977087  10485760    5G Ceph Journal
/dev/nvme0n1p15 213977088 224462847  10485760    5G Ceph Journal

Command (m for help):
```

Delete each Ceph journal partition using the d command, as follows:

```
Command (m for help): d
Partition number (1,2,4, default 4):

Partition 4 has been deleted.

Command (m for help): p
Disk /dev/nvme0n1: 372.6 GiB, 400088457216 bytes, 781422768 sectors
Units: sectors of 1 * 512 = 512 bytes
Sector size (logical/physical): 512 bytes / 512 bytes
I/O size (minimum/optimal): 512 bytes / 512 bytes
Disklabel type: gpt
Disk identifier: 90D14639-8774-4724-A53A-D0011CA3A41A

Device           Start      End   Sectors  Size Type
/dev/nvme0n1p1    2048   976895    974848  476M EFI System
/dev/nvme0n1p2  976896 26781695  25804800 12.3G Linux filesystem
```

Now create all of the new partitions for BlueStore, as shown in the following screenshot:

```
Command (m for help): n
Partition number (3-128, default 3):
First sector (26781696-781422734, default 26781696):
Last sector, +sectors or +size{K,M,G,T,P} (26781696-781422734, default 781422734): +30G

Created a new partition 3 of type 'Linux filesystem' and of size 30 GiB.
```

Add one partition for each OSD you intend to create. When finished, your partition table should look something like the following:

```
Command (m for help): p
Disk /dev/nvme0n1: 372.6 GiB, 400088457216 bytes, 781422768 sectors
Units: sectors of 1 * 512 = 512 bytes
Sector size (logical/physical): 512 bytes / 512 bytes
I/O size (minimum/optimal): 512 bytes / 512 bytes
Disklabel type: gpt
Disk identifier: 90D14639-8774-4724-A53A-D0011CA3A41A

Device            Start       End   Sectors  Size Type
/dev/nvme0n1p1     2048    976895    974848  476M EFI System
/dev/nvme0n1p2   976896  26781695  25804800 12.3G Linux filesystem
/dev/nvme0n1p3 26781696  89696255  62914560   30G Linux filesystem
/dev/nvme0n1p4 89696256 152610815  62914560   30G Linux filesystem
/dev/nvme0n1p5 152610816 215525375 62914560   30G Linux filesystem
/dev/nvme0n1p6 215525376 278439935 62914560   30G Linux filesystem
/dev/nvme0n1p7 278439936 341354495 62914560   30G Linux filesystem
/dev/nvme0n1p8 341354496 404269055 62914560   30G Linux filesystem
/dev/nvme0n1p9 404269056 467183615 62914560   30G Linux filesystem
/dev/nvme0n1p10 467183616 530098175 62914560  30G Linux filesystem
/dev/nvme0n1p11 530098176 593012735 62914560  30G Linux filesystem
/dev/nvme0n1p12 593012736 655927295 62914560  30G Linux filesystem
/dev/nvme0n1p13 655927296 718841855 62914560  30G Linux filesystem
/dev/nvme0n1p14 718841856 781422734 62580879 29.9G Linux filesystem
```

Use the w command to write the new partition table to disk, as shown in the following screenshot. Upon doing so, you'll be informed that the new partition table is not currently in use, and so we need to run sudo partprobe to load the table into the kernel:

```
Command (m for help): w
The partition table has been altered.
Calling ioctl() to re-read partition table.
Re-reading the partition table failed.: Device or resource busy

The kernel still uses the old table. The new table will be used at the next reboot or after you run partprobe(8) or kpart
x(8).

root@mc-8c-osd02:~# partprobe
```

5. Go back to one of your monitors. First, confirm the OSDs we are going to remove and remove the OSDs using the following purge commands:

```
sudo ceph osd tree
```

The preceding command gives the following output:

```
-8          87.30499         host mc-8c-osd02-hdd
36   hdd    7.27499             osd.36          down  1.00000 1.00000
37   hdd    7.27499             osd.37          down  1.00000 1.00000
38   hdd    7.27499             osd.38          down  1.00000 1.00000
39   hdd    7.27499             osd.39          down  1.00000 1.00000
40   hdd    7.27499             osd.40          down  1.00000 1.00000
41   hdd    7.27499             osd.41          down  1.00000 1.00000
42   hdd    7.27499             osd.42          down  1.00000 1.00000
43   hdd    7.27499             osd.43          down  1.00000 1.00000
44   hdd    7.27499             osd.44          down  1.00000 1.00000
45   hdd    7.27499             osd.45          down  1.00000 1.00000
46   hdd    7.27499             osd.46          down  1.00000 1.00000
47   hdd    7.27499             osd.47          down  1.00000 1.00000
```

Now, remove the logical OSD entry from the Ceph cluster—in this example, OSD 36:

```
sudo ceph osd purge x --yes-i-really-mean-it
```

```
sysprosupport@mc-ceph-mon1:~$ sudo ceph osd purge 36 --yes-i-really-mean-it
purged osd.36
```

6. Check the status of your Ceph cluster with the `ceph -s` command. You should now see that the OSD has been removed, as shown in the following screenshot:

```
cluster:
    id:     c1703b54-b4cd-41ab-a3ba-
    health: HEALTH_WARN
            13814187/245143281 objects misplaced (5.635%)
            Degraded data redundancy: 16121791/245143281 objects degraded (6.576%), 2114 pgs degraded, 188 pgs
ersized

services:
    mon: 3 daemons, quorum mc-ceph-mon1,mc-ceph-mon2,mc-ceph-mon3
    mgr: mc-ceph-mon1(active), standbys: mc-ceph-mon2
    mds: cephfs-1/1/1 up  {0=mc-ceph-mds1=up:active}, 1 up:standby-replay
    osd: 180 osds: 179 up, 179 in; 3178 remapped pgs

data:
    pools:   6 pools, 10688 pgs
    objects: 81.71M objects, 311TiB
    usage:   872TiB used, 367TiB / 1.21PiB avail
    pgs:     16121791/245143281 objects degraded (6.576%)
             13814187/245143281 objects misplaced (5.635%)
             7476 active+clean
             1782 active+undersized+degraded+remapped+backfill_wait
             1054 active+remapped+backfill_wait
             321  active+undersized+degraded+remapped+backfilling
             20   active+remapped+backfilling
             16   active+clean+scrubbing+deep
             11   active+recovery_wait+degraded
             7    active+clean+scrubbing
             1    active+recovery_wait+remapped

io:
    client:   996KiB/s rd, 31.0MiB/s wr, 54op/s rd, 187op/s wr
    recovery: 3.94GiB/s, 1.06kobjects/s
```

Note that the number of OSDs has dropped, and that, because the OSDs have been removed from the CRUSH map, Ceph has now started to try and recover the missing data onto the remaining OSDs. It's probably a good idea not to leave Ceph in this state for too long to avoid unnecessary data movement.

7. Now issue the `ceph-volume` command to create the `bluestore` OSD using the following code. In this example, we will be storing the DB on a separate flash device, so we need to specify that option. Also, as per this book's recommendation, the OSD will be encrypted:

```
sudo ceph-volume lvm create --bluestore --data /dev/sd<x> --
block.db /dev/sda<ssd> --dmcrypt
```

The preceding command gives a lot of output, but if successful, we will end with the following:

```
Running command: systemctl enable --runtime ceph-osd@47
Running command: systemctl start ceph-osd@47
--> ceph-volume lvm activate successful for osd ID: 47
--> ceph-volume lvm create successful for: /dev/sdl
```

8. Check the status of ceph again with ceph-s to make sure that the new OSDs have been added and that Ceph is recovering the data onto them, as shown in the following screenshot:

```
cluster:
    id:     c1703b54-b4cd-41ab-a3ba-
    health: HEALTH_WARN
            213263/245143401 objects misplaced (0.087%)
            Degraded data redundancy: 16150505/245143401 objects degraded (6.588%), 2093 pgs
dersized

services:
    mon: 3 daemons, quorum mc-ceph-mon1,mc-ceph-mon2,mc-ceph-mon3
    mgr: mc-ceph-mon1(active), standbys: mc-ceph-mon2
    mds: cephfs-1/1/1 up  {0=mc-ceph-mds1=up:active}, 1 up:standby-replay
    osd: 192 osds: 191 up, 191 in; 2123 remapped pgs

data:
    pools:   6 pools, 10688 pgs
    objects: 81.71M objects, 311TiB
    usage:   873TiB used, 453TiB / 1.30PiB avail
    pgs:     16150505/245143401 objects degraded (6.588%)
             213263/245143401 objects misplaced (0.087%)
             8551 active+clean
             2020 active+undersized+degraded+remapped+backfill_wait
             70   active+undersized+degraded+remapped+backfilling
             33   active+remapped+backfill_wait
             11   active+clean+scrubbing+deep
             3    active+recovering+degraded

io:
    client:   49.1MiB/s rd, 21.2MiB/s wr, 455op/s rd, 506op/s wr
    recovery: 768MiB/s, 233objects/s
```

Note that the number of misplaced objects is now almost zero because of the new OSDs that were placed in the same location in the CRUSH map before they were upgraded. Ceph now only needs to recover the data, not redistribute the data layout.

If further nodes need to be upgraded, wait for the back-filling process to complete and for the Ceph status to return to HEALTH_OK. Then the work can proceed on the next node.

As you can see, the overall procedure is very simple and is identical to the steps required to replace a failed disk.

Summary

In this chapter, we learned about the new object store in Ceph called BlueStore. Hopefully, you have a better understanding of why it was needed and the limitations in the existing filestore design. You should also have a basic understanding of the inner workings of BlueStore and feel confident in how to upgrade your OSDs to BlueStore.

In the next chapter we will look at how Ceph storage can be exported via commonly used storage protocols to enable Ceph storage to be consumed by non-Linux clients.

Questions

1. What object store is the default when creating OSDs in Luminous and newer releases?
2. What database does BlueStore use internally?
3. What is the name of the process for moving data between levels in the database part of BlueStore?
4. What is the name of the method where small writes can be temporarily written to an SSD instead of an HDD?
5. How can you mount BlueFS and browse it as a standard Linux filesystem?
6. What's the default compression algorithm used in BlueStore?
7. Moving up a level in the BlueStore database increases the size by what multiplier?

4
Ceph and Non-Native Protocols

Years of development have enabled Ceph to build an extensive feature set, bringing high quality and performance storage to Linux. However, clients that don't run Linux (and that are therefore unable to natively talk to Ceph) have a limited scope as to where Ceph can be deployed. Recently, a number of new enhancements have been developed to allow Ceph to start to talk to some of these non-Linux-based clients, such as the **Internet Small Computer Systems Interface (iSCSI)** and **Network File System (NFS)**. This chapter will look in detail at the various methods by which Ceph storage can be exported to clients and the strengths and weaknesses of each. In all methods, a Linux server is used as a proxy to translate the I/O requests from these clients into native Ceph I/Os, and as such, a working knowledge of how to use these protocols in Linux is beneficial. Making these proxy servers highly available will also be covered in this chapter, along with the difficulties of doing so.

The two main storage types that will be looked at in this chapter will be file and block storage, as these are the most popular types of storage in legacy enterprise workloads.

Briefly, we'll cover the following topics in this chapter:

- Block
- File
- Examples:
    - Exporting Ceph RBDs via iSCSI
    - Exporting CephFS via Samba
    - Exporting CephFS via NFS
- ESXi hypervisor
- Clustering

Block

Block-level storage mimics the type of storage that would have originally been provided by hard disks and, later, storage arrays. Typically, block storage is exported via storage arrays via fiber channel or iSCSI onto hosts where a local filesystem is then formatted onto the block device. In some cases, this filesytem may be of the clustered type, and can allow the block device to be presented across many hosts at the same time. It's important to note that even though block-based storage allows you to present it to multiple hosts, this should only be done if the filesystem supports it; otherwise, corruption of the filesystem is highly likely.

One use of block storage that has seen a massive expansion in recent years has been through the use of virtualization. Block storage is quite often presented to a hypervisor that's formatted with a filesystem. One or more virtual machines are then stored as files on this filesystem. This differs greatly from the native Ceph approach when using KVM as the hypervisor; as KVM directly supports Ceph **RADOS Block Devices (RBDs)**, it stores each VM's disk directly as an RBD, removing the complexity and overheads associated with the hypervisor's filesystem.

Ceph RBDs, which are a type of block storage, can be exported via iSCSI to allow clients that speak iSCSI to consume Ceph storage. Since the release of Mimic, Ceph has had a basic level of support for configuring iSCSI exports of RBD images. The configuration of Ceph's iSCSI support is all managed through Ansible, which both installs the required software and exports the iSCSI devices.

At the time of writing, there are currently still a few limitations that the reader should be aware of, mainly surrounding the **Highly Available (HA)** capabilities. The issues largely affect ESXi and clustering solutions where multiple hosts try and access the block device concurrently. At the time of writing, it is not recommended for you to use Ceph's iSCSI support for either of these use cases. For users who are interested in exploring the current compatibility further, it's recommended that they consult the upstream Ceph documentation and mailing lists.

File

As the name indicates, file storage is supported by some form of filesystem that stores files and directories. In the traditional storage scenario, file storage is normally provided via servers acting as *file servers* or through the use of **network-attached storage (NAS)**. File-based storage can be provided over several protocols and can sit on several different types of filesystems.

The two most common file-access protocols are SMB and NFS, which are widely supported by many clients. SMB is traditionally seen as a Microsoft protocol, being the native file-sharing protocol in Windows, whereas NFS is seen as the protocol used on Unix-based infrastructures.

As we shall see later, both Ceph's RBDs and its own CephFS filesystem can be used as a basis to export file-based storage to clients. RBDs can be mounted on a proxy server where a local filesystem is then placed on top. From here, the exportation as NFS or SMB is very similar to any other server with local storage. When using CephFS, which in itself is a filesystem, there are direct interfaces to both NFS and SMB server software to minimize the number of levels in the stack.

There are a number of advantages to exporting CephFS instead of a filesystem sitting on top of an RBD. These mainly center around simplifying the number of layers that I/Os have to pass through and the number of components in an HA setup. As was discussed earlier, most local filesystems can only be mounted on one server at a time, otherwise corruption will occur. Therefore, when designing an HA solution involving RBDs and local filesystems, care needs to be taken to ensure that the clustering solution won't try and mount the RBD and filesystem across multiple nodes. This is covered in more detail later in this chapter in the section on clustering.

There is, however, one possible reason for wanting to export RBDs formatted with local filesystems: the RBD component of Ceph is much simpler than CephFS in its operation and has been marked as stable for much longer than CephFS. While CephFS has proved to be very stable, thought should be given to the operational side of the solution, and you should ensure that the operator is happy managing CephFS.

To export CephFS via NFS, there are two possible solutions. One is to use the CephFS kernel client and mount the filesystem into the operating system, and then use the kernel-based NFS kernel server to export it to clients. Although this configuration should work perfectly fine, both the kernel-based NFS server and the CephFS client will typically rely on the operator to run a fairly recent kernel to support the latest features.

A much better idea would be to use `nfs-ganesha`, which has support for directly communicating to CephFS filesystems. As Ganesha runs entirely in user space, there's no requirement for specific kernel versions, and the supported CephFS client functionality can keep up with the current state of the Ceph project. There are also several enhancements in Ganesha that the kernel-based NFS server doesn't support. Additionally, HA NFS should be easier to achieve with Ganesha over the kernel server.

Samba can be used to export CephFS as a Windows-compatible share. Like NFS, Samba also supports the ability to directly communicate with CephFS, and so in most cases, there should be no requirement to have to mount the CephFS filesystem into the OS first. A separate project CTDB can be used to provide HA of the CephFS-backed Samba shares.

Finally, it is worth noting that, although Linux clients can mount CephFS directly, it may still be preferable to export CephFS via NFS or SMB to them. We should do this because, given the way CephFS works, clients are in direct communication with the Ceph cluster, and in some cases, this may not be desirable because of security concerns. By reexporting CephFS via NFS, clients can consume the storage without being directly exposed to the Ceph cluster.

Examples

The following examples will demonstrate how to export RBDs as iSCSI devices, as well as how to export CephFS via NFS and Samba. All these examples assume you already have a working CephFS filesystem ready to export; if that is not the case, then please refer to Chapter 5, *RADOS Pools and Client Access*, for instructions on how to deploy one.

They also assume you have a VM available to act as the proxy server. This could be a Ceph monitor VM for testing purposes, but this is not recommended for production workloads.

Exporting Ceph RBDs via iSCSI

iSCSI is a technology that allows you to export block devices over IP networking. As 10 G networking has been more widely adopted, iSCSI has become extremely popular and is now the dominant technology in the block storage scene.

The device that's exporting the block storage is called the iSCSI target and the client is called the iSCSI initiator, both of which are identified by an IQN name.

At the time of writing, the iSCSI support in Ceph only works with Red Hat-derived distributions. Although the underlying components should all work across any Linux distribution, the glue that holds them together still requires a number of updates to improve compatibility. Therefore, this example will require a VM running CentOS for the iSCSI components to be installed on. If you're testing the functionality in the Vagrant and Ansible lab created in Chapter 2, *Deploying Ceph with Containers*, then you can modify the Vagrant file to provision an additional VM running CentOS.

The official package repository for the iSCSI components is only available via a full RHEL subscription. To obtain the packages for this example, they need to be downloaded from the Ceph's project build server.

The following links will take you to the recent builds of each package:

- `https://shaman.ceph.com/repos/ceph-iscsi/master/`
- `https://shaman.ceph.com/repos/kernel/`
- `https://shaman.ceph.com/repos/ceph-iscsi-cli/`
- `https://shaman.ceph.com/repos/ceph-iscsi-config/`
- `https://shaman.ceph.com/repos/python-rtslib/`
- `https://shaman.ceph.com/repos/tcmu-runner/`

On each page, look at the **arch** column as shown in the following screenshot. This is the directory that you'll need to look in for the packages later:

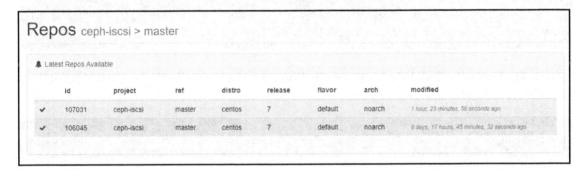

Click the latest (or whatever version you require) build number on the left, which will take you to the following page:

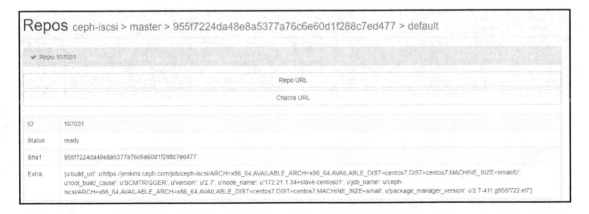

Click on the **Repo URL** link, which will take you to the repository directory tree. Browse to the correct arch type that you saw in the column earlier and you will be presented with the RPM to download, as shown in the following screenshot:

Index of /r/ceph-iscsi/master/955f7224da48e8a5377a76c6e60d1f288c7ed477/centos/7/flavors/default/noarch/

```
../
repodata/                                24-Nov-2018 21:02          -
ceph-iscsi-2.7-411.e955f722.el7.noarch.rpm   24-Nov-2018 21:00      176316
```

Copy the URL and then use `wget` to download the package, as shown in the following screenshot:

```
[root@ceph-iscsi ~]# wget https://2.chacra.ceph.com/r/ceph-iscsi/master/91b10122804f98e76475386366f4b11fe78ceee6/centos/7/flavors/default/noarch/ceph-iscsi-2.
7-393.g91b1012.el7.noarch.rpm
--2018-11-25 20:57:37--  https://2.chacra.ceph.com/r/ceph-iscsi/master/91b10122804f98e76475386366f4b11fe78ceee6/centos/7/flavors/default/noarch/ceph-iscsi-2.7
-393.g91b1012.el7.noarch.rpm
Resolving 2.chacra.ceph.com (2.chacra.ceph.com)... 158.69.78.70
Connecting to 2.chacra.ceph.com (2.chacra.ceph.com)|158.69.78.70|:443... connected.
HTTP request sent, awaiting response... 200 OK
Length: 176156 (172K) [application/x-redhat-package-manager]
Saving to: 'ceph-iscsi-2.7-393.g91b1012.el7.noarch.rpm.1'

100%[===================================================================>] 176,156      1.05MB/s    in 0.2s

2018-11-25 20:57:38 (1.09 MB/s) - 'ceph-iscsi-2.7-393.g91b1012.el7.noarch.rpm.1' saved [176156/176156]
```

Repeat this for every URL listed previously. When you have finished, you should have the following packages:

```
[root@ceph-iscsi ~]# ls *.rpm
ceph-iscsi-2.7-393.g91b1012.el7.noarch.rpm     ceph-iscsi-config-2.6-76.g179cbf4.el7.noarch.rpm    python-rtslib-2.1.fb67-10.g7713d1e.noarch.rpm
ceph-iscsi-cli-2.7-88.gae73930.el7.noarch.rpm  kernel-4.20.0_rc2_ceph_g8691a93268a5-1.x86_64.rpm   tcmu-runner-1.4.0-1.el7.x86_64.rpm
```

Now, install all of the of RPMs by running the following:

```
yum install *.rpm
```

Package	Arch	Version	Repository	Size
Installing:				
ceph-iscsi	noarch	2.7-393.g91b1012.el7	/ceph-iscsi-2.7-393.g91b1012.el7.noarch	662 k
kernel	x86_64	4.20.0_rc2_ceph_g8691a93268a5-1	/kernel-4.20.0_rc2_ceph_g8691a93268a5-1.x86_64	1.4 G
python-rtslib	noarch	2.1.fb67-10.g7713d1e	/python-rtslib-2.1.fb67-10.g7713d1e.noarch	682 k
tcmu-runner	x86_64	1.4.0-1.el7	/tcmu-runner-1.4.0-1.el7.x86_64	431 k

Now that the base iSCSI support is installed, we also require the Ceph packages to be installed using the following code:

```
rpm --import 'https://download.ceph.com/keys/release.asc'
```

Create a new repository file and add the Ceph RPM repositories using the following code:

```
nano /etc/yum.repos.d/ceph.repo
```

```
  GNU nano 2.3.1                                File: /etc/yum.repos.d/ceph.repo

[ceph]
name=Ceph packages
baseurl=http://download.ceph.com/rpm-mimic/el7/$basearch
enabled=1
gpgcheck=1
type=rpm-md
gpgkey=https://download.ceph.com/keys/release.asc
priority=1


[ceph-noarch]
name=Ceph noarch packages
baseurl=http://download.ceph.com/rpm-mimic/el7/noarch
enabled=1
gpgcheck=1
type=rpm-md
gpgkey=https://download.ceph.com/keys/release.asc
priority=1
```

Now add the Fedora EPEL repository, and install and update Ceph using the following code:

```
yum install -y
https://dl.fedoraproject.org/pub/epel/epel-release-latest-7.noarch.rpm
yum update
yum install ceph
```

Create the Ceph configuration directory, if it doesn't already exist, using the following code:

```
mkdir /etc/ceph
```

Copy `ceph.conf` over from a Ceph monitor node using the following code:

```
scp mon1:/etc/ceph/ceph.conf /etc/ceph/ceph.conf
```

Copy the Ceph `keyring` over using the following code:

```
scp mon1:/etc/ceph/ceph.client.admin.keyring
/etc/ceph/ceph.client.admin.keyring
```

Edit the Ceph iSCSI gateway configuration file using the following code:

```
nano /etc/ceph/iscsi-gateway.cfg
```

```
  GNU nano 2.3.1                                  File: /etc/ceph/iscsi-gateway.cfg

[config]
# Name of the Ceph storage cluster. A suitable Ceph configuration file allowing
# access to the Ceph storage cluster from the gateway node is required, if not
# colocated on an OSD node.
cluster_name = ceph

# Place a copy of the ceph cluster's admin keyring in the gateway's /etc/ceph
# drectory and reference the filename here
gateway_keyring = ceph.client.admin.keyring


# API settings.
# The API supports a number of options that allow you to tailor it to your
# local environment. If you want to run the API under https, you will need to
# create cert/key files that are compatible for each iSCSI gateway node, that is
# not locked to a specific node. SSL cert and key files *must* be called
# 'iscsi-gateway.crt' and 'iscsi-gateway.key' and placed in the '/etc/ceph/' directory
# on *each* gateway node. With the SSL files in place, you can use 'api_secure = true'
# to switch to https mode.

# To support the API, the bear minimum settings are:
api_secure = false
minimum_gateways=1
```

Make sure it looks like the code shown in the preceding screenshot. Note the addition on the bottom line to allow the testing of `ceph-iscsi` with only a single server. In a production setting, this line wouldn't be required as you would most likely have redundant iSCSI gateways.

Now enable and start the `ceph-iscsi` daemons using the following code:

```
systemctl daemon-reload
systemctl enable rbd-target-api
systemctl start rbd-target-api
systemctl enable rbd-target-gw
systemctl start rbd-target-gw
```

Note that the configuration stored in `iscsi-gateway.conf` is only to allow the `ceph-iscsi` services to start and connect to the Ceph cluster. The actual iSCSI configuration is stored centrally in RADOS objects.

Now that the iSCSI daemons are running, the `gwcli` tool can be used to administer the iSCSI configuration and present the RBDs as iSCSI devices.

Once `gwcli` has started successfully, we can run the `ls` command to see the structure of the `ceph-iscsi` configuration as shown in the following screenshot:

The `gwcli` tool has connected to the Ceph cluster and retrieved the list of pools and other configuration. We can now configure the iSCSI.

The first item to be configured is the iSCSI gateway, using the following code:

```
cd iscsi-target
create iqn.2003-01.com.redhat.iscsi-gw:iscsi-igw
```

Now, by entering the `iqn` that has been created, the IPs of all of the gateways can be added using the following code:

```
cd iqn.2003-01.com.redhat.iscsi-gw:iscsi-igw
cd gateways
create ceph-iscsi 10.176.20.38
```

```
/iscsi-target> cd iqn.2003-01.com.redhat.iscsi-gw:iscsi-igw
/iscsi-target...-gw:iscsi-igw> cd gateways
/iscsi-target...-igw/gateways> create ceph-iscsi 10.176.20.38
Adding gateway, sync'ing 0 disk(s) and 0 client(s)
ok
```

Now we can create or add the RBDs. If the RBD already exists when running the `create` command, then `ceph-iscsi` will simply add the existing RBD; if no RBD of the given name exists, then a new RBD will be created. A good example of when using a preexisting RBD maybe required is when the RBD contains data or if we need to place the RBD data on an erasure-coded pool.

For this example, a 100 GB RBD called `iscsi-test` will be created in the RBD pool, as shown in the following code:

```
cd /disks
create pool=rbd image=iscsi-test size=100G
```

```
/iscsi-target...-igw/gateways> cd /disks
/disks> create pool=rbd image=iscsi-test size=100G
ok
```

Now the initiator `iqn` needs to be added and chap authentication assigned, as shown in the following code:

```
cd /iscsi-target/iqn.2003-01.com.redhat.iscsi-gw:iscsi-igw
cd hosts
create iqn.2018-11.com.test:my-test-client
auth chap=chapuser/chappassword
```

```
/disks> cd /iscsi-target/iqn.2003-01.com.redhat.iscsi-gw:iscsi-igw
/iscsi-target...-gw:iscsi-igw> cd hosts
/iscsi-target...csi-igw/hosts> create iqn.2018-11.com.test:my-test-client
ok
/iscsi-target...y-test-client> auth chap=chapuser/chappassword
ok
```

Finally, add the disks to the host as LUNs using the following code. The format of the target is `<rados pool>.<RBD name>`:

```
disk add rbd.iscsi-test
```

```
/iscsi-target...y-test-client> disk add rbd.iscsi-test
ok
```

The iSCSI target configuration is now complete and available to be added into any iSCSI initiator's target list. Once added and rescanned, the RBDs will show up as LUNS and can then be treated like normal block devices and formatted with any filesystem, as required.

Exporting CephFS via Samba

The Samba project was originally designed to allow clients and servers to talk to the Microsoft SMB protocol. It has since evolved to be able to act as a full Windows domain controller. As Samba can act as a file server for clients talking to the SMB protocol, it can be used to export CephFS to Windows clients.

There is a separate project called CTDB that's used in conjunction with Samba to create a failover cluster to provide highly available SMB shares. CTDB uses the concept of a recovery lock to detect and handle split-brain scenarios. Traditionally, CTDB has used an area of a clustered filesystem to store the recovery lock file; however, this approach does not work very well with CephFS because of the fact that the timings of the recovery sequence conflict with the timings of the OSDs and CephFS MDS failovers. Hence, a RADOS-specific recovery lock was developed that allowed CTDB to store recovery lock information directly in a RADOS object, which avoids the aforementioned issues.

In this example, a two-proxy node cluster will be used to export a directory on CephFS as an SMB share that can be accessed from Windows clients. CTDB will be used to provide fail over functionality. This share will also make use of CephFS snapshots to enable the previous version's functionality in Windows File Explorer.

For this example, you will need two VMs that have functional networking and can reach your Ceph cluster. The VMs can either be manually created, deployed via Ansible in your lab, or installed on the Ceph monitors for testing the Samba software can be.

Install the `ceph`, `ctdb`, and `samba` packages on both VMs using the following code:

```
sudo apt-get install ceph samba ctdb
```

```
The following NEW packages will be installed:
  attr binutils binutils-common binutils-x86-64-linux-gnu ceph ceph-base ceph-common ceph-mgr
  ceph-mon ceph-osd chrony formencode-i18n ibverbs-providers javascript-common libaio1
  libavahi-client3 libavahi-common-data libavahi-common3 libbabeltrace1 libbinutils libcephfs2
  libcups2 libdw1 libgoogle-perftools4 libgpgme11 libibverbs1 libjansson4 libjs-jquery
  libjs-sphinxdoc libjs-underscore libldb1 libleveldb1v5 libnl-route-3-200 libnspr4 libnss3
  libpython-stdlib libpython2.7 libpython2.7-minimal libpython2.7-stdlib librados2
  libradosstriper1 librbd1 libsnappy1v5 libtalloc2 libtcmalloc-minimal4 libtdb1 libtevent0
  libwbclient0 python python-asn1crypto python-bs4 python-cephfs python-certifi
  python-cffi-backend python-chardet python-cherrypy3 python-crypto python-cryptography
  python-dnspython python-enum34 python-formencode python-html5lib python-idna python-ipaddress
  python-jinja2 python-ldb python-logutils python-lxml python-mako python-markupsafe
  python-minimal python-openid python-openssl python-paste python-pastedeploy
  python-pastedeploy-tpl python-pastescript python-pecan python-pkg-resources python-prettytable
  python-pyinotify python-rados python-rbd python-repoze.lru python-requests python-routes
  python-samba python-scgi python-setuptools python-simplegeneric python-simplejson
  python-singledispatch python-six python-talloc python-tdb python-tempita python-urllib3
  python-waitress python-webencodings python-webob python-webtest python-werkzeug python2.7
  python2.7-minimal samba samba-common samba-common-bin samba-dsdb-modules samba-libs
  samba-vfs-modules tdb-tools
upgraded, 111 newly installed, 0 to remove and 123 not upgraded.
eed to get 61.1 MB of archives.
fter this operation, 264 MB of additional disk space will be used.
o you want to continue? [Y/n] _
```

Copy `ceph.conf` over from a Ceph monitor node using the following code:

```
scp mon1:/etc/ceph/ceph.conf /etc/ceph/ceph.conf
```

Copy the Ceph keyring over from a monitor node using the following code:

```
scp mon1:/etc/ceph/ceph.client.admin.keyring
/etc/ceph/ceph.client.admin.keyring
```

Your Samba gateways should now be able to act as clients to your Ceph cluster. This can be confirmed by checking that you can query the Ceph clusters status.

As mentioned previously, CTDB has a Ceph plugin to store the recovery lock directly in a RADOS pool. In some Linux distributions, this plugin may not be distributed along with the Samba and CTDB packages; certainly, in Debian-based distributions, it is not currently included. To work around this and save on having to manually compile, we will borrow a precompiled version from another distribution.

Download the `samba-ceph` package from the SUSE repositories using the following code:

```
wget
http://widehat.opensuse.org/opensuse/update/leap/42.3/oss/x86_64/samba-ceph
-4.6.7+git.51.327af8d0a11-6.1.x86_64.rpm
```

```
root@ceph-smb01:~# wget http://widehat.opensuse.org/opensuse/update/leap/42.3/oss/x86_64/samba-ceph-4.6.7+git.51.327af8d0a11-6.1.x86_64.rpm
--2018-12-03 22:50:36--  http://widehat.opensuse.org/opensuse/update/leap/42.3/oss/x86_64/samba-ceph-4.6.7+git.51.327af8d0a11-6.1.x86_64.rpm
Resolving widehat.opensuse.org [widehat.opensuse.org]... 62.146.92.202
Connecting to widehat.opensuse.org [widehat.opensuse.org]|62.146.92.202|:80... connected.
HTTP request sent, awaiting response... 200 OK
Length: 250093 (244K) [application/x-redhat-package-manager]
Saving to: 'samba-ceph-4.6.7+git.51.327af8d0a11-6.1.x86_64.rpm'

samba-ceph-4.6.7+git.51.327af8d0a11-6.1.x86_ 100%[===================================================================>] 244.23K  --.-KB/s    in 0.1s
```

Install a utility that will extract the contents of RPM packages using the following code:

```
apt-get install rpm2cpio
```

```
root@ceph-smb01:~# sudo apt-get install rpm2cpio
Reading package lists... Done
Building dependency tree
Reading state information... Done
The following additional packages will be installed:
  libarchive13 liblua5.2-0 librpm8 librpmio8 rpm-common
Suggested packages:
  lrzip rpm-i18n
The following NEW packages will be installed:
  libarchive13 liblua5.2-0 librpm8 librpmio8 rpm-common rpm2cpio
0 upgraded, 6 newly installed, 0 to remove and 123 not upgraded.
Need to get 681 kB of archives.
After this operation, 2,414 kB of additional disk space will be used.
Do you want to continue? [Y/n] y
```

Use the `rpm2cpio` utility to extract the contents of the RPM package that has just been downloaded using the following code:

```
rpm2cpio samba-ceph-4.6.7+git.51.327af8d0a11-6.1.x86_64.rpm | cpio -i --
make-directories
```

```
root@ceph-smb01:~# rpm2cpio samba-ceph-4.6.7+git.51.327af8d0a11-6.1.x86_64.rpm | cpio -i --make-directories
137 blocks
```

Finally, copy the CTDB RADOS helper into the `bin` folder on the VM using the following code:

```
cp usr/lib64/ctdb/ctdb_mutex_ceph_rados_helper /usr/local/bin/
```

Make sure all of the steps are carried out on both VMs. Now all of the required software is installed, we can proceed with the configuration of Samba and CTDB. Both CTDB and Samba come with example contents in their configuration files. For the purpose of this example, only the bare minimum contents will be shown; it is left as an exercise for the reader if they wish to further explore the range of configuration options available:

```
nano /etc/samba/smb.conf
```

```
[global]
netbios name = CephFS_SMB
server string = Samba Version %v on $h
workgroup = Workgroup
clustering = yes

[cephfs]
vfs objects = ceph
path = /
kernel share modes = no
valid users = test
writable = yes
```

```
nano /etc/ctdb/ctdbd.conf
```

```
CTDB_RECOVERY_LOCK="!/usr/local/bin/ctdb_mutex_ceph_rados_helper ceph client.admin rbd ctdb"
CTDB_NODES=/etc/ctdb/nodes
CTDB_MANAGES_SAMBA=yes
CTDB_SAMBA_SKIP_SHARE_CHECK=yes
```

```
nano /etc/ctdb/nodes
```

On each line, enter the IP address of each node participating in the CTDB Samba cluster, as shown in the following screenshot:

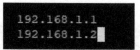

```
192.168.1.1
192.168.1.2
```

The last step is to create a Samba user that can be used to access the share. To do this, use the following code:

```
smbpasswd -a test
```

```
root@ceph-smb02:~# smbpasswd -a test
New SMB password:
Retype new SMB password:
Added user test.
```

Again, make sure this configuration is repeated across both Samba nodes. Once complete, the CTDB service can be started, which should hopefully form quorum and then launch Samba. You can start the CTDB service using the following code:

```
systemctl restart ctdb
```

After a few seconds, CTDB will start to mark the nodes as healthy; this can be confirmed by running the following code:

```
ctdb status
```

This should hopefully display a status similar to the following screenshot:

```
root@ceph-smb01:~# ctdb status
Number of nodes:2
pnn:0 10.253.1.182      OK (THIS NODE)
pnn:1 10.253.1.183      OK
Generation:1176937011
Size:2
hash:0 lmaster:0
hash:1 lmaster:1
Recovery mode:NORMAL (0)
Recovery master:0
```

It's normal for the status to be unhealthy for a short period after being started, but if the status stays in this state, check the CTDB logs located at /var/log/ctdb for a possible explanation as to what has gone wrong.

Once CTDB enters a healthy state, you should be able to access the CephFS share from any Windows client.

To provide true HA, you would need a mechanism to steer clients to the active node's IP addresses using something like a load balancer. This is outside the scope of this example.

Exporting CephFS via NFS

NFS is a file-sharing protocol that's supported on Linux, Windows, and ESXi operating systems. Being able to export CephFS filesystems as NFS shares therefore opens the door to being able to make use of CephFS across many different types of clients.

Ganesha is a user space NFS server that has a native CephFS plugin, so it is able to directly communicate with CephFS filesystems without having to mount them to the local server first. It also has support for storing its configuration and recovery information directly in RADOS objects, which helps to allow the NFS server to be run in a stateless fashion.

Go through the following steps to install and configure the export of CephFS via Ganesha:

1. Using the following code, install the Ganesha PPA (Ganesha 2.7 was the newest release at the time of writing):

   add-apt-repository ppa:nfs-ganesha/nfs-ganesha-2.7

```
root@nfs1:~# add-apt-repository ppa:nfs-ganesha/nfs-ganesha-2.7
 NFS-Ganesha 2.7
 More info: https://launchpad.net/~nfs-ganesha/+archive/ubuntu/nfs-ganesha-2.7
Press [ENTER] to continue or Ctrl-c to cancel adding it.

Hit:1 http://archive.ubuntu.com/ubuntu bionic InRelease
Hit:2 http://archive.ubuntu.com/ubuntu bionic-updates InRelease
Hit:3 http://archive.ubuntu.com/ubuntu bionic-backports InRelease
Get:4 http://ppa.launchpad.net/nfs-ganesha/nfs-ganesha-2.7/ubuntu bionic InRelease [21.3 kB]
Hit:5 http://security.ubuntu.com/ubuntu bionic-security InRelease
Get:6 http://ppa.launchpad.net/nfs-ganesha/nfs-ganesha-2.7/ubuntu bionic/main amd64 Packages [2,140 B]
Get:7 http://ppa.launchpad.net/nfs-ganesha/nfs-ganesha-2.7/ubuntu bionic/main Translation-en [1,176 B]
Fetched 24.6 kB in 1s (17.8 kB/s)
Reading package lists... Done
root@nfs1:~# 
```

2. Install the PPA for `libntirpc-1.7`, which is required by Ganesha, using the following code:

   add-apt-repository ppa:gluster/libntirpc-1.7

```
root@nfs1:~# add-apt-repository ppa:gluster/libntirpc-1.7
 This PPA is deprecated, please use https://launchpad.net/~nfs-ganesha
 More info: https://launchpad.net/~gluster/+archive/ubuntu/libntirpc-1.7
Press [ENTER] to continue or Ctrl-c to cancel adding it.

Hit:1 http://archive.ubuntu.com/ubuntu bionic InRelease
Hit:2 http://archive.ubuntu.com/ubuntu bionic-updates InRelease
Hit:3 http://archive.ubuntu.com/ubuntu bionic-backports InRelease
Get:4 http://ppa.launchpad.net/gluster/libntirpc-1.7/ubuntu bionic InRelease [21.3 kB]
Hit:5 http://ppa.launchpad.net/nfs-ganesha/nfs-ganesha-2.7/ubuntu bionic InRelease
Hit:6 http://security.ubuntu.com/ubuntu bionic-security InRelease
Get:7 http://ppa.launchpad.net/gluster/libntirpc-1.7/ubuntu bionic/main amd64 Packages [700 B]
Get:8 http://ppa.launchpad.net/gluster/libntirpc-1.7/ubuntu bionic/main Translation-en [448 B]
Fetched 22.4 kB in 1s (42.6 kB/s)
Reading package lists... Done
```

3. Install Ganesha using the following code:

```
apt-get install ceph nfs-ganesha nfs-ganesha-ceph liburcu6
```

```
root@nfs1:~# apt-get install nfs-ganesha nfs-ganesha-ceph
Reading package lists... Done
Building dependency tree
Reading state information... Done
The following additional packages will be installed:
  daemon ibverbs-providers keyutils libcephfs2 libibverbs1 libnfsidmap2 libnl-route-3-200 libnspr4 libnss3 libntirpcl librados2
  libtirpcl libwbclient0 nfs-common rpcbind
Suggested packages:
  watchdog
The following NEW packages will be installed:
  daemon ibverbs-providers keyutils libcephfs2 libibverbs1 libnfsidmap2 libnl-route-3-200 libnspr4 libnss3 libntirpcl librados2
  libtirpcl libwbclient0 nfs-common nfs-ganesha nfs-ganesha-ceph rpcbind
0 upgraded, 17 newly installed, 0 to remove and 0 not upgraded.
Need to get 5,975 kB of archives.
After this operation, 22.9 MB of additional disk space will be used.
Do you want to continue? [Y/n] y
```

4. Copy `ceph.conf` over from a Ceph monitor node using the following code:

```
scp mon1:/etc/ceph/ceph.conf /etc/ceph/ceph.conf
```

5. Copy the Ceph keyring over from a monitor node using the following code:

```
scp mon1:/etc/ceph/ceph.client.admin.keyring
/etc/ceph/ceph.client.admin.keyring
```

Now that Ganesha is installed, it needs to be configured to point at your CephFS
filesystem. A sample configuration file is provided with the Ganesha packages;
you can use this file as a basis for this. Firstly, copy the sample Ganesha Ceph
config file to become the main Ganesha config file using the following code:

```
mv /etc/ganesha/ceph.conf /etc/ganesha/ganesha.conf
```

The configuration file is well commented, but the following screenshot shows a condensed version with all of the necessary options configured. It's recommended that the default configuration file is kept and options adjusted where necessary instead of pasting over the top, as the included comments are very useful in gaining a better understanding of the configuration options:

```
NFS_CORE_PARAM
{
        Enable_NLM = false;
        Enable_RQUOTA = false;
        Protocols = 4;
}
NFSv4
{
        RecoveryBackend = rados_ng;
        Minor_Versions = 1,2;
}
CACHEINODE {
        Dir_Chunk = 0;
        NParts = 1;
        Cache_Size = 1;
}
EXPORT
{
        Export_ID=100;
        Protocols = 4;
        Transports = TCP;
        Path = /;
        Pseudo = /ceph/;
        Access_Type = RW;
        Attr_Expiration_Time = 0;
        FSAL {
                Name = CEPH;
                User_Id = "admin";
        }
}
CEPH
{
        Ceph_Conf = /etc/ceph/ceph.conf;
}
RADOS_KV
{
        Ceph_Conf = /etc/ceph/ceph.conf;
        UserId = "admin";
        pool = "rbd";
        nodeid = "ceph-nfs";
}
```

The `path config` variable needs to be set to the root of the CephFS filesystem as CephFS doesn't currently correctly support exporting subdirectories via NFS.

6. Now enable and start the `nfs-ganesha` service using the following code:

```
systemctl enable nfs-ganesha
systemctl start nfs-ganesha
```

You should now be able to mount the NFS share into any compatible client. The NFS share name will be CephFs.

ESXi hypervisor

A reasonably frequent requirement is to be able to export Ceph storage and consume it via VMware's ESXi hypervisor. ESXi supports iSCSI block storage that's formatted with its own VMFS clustered filesystem and file-based NFS storage. Both are fully functional and supported, meaning that it is normally a matter of user preference as to which is implemented or what's best supported by their storage array.

When exporting Ceph storage to ESXi, there are a number of additional factors that may need to be taken into consideration when using Ceph as a storage provider and when deciding between iSCSI and NFS. As such, this section of this chapter is dedicated to explaining the additional factors that should be taken into consideration when presenting Ceph storage to ESXi.

The first thing to consider is that ESXi was developed with enterprise storage arrays in mind, and a couple of the design decisions during its development have been made around the operation of these storage arrays. As discussed in the opening chapter, direct attached, fiber channel, and iSCSI arrays will have much lower latency than distributed network storage. With Ceph, an additional hop will be required, acting as the NFS or iSCSI proxy; this often results in a write latency that's several times that of a good block storage array.

To assist with storage vendors' QOS attempts (ignoring VAAI accelerations for now), ESXi will break up any clone or migration operations into smaller 64 KB I/Os, with the reasoning being that a large number of parallel 64 KBs are easier to schedule for disk time than large multi MB I/Os, which would block disk operations for a longer time. Ceph, however, tends to favor larger I/O sizes, and so tends to perform worse when cloning or migrating VMs. Additionally, depending on the exportation method, Ceph may not provide read ahead, and so might harm sequential read performance.

Another area in which care needs to be taken is in managing the impact of Ceph's PG locking. When accessing an object stored in Ceph, the PG containing that object is locked to preserve data consistency. All other I/Os to that PG have to queue until the lock is released. For most scenarios, this presents minimal issues; however, when exporting Ceph to ESXi, there are a number of things that ESXi does that can cause contention around this PG locking.

As mentioned previously, ESXi migrates VMs by submitting the I/Os as 64 KB. It also tries to maintain a stream of 32 of these operations in parallel to keep performance acceptable. This causes issues when using Ceph as the underlying storage, as a high percentage of these 64 KB I/Os will all be hitting the same 4 MB object, which means that out of the 32 parallel requests, each one ends up being processed in an almost serial manner. RBD striping may be used to try and ensure that these highly parallel but also highly localized I/Os are distributed across a number of objects, but your mileage may vary. VAAI accelerations may help with some of the migration and cloning operations but, in some cases, these aren't always possible to use, and so ESXi will fall back to the default method.

In relation to VM migration, if you are using a VMFS over iSCSI over RBD configuration, you can also experience PG lock contention upon updating the VMFS metadata, which is stored in only a small area of the disk. The VMFS metadata will often be updated heavily when growing a thinly provisioned VMDK or writing into snapshotted VM files. PG lock contention can limit throughput when a number of VMs on the VMFS filesystem are all trying to update the VMFS metadata at once.

At the time of writing, the official Ceph iSCSI support disables RBD caching. For certain operations, the lack of read-ahead caching has a negative impact on I/O performance. This is especially seen when you have to read sequentially through VMDK files, such as when you are migrating a VM between datastores or removing snapshots.

Regarding HA support, at the time of writing, the official Ceph iSCSI support only uses implicit ALUA to manage the active iSCSI paths. This causes issues if an ESXi host fails over to another path and other hosts in the same vSphere cluster stay on the original path. The long-term solution will be to switch to explicit ALUA, which allows the iSCSI initiator to control the active paths on the target, thereby ensuring that all hosts talk down the same path. The only current workaround to enable a full HA stack is to only run one VM per datastore.

The NFS–XFS–RBD configuration shares a lot of the PG lock contention issues as the iSCSI configuration, and suffers from the contention caused by the XFS journal. The XFS journal is a small circular buffer measured in 10s of MBs, covering only a few underlying RADOS objects. As ESXi is sending sync writes via NFS, parallel writes to XFS queue up, waiting on journal writes to complete. Because XFS is not a distributed filesystem, extra steps need to be implemented when building an HA solution to manage the mounting of the RBDs and XFS filesystems.

Finally, we have the NFS and CephFS method. As CephFS is a filesystem, it can be directly exported, meaning that there is one less layer than there is with the other two methods. Additionally, as CephFS is a distributed filesystem, it can be mounted across multiple proxy nodes at the same time, meaning that there are two fewer cluster objects to track and manage.

It's also likely that a single CephFS filesystem will be exported via NFS, providing a single large ESXi datastore, meaning that there is no need to worry about migrating VMs between datastores, as is the case with RBDs. This greatly simplifies the operation, and works around a lot of the limitations that we've discussed so far.

Although CephFS still requires metadata operations, these are carried out in parallel far better than they are in the way metadata operations in XFS or VMFS are handled, and so there is only minimal impact on performance. The CephFS metadata pool can also be placed on flash storage to further increase performance. The way metadata updates are handled also greatly lowers the occurrence of PG locking, meaning that parallel performance on the datastore is not restricted.

As mentioned previously in the NFS section, CephFS can be exported both directly via the Ganesha FSAL or by being mounted through the Linux kernel and then exported. For performance reasons, mounting CephFS via the kernel and then exporting is the current preferred method.

Before deciding on which method suits your environment the best, it is recommended that you investigate each method further and make sure that you are happy administering the solution.

Clustering

The aim of clustering is to take a single point of failure and, by letting it run across multiple servers, make the service more reliable. In theory this sounds relatively simple: if server A goes down, start the service on server B. In practice, however, there are several considerations that need to be taken into account; otherwise, there is a risk that availability will likely be worse than a single server, or even worse, that data corruption may occur. High availability is very hard to get right and very easy to get wrong.

Split brain

The first issue that needs to be dealt with in clustering is the scenario where nodes of the cluster become disconnected and unaware of each other's status. This condition is known as split brain. In a two-node cluster, each node has no way of knowing whether the reason that it has lost communication with the other node is because the other node has gone offline or because there is some form of networking interruption. In the latter case, making the incorrect assumption and starting resources on both nodes would lead to data corruption. The way to work around split brain is to make sure a cluster always has an odd number of nodes; that way, at least two nodes should always be able to form quorum and agree that the third node is the one that has had the failure.

However, even when nodes have formed quorum, it isn't still safe to restart resources on the remaining nodes. Take the case where a node appears offline, possibly because of a networking partition, or maybe the server is under high load and stops responding in time. If the remaining nodes where to restart services on themselves, what would happen if and when this unresponsive node comes back online? In order to deal with this scenario, we need to ensure that the cluster can be 100% sure of the state of all of the nodes and resources at all times. This is accomplished with fencing.

Fencing

Fencing is a process of restricting the running of resources unless there is a consistent view of the cluster state. It also plays a part in trying to return the cluster to a known state by controlling the power state of cluster nodes or other methods. As mentioned previously, if the cluster can't be sure of the current state of a cluster node, services cannot simply be restarted on other nodes, as there is no way of knowing whether the affected node is actually dead or is still running those resources. Unless configured to risk data consistency, the cluster will simply wait indefinitely until it can be sure of the state, and unless the affected node returns by itself, the cluster resources will remain offline.

The solution is to employ fencing with a method such as **Shoot The Other Node In The Head (STONITH)**, which is designed to be able to return the cluster to a normal state by manipulating an external control mechanism. The most popular approach is to use a server's bulit-in IPMI functionality to power cycle the node. As the server's IPMI is external to the operating system and usually connected to a different network than the server's LAN, it is highly unlikely that it would be affected by whatever has caused the server to appear offline. By power cycling the server and getting confirmation from IPMI that this has happened, the cluster can now be 100% certain that the the cluster resources are no longer running on that node. The cluster is then OK to restart resources on other nodes, without risk of conflict or corruption.

Pacemaker and corosync

The most widely used clustering solution on Linux is the combination of pacemaker and corosync. Corosync is responsible for messaging between nodes and ensuring a consistent cluster state, and pacemaker is responsible for managing the resources on top of this cluster state. There are a large number of resource agents available for pacemaker that enable the clustering of a wide range of services, including a number of STONITH agents for common-server IPMIs.

They can both be managed by a number of different client tools, the most common being pcs and crmsh. The following tutorial will focus on the crmsh toolset.

Creating a highly available NFS share backed by CephFS

In this example, three VMs will be required to form the cluster nodes. Go through the following steps across all three VMs:

1. Install the corosync, pacemaker, and cmrsh toolsets using the following code:

```
apt-get install corosync pacemaker crmsh
```

```
root@nfs3:~# apt-get install corosync pacemaker crmsh
Reading package lists... Done
Building dependency tree
Reading state information... Done
The following additional packages will be installed:
    cluster-glue libcfg6 libcib4 libcmap4 libcorosync-common4 libcpg4 libcrmcluster4 libcrmcommon3 libcrmservice3 libesmtp6 liblrm2
    liblrmd1 libltd17 libnetl libopenhpi3 libopenipmi0 libpe-rules2 libpe-status10 libpengine10 libpils2 libplumb2 libplumbgp12
    libqb0 libquorum5 librdmacml libsensors4 libsnmp-base libsnmp30 libstatgrab10 libstonith1 libstonithd2 libtimedate-perl
    libtotem-pg5 libtransitioner2 libvotequorum8 libxml2-utils openhpid pacemaker-cli-utils pacemaker-common
    pacemaker-resource-agents python-dateutil python-parallax python-yaml resource-agents xsltproc
Suggested packages:
    ipmitool esyncl osfsl tools sbd lm sensors snmp mibs downloader fence agents
The following NEW packages will be installed:
    cluster-glue corosync crmsh libcfg6 libcib4 libcmap4 libcorosync-common4 libcpg4 libcrmcluster4 libcrmcommon3 libcrmservice3
    libesmtp6 liblrm2 liblrmd1 libltd17 libnetl libopenhpi3 libopenipmi0 libpe-rules2 libpe-status10 libpengine10 libpils2 libplumb2
    libplumbgp12 libqb0 libquorum5 librdmacml libsensors4 libsnmp-base libsnmp30 libstatgrab10 libstonith1 libstonithd2
    libtimedate-perl libtotem-pg5 libtransitioner2 libvotequorum8 libxml2-utils openhpid pacemaker pacemaker-cli-utils
    pacemaker-common pacemaker-resource-agents python-dateutil python-parallax python-yaml resource-agents xsltproc
0 upgraded, 48 newly installed, 0 to remove and 119 not upgraded.
Need to get 5,326 kB of archives.
After this operation, 24.0 MB of additional disk space will be used.
Do you want to continue? [Y/n]
```

2. Edit the `corosync` configuration file and change the bind address (`bindnetaddr`) to match the IP configured on the VM using the following code:

```
nano /etc/corosync/corosync.conf
```

```
interface {
        # Rings must be consecutively numbered, starting at 0.
        ringnumber: 0
        # This is normally the *network* address of the
        # interface to bind to. This ensures that you can use
        # identical instances of this configuration file
        # across all your cluster nodes, without having to
        # modify this option.
        bindnetaddr: 192.168.1.1
        # However, if you have multiple physical network
        # interfaces configured for the same subnet, then the
        # network address alone is not sufficient to identify
        # the interface Corosync should bind to. In that case,
        # configure the *host* address of the interface
        # instead:
```

3. Enable and start the `corosync` service using the code shown in the following screenshot:

```
root@nfs1:~# systemctl enable corosync
Synchronizing state of corosync.service with SysV service script with /lib/systemd/systemd-sysv-install.
Executing: /lib/systemd/systemd-sysv-install enable corosync
root@nfs1:~# systemctl start corosync
```

4. After these steps have been completed on all nodes, check the status of the cluster. You should see that all three nodes have joined the cluster, as shown in the following screenshot:

```
root@nfs1:~# crm status
Stack: corosync
Current DC: nfs2 (version 1.1.18-2b07d5c5a9) - partition with quorum
Last updated: Sun Dec  9 21:23:18 2018
Last change: Sun Dec  9 21:19:01 2018 by hacluster via crmd on nfs2

3 nodes configured
0 resources configured

Online: [ nfs1 nfs2 nfs3 ]

No resources
```

Note that it says `No resources`. This is because, although the cluster is running and nodes have become members, no resources have yet to be configured. A virtual IP resource will be required, which is what NFS clients will connect to. A resource to control the Ganesha service will also be needed. Resources are managed by resource agents. These are normally scripts that contain a set of standard functions that pacemaker calls to start, stop, and monitor the resource. There are a large number of resource agents that are included with the standard pacemaker installation, but writing custom ones is not too difficult if required.

5. As discussed at the start of this section, fencing and STONITH are essential parts of an HA cluster; however, when building test environments, it can be hard to implement STONITH. By default, if a STONITH configuration has not been configured, pacemaker will not let you start any resources, so for the purpose of this example, STONITH should be disabled with the following command:

```
crm configure property stonith-enabled=false
```

```
root@nfs1:~# crm configure property stonith-enabled=false
```

6. Now that the cluster is ready to have resources created, let's create the virtual IP resource using the following code:

```
crm configure primitive p_VIP-NFS ocf:heartbeat:IPaddr params
ip=192.168.1.1 op monitor interval=10s
```

```
root@nfs1:~# crm status
Stack: corosync
Current DC: nfs2 (version 1.1.18-2b07d5c5a9) - partition with quorum
Last updated: Sun Dec  9 23:11:53 2018
Last change: Sun Dec  9 23:11:50 2018 by root via cibadmin on nfs1

3 nodes configured
1 resource configured

Online: [ nfs1 nfs2 nfs3 ]

Full list of resources:

 p_VIP-NFS      (ocf::heartbeat:IPaddr):        Started nfs1
```

From the preceding screenshot, you can see that the virtual IP has been started and is now running on node `nfs1`. If node `nfs1` becomes unavailable, then the cluster will try and keep the resource running by moving it to another node.

Now, as we did with the previous NFS section, let's install the latest version of Ganesha by going through the following steps:

1. Install the Ganesha PPA using the following code (`ganesha 2.7` was the newest release at the time of writing):

    add-apt-repository ppa:nfs-ganesha/nfs-ganesha-2.7

```
root@nfs1:~# add-apt-repository ppa:nfs-ganesha/nfs-ganesha-2.7
 NFS-Ganesha 2.7
 More info: https://launchpad.net/~nfs-ganesha/+archive/ubuntu/nfs-ganesha-2.7
Press [ENTER] to continue or Ctrl-c to cancel adding it.

Hit:1 http://archive.ubuntu.com/ubuntu bionic InRelease
Hit:2 http://archive.ubuntu.com/ubuntu bionic-updates InRelease
Hit:3 http://archive.ubuntu.com/ubuntu bionic-backports InRelease
Get:4 http://ppa.launchpad.net/nfs-ganesha/nfs-ganesha-2.7/ubuntu bionic InRelease [21.3 kB]
Hit:5 http://security.ubuntu.com/ubuntu bionic-security InRelease
Get:6 http://ppa.launchpad.net/nfs-ganesha/nfs-ganesha-2.7/ubuntu bionic/main amd64 Packages [2,140 B]
Get:7 http://ppa.launchpad.net/nfs-ganesha/nfs-ganesha-2.7/ubuntu bionic/main Translation-en [1,176 B]
Fetched 24.6 kB in 1s (17.8 kB/s)
Reading package lists... Done
root@nfs1:~#
```

2. Using the following code, install the PPA for `libntirpc-1.7`, which is required by Ganesha:

    add-apt-repository ppa:gluster/libntirpc-1.7

```
root@nfs1:~# add-apt-repository ppa:gluster/libntirpc-1.7
 This PPA is deprecated, please use https://launchpad.net/~nfs-ganesha
 More info: https://launchpad.net/~gluster/+archive/ubuntu/libntirpc-1.7
Press [ENTER] to continue or Ctrl-c to cancel adding it.

Hit:1 http://archive.ubuntu.com/ubuntu bionic InRelease
Hit:2 http://archive.ubuntu.com/ubuntu bionic-updates InRelease
Hit:3 http://archive.ubuntu.com/ubuntu bionic-backports InRelease
Get:4 http://ppa.launchpad.net/gluster/libntirpc-1.7/ubuntu bionic InRelease [21.3 kB]
Hit:5 http://ppa.launchpad.net/nfs-ganesha/nfs-ganesha-2.7/ubuntu bionic InRelease
Hit:6 http://security.ubuntu.com/ubuntu bionic-security InRelease
Get:7 http://ppa.launchpad.net/gluster/libntirpc-1.7/ubuntu bionic/main amd64 Packages [700 B]
Get:8 http://ppa.launchpad.net/gluster/libntirpc-1.7/ubuntu bionic/main Translation-en [448 B]
Fetched 22.4 kB in 1s (42.6 kB/s)
Reading package lists... Done
```

3. Install Ganesha using the following code:

```
apt-get install ceph nfs-ganesha nfs-ganesha-ceph liburcu6
```

```
root@nfs1:~# apt-get install nfs-ganesha nfs-ganesha-ceph
Reading package lists... Done
Building dependency tree
Reading state information... Done
The following additional packages will be installed:
  daemon ibverbs-providers keyutils libcephfs2 libibverbs1 libnfsidmap2 libnl-route-3-200 libnspr4 libnss3 libntirpc1 librados2
  libtirpc1 libwbclient0 nfs-common rpcbind
Suggested packages:
  watchdog
The following NEW packages will be installed:
  daemon ibverbs-providers keyutils libcephfs2 libibverbs1 libnfsidmap2 libnl-route-3-200 libnspr4 libnss3 libntirpc1 librados2
  libtirpc1 libwbclient0 nfs-common nfs-ganesha nfs-ganesha-ceph rpcbind
0 upgraded, 17 newly installed, 0 to remove and 0 not upgraded.
Need to get 5,975 kB of archives.
After this operation, 22.9 MB of additional disk space will be used.
Do you want to continue? [Y/n] y
```

4. Copy `ceph.conf` over from a Ceph monitor node using the following code:

```
scp mon1:/etc/ceph/ceph.conf /etc/ceph/ceph.conf
```

5. Copy the Ceph keyring over from a monitor node using the following code:

```
scp mon1:/etc/ceph/ceph.client.admin.keyring
/etc/ceph/ceph.client.admin.keyring
```

6. Now that Ganesha is installed, the configuration can be applied. The same configuration can be used from the standalone Ganesha section, as shown in the following screenshot:

```
NFS_CORE_PARAM
{
        Enable_NLM = false;
        Enable_RQUOTA = false;
        Protocols = 4;
}
NFSv4
{
        RecoveryBackend = rados_ng;
        Minor_Versions =  1,2;
}
CACHEINODE {
        Dir_Chunk = 0;
        NParts = 1;
        Cache_Size = 1;
}
EXPORT
{
        Export_ID=100;
        Protocols = 4;
        Transports = TCP;
        Path = /;
        Pseudo = /ceph/;
        Access_Type = RW;
        Attr_Expiration_Time = 0;
        FSAL {
                Name = CEPH;
                User_Id = "admin";
        }
}
CEPH
{
        Ceph_Conf = /etc/ceph/ceph.conf;
}
RADOS_KV
{
        Ceph_Conf = /etc/ceph/ceph.conf;
        UserId = "admin";
        pool = "rbd";
        nodeid = "ceph-nfs";
}
```

Unlike in the standalone example, we must ensure that Ganesha is not set to run by itself, and only pacemaker should launch it.

Now that all of the configuration work is completed, the pacemaker resource can be added to control the running of Ganesha using the following code:

```
crm configure primitive p_ganesha systemd:nfs-ganesha op monitor
interval=10s
```

Finally, we need to make sure that the Ganesha service is running on the same node as the virtual IP. We can do this by creating a group resource using the following code. A group resource ensures that all resources are run together on the same node, and that they're started in the order in which they are defined:

```
crm configure group g_NFS p_VIP-NFS p_ganesha
```

Now, if we check the status of the cluster, we can see that the Ganesha service is now being run, and because of the grouping, it is running on the same node as the virtual IP, as shown in the following screenshot:

```
root@nfs1:~# crm status
Stack: corosync
Current DC: nfs2 (version 1.1.18-2b07d5c5a9) - partition with quorum
Last updated: Tue Dec 11 21:08:57 2018
Last change: Tue Dec 11 21:05:23 2018 by root via cibadmin on nfs1

3 nodes configured
2 resources configured

Online: [ nfs1 nfs2 nfs3 ]

Full list of resources:

 Resource Group: g_NFS
     p_VIP-NFS   (ocf::heartbeat:IPaddr):         Started nfs2
     p_ganesha   (systemd:nfs-ganesha):   Started nfs2
```

NFS clients should now be able to connect to the virtual IP and map the NFS share. If a cluster node fails, the virtual IP and Ganesha service will migrate to another cluster node, and clients should only see a brief interruption to service.

To check the failover capability, we can put the running cluster node into standby mode to force pacemaker to run the resources on another node.

In the current example, the resources are running on node `nfs2`, so the command is as follows:

```
crm node standby nfs2
```

```
root@nfs1:~# crm status
Stack: corosync
Current DC: nfs2 (version 1.1.18-2b07d5c5a9) - partition with quorum
Last updated: Tue Dec 11 21:30:05 2018
Last change: Tue Dec 11 21:29:58 2018 by root via crm_attribute on nfs1

3 nodes configured
2 resources configured

Node nfs2: standby
Online: [ nfs1 nfs3 ]

Full list of resources:

 Resource Group: g_NFS
     p_VIP-NFS   (ocf::heartbeat:IPaddr):        Started nfs3
     p_ganesha   (systemd:nfs-ganesha):  Started nfs3
```

We can see now that node `nfs2` is now in `standby` mode and the resources have moved across to running on node `nfs3`.

Summary

In this chapter, you learned about the different storage protocols that exist and how they match to Ceph's capabilities. You also learned the protocols that are best suited for certain roles, and should be able to make informed decisions when selecting them.

Having worked through the examples, you should also have a firm understanding of how to export Ceph storage via iSCSI, NFS, and SMB to enable non-native Ceph clients to consume Ceph storage.

Finally, you should also understand the requirements for being able to design and build a resilient failover cluster that can be used to deliver highly available Ceph storage to non-native clients.

In the next chapter we will look at the different types of RADOS pool types and the different types of Ceph storage which can be provisioned.

Questions

1. Name the three storage protocols discussed in this chapter.
2. What storage protocol is typically used to provide block storage over an IP network?
3. Which storage protocol is primarily used by Windows clients?
4. What's the user space NFS server called?
5. What two pieces of software are used to build a failover cluster?
6. Why might you want to export CephFS via NFS to Linux clients?

Section 2: Operating and Tuning

2

By the end of this section, the reader will be able to take a vanilla Ceph installation and configure it to best serve their use case's requirements.

The following chapters are in this section:

5
RADOS Pools and Client Access

Ceph provides a variety of different pool types and configurations. It also supports several different data-storage types to offer storage to clients. This chapter will look at the differences between replicated and erasure-coded pools, giving examples of the creation and maintenance of both. We will then move on to how to use these pools for the three data-storage methods: **RADOS Block Device (RBD)**, object, and CephFS. Finally, we will finish with a look at how to take snapshots of the different types of storage methods. The following topics are covered in this chapter:

- Pools
- Ceph storage types

Pools

RADOS pools are the core part of a Ceph cluster. Creating a RADOS pool is what drives the creation and distribution of the placement groups, which themselves are the autonomous part of Ceph. Two types of pools can be created, replicated, and erasure-coded, offering different usable capacities, durability, and performance. RADOS pools can then be used to provide different storage solutions to clients via RBS, CephFS, and RGW, or they can be used to enable tiered performance overlaying other RADOS pools.

Replicated pools

Replicated RADOS pools are the default pool type in Ceph; data is received by the primary OSD from the client and then replicated to the remaining OSDs. The logic behind the replication is fairly simple and requires minimal processing to calculate and replicate the data between OSDs. However, as the data is replicated in whole, there is a large write penalty, as the data has to be written multiple times across the OSDs. By default, Ceph will use a replication factor of 3x, so all data will be written three times; this does not take into account any other write amplification that may be present further down in the Ceph stack. This write penalty has two main drawbacks: It obviously puts further I/O load on your Ceph cluster, as there is more data to be written, and in the case of SSDs, these extra writes will wear out the flash cells more quickly. However, as we will see in the section, *Erasure-code pools*, for smaller I/Os, the simpler replication strategy actually results in lower total required operations—there is always a fixed 3x write penalty, no matter the I/O size.

It should also be noted that although all replicas of an object are written to during a client write operation, when an object is read, only the primary OSD holding a copy of the object is involved. A client also only sends the write operation to the primary OSD, which then sends the operation to the remaining replicas. There are a number of reasons for this behavior, but they largely center around ensuring the consistency of reads.

As mentioned, the default replication size is 3, with a required minimum size of two replicas to accept client I/O. Decreasing either of these values is not recommended, and increasing them will likely have minimal effects on increasing data durability, as the chance of losing three OSDs that all share the same PG is highly unlikely. As Ceph will prioritize the recovery of PGs that have the fewest copies, this further minimizes the risk of data loss, therefore, increasing the number of replica copies to four is only beneficial when it comes to improving data availability, where two OSDs sharing the same PG can be lost and allow Ceph to keep servicing client I/O. However, due to the storage overhead of four copies, it would be recommended to look at erasure coding at this point. With the introduction of NVMes, which due to their faster performance reduce rebuild times, using a replica size of 2 can still offer reasonable data durability.

To create a replicated pool, issue a command, such as the one in the following example:

```
ceph osd pool create MyPool 128 128 replicated
```

This would create a replicated pool with 128 placement groups, called MyPool.

Erasure code pools

Ceph's default replication level provides excellent protection against data loss by storing three copies of your data on different OSDs. However, storing three copies of data vastly increases both the purchase cost of the hardware and the associated operational costs, such as power and cooling. Furthermore, storing copies also means that for every client write, the backend storage must write three times the amount of data. In some scenarios, either of these drawbacks may mean that Ceph is not a viable option.

Erasure codes are designed to offer a solution. Much like how RAID 5 and 6 offer increased usable storage capacity over RAID 1, erasure coding allows Ceph to provide more usable storage from the same raw capacity. However, also like the parity-based RAID levels, erasure coding brings its own set of disadvantages.

What is erasure coding?

Erasure coding allows Ceph to achieve either greater usable storage capacity or increase resilience to disk failure for the same number of disks, versus the standard replica method. Erasure coding achieves this by splitting up the object into a number of parts and then also calculating a type of **cyclic redundancy check (CRC)**, the erasure code, and then storing the results in one or more extra parts. Each part is then stored on a separate OSD. These parts are referred to as K and M chunks, where K refers to the number of data shards and M refers to the number of erasure code shards. As in RAID, these can often be expressed in the form $K+M$, or 4+2, for example.

In the event of an OSD failure that contains an object's shard, which is one of the calculated erasure codes, data is read from the remaining OSDs that store data with no impact. However, in the event of an OSD failure that contains the data shards of an object, Ceph can use the erasure codes to mathematically recreate the data from a combination of the remaining data and erasure code shards.

K+M

The more erasure code shards you have, the more OSD failures you can tolerate and still successfully read data. Likewise, the ratio of K to M shards each object is split into has a direct effect on the percentage of raw storage that is required for each object.

A 3+1 configuration will give you 75% usable capacity but only allows for a single OSD failure, and so would not be recommended. In comparison, a three-way replica pool only gives you 33% usable capacity.

4+2 configurations would give you 66% usable capacity and allows for two OSD failures. This is probably a good configuration for most people to use.

At the other end of the scale, *18+2* would give you 90% usable capacity and still allow for two OSD failures. On the surface, this sounds like an ideal option, but the greater total number of shards comes at a cost. A greater number of total shards has a negative impact on performance and also an increased CPU demand. The same 4 MB object that would be stored as a whole single object in a replicated pool would now be split into 20 x 200-KB chunks, which have to be tracked and written to 20 different OSDs. Spinning disks will exhibit faster bandwidth, measured in MBps with larger I/O sizes, but bandwidth drastically tails off at smaller I/O sizes. These smaller shards will generate a large amount of small I/O and cause an additional load on some clusters.

Also, it's important not to forget that these shards need to be spread across different hosts according to the CRUSH map rules: no shard belonging to the same object can be stored on the same host as another shard from the same object. Some clusters may not have a sufficient number of hosts to satisfy this requirement. If a CRUSH rule cannot be satisfied, the PGs will not become active, and any I/O destined for these PGs will be halted, so it's important to understand the impact on a cluster's health of making CRUSH modifications.

Reading back from these high-chunk pools is also a problem. Unlike in a replica pool, where Ceph can read just the requested data from any offset in an object, in an erasure pool, all shards from all OSDs have to be read before the read request can be satisfied. In the *18+2* example, this can massively amplify the amount of required disk read ops, and average latency will increase as a result. This behavior is a side-effect that tends to only cause a performance impact with pools that use a lot of shards. A 4+2 configuration in some instances will get a performance gain compared to a replica pool, from the result of splitting an object into shards. As the data is effectively striped over a number of OSDs, each OSD has to write less data, and there are no secondary and tertiary replicas to write.

Erasure coding can also be used to improve durability rather than to maximize available storage space. Take, for example, a 4+4 pool: it has a storage efficiency of 50%, so it's better than a 3x replica pool, yet it can sustain up to four OSD losses without data loss.

How does erasure coding work in Ceph?

As with replication, Ceph has a concept of a primary OSD, which also exists when using erasure-coded pools. The primary OSD has the responsibility of communicating with the client, calculating the erasure shards, and sending them out to the remaining OSDs in the PG set. This is illustrated in the following diagram:

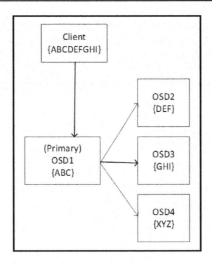

If an OSD in the set is down, the primary OSD can use the remaining data and erasure shards to reconstruct the data, before sending it back to the client. During read operations, the primary OSD requests all OSDs in the PG set to send their shards. The primary OSD uses data from the data shards to construct the requested data, and the erasure shards are discarded. There is a fast read option that can be enabled on erasure pools, which allows the primary OSD to reconstruct the data from erasure shards if they return quicker than data shards. This can help to lower average latency at the cost of a slightly higher CPU usage. The following diagram shows how Ceph reads from an erasure-coded pool:

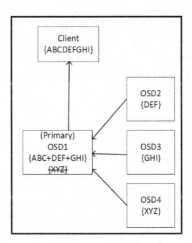

The following diagram shows how Ceph reads from an erasure pool when one of the data shards is unavailable. Data is reconstructed by reversing the erasure algorithm, using the remaining data and erasure shards:

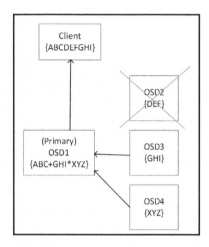

Algorithms and profiles

There are a number of different erasure plugins you can use to create your erasure-coded pool.

Jerasure

The default erasure plugin in Ceph is the jerasure plugin, which is a highly-optimized open source erasure-coding library. The library has a number of different techniques that can be used to calculate the erasure codes. The default is Reed-Solomon, and this provides good performance on modern processors, which can accelerate the instructions that the technique uses.

There are also a number of other jerasure techniques that can be used, which all have a fixed number of M shards. If you are intending on only having two M shards, they can be a good candidate, as their fixed size means that optimizations are possible, lending to increased performance. Each optimized technique, aside from only supporting two erasure shards, also tends to have certain requirements around the total number of shards. Here is a brief description of each optimized technique:

- reed_sol_van: The default technique, complete flexibility on number of $k+m$ shards, also the slowest.

- `reed_sol_r6_op`: Optimized version of default technique for use cases where $m=2$. Although it is much faster than the unoptimized version, it's not as fast as other versions. However, the number of k shards is flexible.
- `cauchy_orig`: Better than the default, but it's better to use `cauchy_good`.
- `cauchy_good`: Middle-of-the-road performance while maintaining full flexibility of the shard configuration.
- `liberation`: Total number of shards must be equal to a prime number and $m=2$, so 3+2, 5+2, or 9+2 are all good candidates, excellent performance.
- `liber8tion`: Total number of shards must be equal to 8 and $m=2$, only 6+2 is possible, but excellent performance.
- `blaum_roth`: Total number of shards must be one less than a prime number and $m=2$, so the ideal is 4+2, excellent performance.

As always, benchmarks should be conducted before storing any production data on an erasure-coded pool to identify which technique best suits your workload.

In general, the jerasure profile should be preferred in most cases, unless another profile has a major advantage, as it offers well-balanced performance and is well-tested.

ISA

The ISA library is designed to work with Intel processors and offers enhanced performance. It supports both the Reed-Solomon and Cauchy techniques.

LRC

One of the disadvantages of using erasure coding in a distributed storage system is that recovery can be very intensive on networking between hosts. As each shard is stored on a separate host, recovery operations require multiple hosts to participate in the process. When the CRUSH topology spans multiple racks, this can put pressure on the inter-rack networking links. The **Locally Repairable erasure Code (LRC)** erasure plugin adds an additional parity shard, which is local to each OSD node. This allows recovery operations to remain local to the node where an OSD has failed and remove the need for nodes to receive data from all other remaining shard-holding nodes.

However, the addition of these local recovery codes does impact the amount of usable storage for a given number of disks. In the event of multiple disk failures, the LRC plugin has to resort to using global recovery, as would happen with the jerasure plugin.

SHEC

The SHEC profile is designed with similar goals to the LRC plugin, in that it reduces the networking requirements during recovery. However, instead of creating extra parity shards on each node, SHEC shingles the shards across OSDs in an overlapping fashion.

The shingle part of the plugin name represents the way the data distribution resembles shingled tiles on a roof of a house. By overlapping the parity shards across OSDs, the SHEC plugin reduces recovery resource requirements for both single and multiple disk failures.

Overwrite support in erasure-coded pools

Although erasure-coded pool support has been in Ceph for several releases now, before the arrival of BlueStore in the Luminous release, it had not supported partial writes. This limitation meant that erasure pools could not directly be used with RBD and CephFS workloads. With the introduction of BlueStore in Luminous, it provided the groundwork for partial write support to be implemented. With partial write support, the number of I/O types that erasure pools can support almost matches replicated pools, enabling the use of erasure-coded pools directly with RBD and CephFS workloads. This dramatically lowers the cost of storage capacity for these use cases.

For full-stripe writes, which occur either for new objects or when the entire object is rewritten, the write penalty is greatly reduced. A client writing a 4 MB object to a 4+2 erasure-coded pool would only have to write 6 MB of data, 4 MB of data chunks, and 2 MB of erasure-coded chunks. This is compared to 12 MB of data written in a replicated pool. It should, however, be noted that each chunk of the erasure stripe will be written to a different OSD. For smaller erasure profiles, such as 4+2, this will tend to offer a large performance boost for both spinning disks and SSDs, as each OSD is having to write less data. However, for larger erasure stripes, the overhead of having to write to an ever-increasing number of OSDs starts to outweigh the benefit of reducing the amount of data to be written, particularly on spinning disks whose latency does not have a linear relationship to the I/O size.

Ceph's userspace clients, such as `librbd` and `libcephfs`, are clever enough to try to batch together smaller I/Os and submit a full stripe write if possible; this can help when the application residing previously is submitting sequential I/O but not aligned to the 4 MB object boundaries.

Partial write support allows overwrites to be done to an object; this introduces a number of complexities, as, when a partial write is done, the erasure chunks also require updating to match the new object contents. This is very similar to the challenges faced by RAID 5 and 6, although having to coordinate this process across several OSDs in a consistent manor increases the complexity. When a partial write is performed, Ceph first reads the entire existing object off the disk, and then it must merge in memory the new writes, calculate the new erasure-coded chunks, and write everything back to the disk. So, not only is there both a read and a write operation involved, but each of these operations will likely touch several disks making up the erasure stripe. As you can see, a single I/O can end up having a write penalty several times higher than that of a replicated pool. For a 4+2 erasure-coded pool, a small 4 KB write could end up submitting 12 I/Os to the disks in the cluster, not taking into account any additional Ceph overheads.

Creating an erasure-coded pool

Let's bring our test cluster up again and switch into super-user mode in Linux, so we don't have to keep prepending sudo to our commands.

Erasure-coded pools are controlled by the use of erasure profiles; these control how many shards each object is broken up into including the split between data and erasure shards. The profiles also include configuration to determine what erasure code plugin is used to calculate the hashes.

The following plugins are available to use:

- Jerasure
- ISA
- LRC
- **Shingled Erasure Coding (SHEC)**

To see a list of the erasure profiles, run the following command:

```
# ceph osd erasure-code-profile ls
```

You can see there is a default profile in the fresh installation of Ceph:

```
vagrant@mon1:~$ sudo ceph osd erasure-code-profile ls
default
```

Let's see what configuration options it contains, using the following command:

```
# ceph osd erasure-code-profile get default
```

The `default` profile specifies that it will use the jerasure plugin with the Reed-Solomon error-correcting codes and will split objects into 2 data shards and 1 erasure shard:

```
vagrant@mon1:~$ sudo ceph osd erasure-code-profile get default
k=2
m=1
plugin=jerasure
technique=reed_sol_van
```

This is almost perfect for our test cluster; however, for the purpose of this exercise, we will create a new profile, using the following commands:

```
# ceph osd erasure-code-profile set example_profile k=2 m=1
plugin=jerasure technique=reed_sol_van
# ceph osd erasure-code-profile ls
```

You can see our new `example_profile` has been created:

```
vagrant@mon1:~$ sudo ceph osd erasure-code-profile ls
default
example_profile
```

Now, let's create our erasure-coded pool with this profile:

```
# ceph osd pool create ecpool 128 128 erasure example_profile
```

The preceding command gives the following output:

```
vagrant@mon1:~$ sudo ceph osd pool create ecpool 128 128 erasure example_profile
pool 'ecpool' created
```

The preceding command instructs Ceph to create a new pool called `ecpool` with 128 PGs. It should be an erasure-coded pool and should use the `example_profile` we previously created.

Let's create an object with a small text string inside it and then prove the data has been stored by reading it back:

```
# echo "I am test data for a test object" | rados --pool
ecpool put Test1 -
# rados --pool ecpool get Test1 -
```

That proves that the erasure-coded pool is working, but it's hardly the most exciting of discoveries:

```
root@mon1:/home/vagrant# echo "I am test data for a test object" | rados --pool ecpool put Test1 -
root@mon1:/home/vagrant# rados --pool ecpool get Test1 -
I am test data for a test object
```

Let's check whether we can see what's happening at a lower level.

First, find out what PG is holding the object we just created:

```
# ceph osd map ecpool Test1
```

The result of the preceding command tells us that the object is stored in PG 3.40 on OSDs 1, 2, and 0 in this example Ceph cluster. That's pretty obvious, as we only have three OSDs, but in larger clusters, that is a very useful piece of information:

```
root@mon1:/home/vagrant# ceph osd map ecpool Test1
osdmap e114 pool 'ecpool' (3) object 'Test1' -> pg 3.ae48bdc0 (3.40) -> up ([1,2,0], p1) acting ([1,2,0
], p1)
```

The PGs will likely be different on your test cluster, so make sure the PG folder structure matches the output of the preceding `ceph osd map` command.

If you are using BlueStore, the file structure of the OSD is no longer viewable by default. However, you can use the following command on a stopped OSD to mount the BlueStore OSD as a Linux filesystem.

We can now look at the folder structure of the OSDs and see how the object has been split using the following commands:

```
ceph-objectstore-tool --op fuse --data-path /var/lib/ceph/osd/ceph-0 --
mountpoint /mnt
```

The following examples are shown using filestore; if using BlueStore, replace the OSD path with the contents of the /mnt mount point from the preceding command:

```
ls -l /var/lib/ceph/osd/ceph-2/current/1.40s0_head/
```

The preceding command gives the following output:

```
root@osd1:/home/vagrant# ls -l /var/lib/ceph/osd/ceph-0/current/3.40s2_head/
total 4
-rw-r--r-- 1 ceph ceph    0 Feb 12 19:53 __head_00000040__3_ffffffffffffffff_2
-rw-r--r-- 1 ceph ceph 2048 Feb 12 19:56 Test1__head_AE48BDC0__3_ffffffffffffffff_2
```

```
# ls -l /var/lib/ceph/osd/ceph-1/current/1.40s1_head/
```

The preceding command gives the following output:

```
root@osd2:/home/vagrant# ls -l /var/lib/ceph/osd/ceph-2/current/3.40s1_head/
total 4
-rw-r--r-- 1 ceph ceph    0 Feb 12 19:53 __head_00000040__3_ffffffffffffffff_1
-rw-r--r-- 1 ceph ceph 2048 Feb 12 19:56 Test1__head_AE48BDC0__3_ffffffffffffffff_1
```

```
# ls -l /var/lib/ceph/osd/ceph-0/current/1.40s2_head/
total 4
```

The preceding command gives the following output:

```
root@osd3:/home/vagrant# ls -l /var/lib/ceph/osd/ceph-1/current/3.40s0_head/
total 4
-rw-r--r-- 1 ceph ceph    0 Feb 12 19:53 __head_00000040__3_ffffffffffffffff_0
-rw-r--r-- 1 ceph ceph 2048 Feb 12 19:56 Test1__head_AE48BDC0__3_ffffffffffffffff_0
```

Notice how the PG directory names have been appended to the shard number and that replicated pools just have the PG number as their directory name. If you examine the contents of the object files, you will see our text string that we entered into the object when we created it. However, due to the small size of the text string, Ceph has padded out the second shard with null characters and the erasure shard; hence, it will contain the same as the first. You can repeat this example with a new object that contains larger amounts of text to see how Ceph splits the text into the shards and calculates the erasure code.

Troubleshooting the 2147483647 error

This small section is included within the erasure-coding, rather than in Chapter 11, *Troubleshooting*, of this book, as it's commonly seen with erasure-coded pools and so is very relevant to this chapter. An example of this error is shown in the following screenshot, when running the `ceph health detail` command:

```
pg 2.7a is creating+incomplete, acting [0,2,1,2147483647] (reducing pool broken_ecpool min_size from 4
may help; search ceph.com/docs for 'incomplete')
pg 2.79 is creating+incomplete, acting [1,0,2,2147483647] (reducing pool broken_ecpool min_size from 4
may help; search ceph.com/docs for 'incomplete')
pg 2.78 is creating+incomplete, acting [1,0,2147483647,2] (reducing pool broken_ecpool min_size from 4
may help; search ceph.com/docs for 'incomplete')
pg 2.7f is creating+incomplete, acting [0,2,1,2147483647] (reducing pool broken_ecpool min_size from 4
may help; search ceph.com/docs for 'incomplete')
```

If you see 2147483647 listed as one of the OSDs for an erasure-coded pool, this normally means that CRUSH was unable to find a sufficient number of OSDs to complete the PG peering process. This is normally due to the number of K+M shards being larger than the number of hosts in the CRUSH topology. However, in some cases, this error can still occur even when the number of hosts is equal to or greater than the number of shards. In this scenario, it's important to understand how CRUSH picks OSDs as candidates for data placement. When CRUSH is used to find a candidate OSD for a PG, it applies the CRUSH map to find an appropriate location in the CRUSH topology. If the result comes back as the same as a previously-selected OSD, Ceph will retry to generate another mapping by passing slightly different values into the CRUSH algorithm. In some cases, if there is a similar number of hosts to the number of erasure shards, CRUSH may run out of attempts before it can suitably find the correct OSD mappings for all the shards. Newer versions of Ceph have mostly fixed these problems by increasing the CRUSH tuneable, `choose_total_tries`.

Reproducing the problem

To aid our understanding of the problem in more detail, the following steps will demonstrate how to create an `erasure-code-profile` that will require more shards than our three-node cluster can support.

Like earlier in the chapter, create a new erasure profile but modify the K/M parameters to be k=3 and m=1:

```
$ ceph osd erasure-code-profile set broken_profile k=3 m=1
plugin=jerasure technique=reed_sol_van
```

Now create a pool with it:

```
$ ceph osd pool create broken_ecpool 128 128 erasure broken_profile
```

If we look at the output from `ceph -s`, we will see that the PGs for this new pool are stuck in the creating state:

```
cluster d9f58afd-3e62-4493-ba80-0356290b3d9f
 health HEALTH_ERR
        128 pgs are stuck inactive for more than 300 seconds
        128 pgs incomplete
        128 pgs stuck inactive
        128 pgs stuck unclean
        all OSDs are running kraken or later but the 'require_kraken_osds' osdmap flag is not set
 monmap e2: 3 mons at {mon1=192.168.0.41:6789/0,mon2=192.168.0.42:6789/0,mon3=192.168.0.43:6789/0}
        election epoch 64, quorum 0,1,2 mon1,mon2,mon3
   mgr active: mon1 standbys: mon2, mon3
 osdmap e98: 3 osds: 3 up, 3 in
        flags sortbitwise,require_jewel_osds
  pgmap v695: 192 pgs, 2 pools, 3920 bytes data, 2 objects
        112 MB used, 26782 MB / 26894 MB avail
             128 creating+incomplete
              64 active+clean
```

The output of `ceph health detail` shows the reason, and we see the `2147483647` error:

```
pg 2.7a is creating+incomplete, acting [0,2,1,2147483647] (reducing pool broken_ecpool min_size from 4
may help; search ceph.com/docs for 'incomplete')
pg 2.79 is creating+incomplete, acting [1,0,2,2147483647] (reducing pool broken_ecpool min_size from 4
may help; search ceph.com/docs for 'incomplete')
pg 2.78 is creating+incomplete, acting [1,0,2147483647,2] (reducing pool broken_ecpool min_size from 4
may help; search ceph.com/docs for 'incomplete')
pg 2.7f is creating+incomplete, acting [0,2,1,2147483647] (reducing pool broken_ecpool min_size from 4
may help; search ceph.com/docs for 'incomplete')
```

If you encounter this error and it is a result of your erasure profile being larger than your number of hosts or racks, depending on how you have designed your CRUSH map, then the only real solution is to either drop the number of shards or increase the number of hosts.

To create an erasure-coded pool, issue a command, as shown in the following example:

```
ceph osd pool create MyECPool 128 128 erasure MyECProfile
```

This would create an erasure-coded pool with 128 placement groups, called `MyECPool`, using the erasure-coding profile, called `MyECProfile`.

Although partial writes bring erasure-coded pools to near parity with replicated pools in terms of supported features, they still cannot store all the required data for RBDs. Therefore, when creating an RBD, you must place the RBD header object on a replicated RADOS pool and then specify that the data objects for that RBD should be stored in the erasure-coded pool.

Scrubbing

To protect against bit-rot, Ceph periodically runs a process called scrubbing to verify the data stored across the OSDs. The scrubbing process works at the PG level and compares the contents of each of the PGs across all of the participating OSDs to check that each OSD has identical contents. If an OSD is found to have an object copy that differs to the others or is even missing the object, the PG is marked as inconsistent. Inconsistent PGs can be repaired by instructing Ceph to repair the PG; this is covered in further detail in Chapter 11, *Troubleshooting*.

There are two types of scrubbing: normal and deep. Normal scrubbing simply checks for the existence of the object and that its metadata is correct; deep scrubbing is when the actual data is compared. Deep scrubbing tends to be much more I/O-intensive than normal scrubbing.

Although BlueStore now supports checksums, the need for scrubbing is not completely redundant. BlueStore only compares the checksums against the data being actively read, and so for cold data that is very rarely written, data loss or corruption could occur and only the scrubbing process would detect this.

There are a number of scrubbing tuning options that are covered later in Chapter 9, *Tuning Ceph*; they influence the scheduling of when scrubbing takes place and the impact on client I/O.

Ceph storage types

Although Ceph provides basic object storage via the RADOS layer, on its own this is not very handy, as the scope of applications that could consume RADOS storage directly is extremely limited. Therefore, Ceph builds on the base RADOS capabilities and provides higher-level storage types that can be more easily consumed by clients.

RBD

RBD for short, is how Ceph storage can be presented as standard Linux block devices. RBDs are composed of a number of objects, 4 MB by default, which are concatenated together. A 4 GB RBD would contain a 1,000 objects by default.

Thin provisioning

Due to the way RADOS works, RBDs are thin provisioned; that is to say, the underlying objects are only provisioned once data is written to the logical block address that corresponds to that object. There are no safeguards around this; Ceph will quite happily let you provision a 1 PB block device on a 1 TB disk, and, as long as you never place more than 1 TB of data on it, everything will work as expected. If used correctly, thin provisioning can greatly increase the usable capacity of a Ceph cluster as VMs, which are typically one of the main use cases for RBDs, likely have a large amount of whitespace contained within them. However care should be taken to monitor the growth of data on the Ceph cluster; if the underlying usable capacity is filled, the Ceph cluster will effectively go offline until space is freed.

Snapshots and clones

RBDs support having snapshots taken of them. Snapshots are a read-only copy of the RBD image that persists its state from the point in time in which it was taken. Multiple snapshots can be taken to retain the RBDs history through time, if desired. The process of taking a snapshot of an RBD is extremely quick, and there is no performance penalty for reads going to the source RBD. However, when a write hits the source RBD for the first time, the existing contents of the object will be cloned for us by the snapshot, further I/O will have no further impact. This process is called **copy-on-write** and is a standard way of performing snapshots in storage products. It should be noted that this process is greatly accelerated in BlueStore, as a full object copy is not required as it was in filestore, although care should still be taken to make sure that RBDs that experience heavy write I/O are not left with open snapshots for long periods of time. As well as snapshots that require extra I/O during writes—as the copy-on-write process creates clones of the objects, additional cluster space is consumed—care should be taken to monitor space consumption when snapshots are in use.

During the removal of a snapshot, the PGs containing snapshot objects enter a snaptrim state. In this state, the objects that had been cloned as part of the copy-on-write process are removed. Again, on BlueStore, this process has much less impact on the cluster load.

RBDs also support snapshot layering; this is a process where a writable clone is made of an existing snapshot, which is itself a snapshot of an existing RBD. This process is typically used to create cloned VMs of master images; an initial RBD is created for a VM, to which an OS is installed. Snapshots are then taken throughout the master image's life to capture changes. These snapshots are then used as the basis for cloning new VMs. When an RBD snapshot is cloned initially, non objects of the objects in the RBD are required to be duplicated, as since they are identical to the source, they can simply be referenced by the clone. Once the cloned RBD starts getting data written to it, each object that is modified is then written out as a new object that belongs to the clone.

This process of object referencing means that a large number of VMs that share the same OS template will likely consume less space than if each VM was individually deployed to fresh RBDs. In some cases, it may be desired to force a full clone where all the RBDs objects are duplicated; this process in Ceph is called flattening a clone.

First, create a snapshot, called `snap1`, of a RBD image, called `test`, in the default RBD pool:

```
rbd snap create rbd/test@snap1
```

Confirm that the snapshot has been created by viewing all snapshots of the RBD:

```
rbd snap ls rbd/test
```

```
$rbd snap ls rbd/test
SNAPID NAME     SIZE TIMESTAMP
    14 snap1 10 GiB Sat Jan  5 21:39:27 2019
```

For the snapshot to be cloned, it needs to be protected. As the clones are dependent on the snapshot, any modification to the snapshot would likely cause corruption in the clones:

```
rbd snap protect rbd/test@snap1
```

View the info of the snapshot; it can be seen that the snapshot is now protected:

```
rbd info rbd/test@snap1
```

```
rbd image 'test':
        size 10 GiB in 2560 objects
        order 22 (4 MiB objects)
        id: 26ad9632ae8944a
        block_name_prefix: rbd_data.26ad9632ae8944a
        format: 2
        features: layering, exclusive-lock, object-map, fast-diff, deep-flatten
        op_features:
        flags:
        create_timestamp: Fri Sep 14 17:18:53 2018
        protected: True
```

Now a clone of the snapshot can be taken:

```
rbd clone rbd/test@snap1 rbd/CloneOfTestSnap1
```

You can confirm the relationship of the clone to the snapshot by viewing the `rbd info` of the clone:

```
rbd info rbd/CloneOfTestSnap1
```

```
$rbd info rbd/CloneOfTestSnap1
rbd image 'CloneOfTestSnap1':
        size 10 GiB in 2560 objects
        order 22 (4 MiB objects)
        id: de6f0a6b8b4567
        block_name_prefix: rbd_data.de6f0a6b8b4567
        format: 2
        features: layering, exclusive-lock, object-map, fast-diff, deep-flatten
        op_features:
        flags:
        create_timestamp: Sat Jan  5 21:53:18 2019
        parent: rbd/test@snap1
        overlap: 10 GiB
```

Or you can do so by viewing the list of children of the snapshot:

```
rbd children rbd/test@snap1
```

```
$rbd children rbd/test@snap1
rbd/CloneOfTestSnap1
```

Now flatten the clone; this will make it a completely independent RBD image no longer dependent on the snapshot:

```
rbd flatten rbd/CloneOfTestSnap1
```

```
$rbd flatten rbd/CloneOfTestSnap1
Image flatten: 8% complete...
```

Confirm that the clone is now no longer attached to the snapshot; note the parent field is now missing:

```
rbd info rbd/CloneOfTestSnap1
```

```
$rbd info rbd/CloneOfTestSnap1
rbd image 'CloneOfTestSnap1':
        size 10 GiB in 2560 objects
        order 22 (4 MiB objects)
        id: de6f0a6b8b4567
        block_name_prefix: rbd_data.de6f0a6b8b4567
        format: 2
        features: layering, exclusive-lock, object-map, fast-diff, deep-flatten
        op_features:
        flags:
        create_timestamp: Sat Jan  5 21:53:18 2019
```

Unprotect the snapshot:

```
rbd snap unprotect rbd/test@snap1
```

And finally delete it:

```
rbd snap rm rbd/test@snap1
```

Object maps

As RBDs support thin provisioning and are composed of a large number of 4 MB objects, tasks such as determining what space the RBD is consuming, or cloning the RBD, would involve a large number of read requests to determine whether a certain object that is part of the RBD exists. To solve this problem, RBDs support object maps; these maps indicate which logical blocks of an RBD have been allocated and so greatly speed up the process of calculating which objects exist. The object map is stored as an object itself in the RADOS pool and should not be manipulated directly.

Exclusive locking

To try to prevent corruption from two clients writing to the same RBD at the same time, exclusive locking allows the client to acquire a lock to disallow any other client from writing to the RBD. It's important to note that clients can always request the lock to be transferred to themselves and so the lock is only to protect the RBD device itself; a non-clustered filesystem will still likely be corrupted if two clients try to mount it, regardless of the exclusive locking.

CephFS

CephFS is a POSIX-compatible filesystem that sits on top of RADOS pools. Being POSIX-compliment means that it should be able to function as a drop-in replacement for any other Linux filesystem and still function as expected. There is both a kernel and userspace client to mount the filesystem on to a running Linux system. The kernel client, although normally faster, tends to lag behind the userspace client in terms of supported features and will often require you to be running the latest kernel to take advantage of certain features and bug fixes. A CephFS filesystem can also be exported via NFS or Samba to non-Linux-based clients, both software have direct support for talking to CephFS. This subject will be covered in more detail in the next chapter.

CephFS stores each file as one or more RADOS objects. If an object is larger than 4 MB, it will be striped across multiple objects. This striping behavior can be controlled by the use of XATTRs, which can be associated with both files and directories, and can control the object size, stripe width, and stripe count. The default striping policy effectively concatenates multiple 4 MB objects together, but by modifying the stripe count and width, a RAID 0 style striping can be achieved.

MDSes and their states

CephFS requires an additional component to coordinate client access and metadata; this component is called the **Metadata Server**, or **MDS** for short. Although the MDS is used to serve metadata requests to and from the client, the actual data read and written still goes directly via the OSDs. This approach minimizes the impact of the MDS on the filesystem's performance for more bulk data transfers, although smaller I/O-intensive operations can start to be limited by the MDS performance. The MDS currently runs as a single-threaded process and so it is recommended that the MDS is run on hardware with the highest-clocked CPU as possible.

The MDS has a local cache for storing hot portions of the CephFS metadata to reduce the amount of I/O going to the metadata pool; this cache is stored in local memory for performance and can be controlled by adjusting the MDS cache memory-limit configuration option, which defaults to 1 GB.

CephFS utilizes a journal stored in RADOS mainly for consistency reasons. The journal stores the stream of metadata updates from clients and then flushes them into the CephFS metadata store. If an MDS is terminated, the MDS that takes over the active role can then replay these metadata events stored in the journal. This process of replaying the journal is an essential part of the MDS becoming active and therefore will block until the process is completed. The process can be sped up by having a standby-replay MDS that is constantly replaying the journal that is ready to take over the primary active role in a much shorter amount of time. If you have multiple active MDSes, whereas a pure standby MDS can be a standby for any active MDS, standby-replay MDSes have to be assigned to a specific MDS rank.

As well as the active and replaying states, an MDS can also be in several other states; the ones you are likely to see in the ceph status are listed for reference for when operating a Ceph cluster with a CephFS filesystem. The states are split into two parts: the part on the left side of the colon shows whether the MDS is up or down. The part on the right side of the colon represents the current operational state:

- `up:active`: This is the normal desired state, as long as one MDS is in this state, clients can access the CephFS filesystem.
- `up:standby`: This can be a normal state as long as one MDS is `up:active`. In this state, an MDS is online but not playing any active part in the CephFS infrastructure. It will come online and replay the CephFS journal in the event that the active MDS goes online.
- `up:standby_replay`: Like the `up:standby` state, an MDS in this state is available to become active in the event of an active MDS going offline. However, a `standby_replay` MDS is continuously replaying the journal of MDS it has been configured to follow, meaning the failover time is greatly reduced. It should be noted that while a standby MDS can replace any active MDS, a `standby_replay` MDS can only replace the one it has been configured to follow.
- `up:replay`: In this state, an MDS has begun taking over the active role and is currently replaying the metadata stored in the CephFS journal.
- `up:reconnect`: If there were active client sessions active when the active MDS went online, the recovering MDS will try to re-establish client connections in this state until the client timeout is hit.

Although there are other states an MDS can be in, it is likely that during normal operations they will not be seen and so have not been included here. Please consult the official Ceph documentation for more details on all available states.

Creating a CephFS filesystem

To create a CephFS filesystem, two RADOS pools are required: one to store the metadata and another to store the actual data objects. Although technically any existing RADOS pools can be used, it's highly recommended that dedicated pools are created. The metadata pool will typically contain only a small percentage of data when compared to the data pool and, so the number of PGs required when provisioning this pool can typically be set in the 64 - 128 range. The data pool should be provisioned much like an RBD pool and the number of PGs calculated to match the number of OSDs in the cluster and the share of data that the CephFS filesystem will store.

At least one MDS will also need to be deployed, but it is recommended that, for any production deployment, at least two MDSes are deployed with one running as a standby or standby-replay.

Edit the `/etc/ansible/hosts` file and add the server that will hold the mds role. The following example is using the `mon2` VM from the test lab in Chapter 2, *Deploying Ceph with Containers*:

```
[rgws]
mon3

[ceph:children]
mons
osds
rgws
```

Now run the Ansible playbook again and it will deploy the mds:

```
INSTALLER STATUS ***************************************************************
Install Ceph Monitor      : Complete (0:01:46)
Install Ceph Manager      : Complete (0:00:17)
Install Ceph OSD          : Complete (0:00:49)
Install Ceph RGW          : Complete (0:00:16)
```

Once the playbook has finished running, check that the mds is up and running; this can be viewed via the ceph-s output:

```
vagrant@mon3:~$ sudo ceph -s
  cluster:
    id:     66fd555c-7a6c-40e9-b775-9d712b4256e1
    health: HEALTH_WARN
            application not enabled on 1 pool(s)
            clock skew detected on mon.mon2, mon.mon3

  services:
    mon: 3 daemons, quorum mon1,mon2,mon3
    mgr: mon1(active)
    osd: 3 osds: 3 up, 3 in
    rgw: 1 daemon active
```

Ansible should have provisioned data pools and metadata pools as part of the deployment process; this can be confirmed by running the following command from one of the monitor nodes:

```
sudo ceph osd lspools
```

```
vagrant@mon1:~$ sudo ceph osd lspools
1 rbd
2 .rgw.root
3 default.rgw.control
4 default.rgw.meta
5 default.rgw.log
6 cephfs_data
7 cephfs_metadata
```

From the preceding screenshot, we can see that pools 6 and 7 have been created for CephFS. If the pools have not been created, follow the steps at the start of this chapter on how to create RADOS pools. While the data pools may be created as erasure-coded pools, the metadata pool must be of the replicated type.

The final step in creating a CephFS filesystem is to instruct Ceph to use the two created RADOS pools to build the filesystem. However, as in the previous steps, the Ansible deployment should have handled this. We can confirm by running the following command:

```
sudo ceph fs status
```

It will show the following if the CephFS filesystem has been created and is ready for service:

```
vagrant@mon1:~$ sudo ceph fs status
cephfs - 0 clients
======
+------+--------+------+---------------+-------+-------+
| Rank | State  | MDS  |   Activity    |  dns  | inos  |
+------+--------+------+---------------+-------+-------+
|  0   | active | mon2 | Reqs:    0 /s |  10   |  13   |
+------+--------+------+---------------+-------+-------+
+-----------------+----------+-------+-------+
|      Pool       |   type   | used  | avail |
+-----------------+----------+-------+-------+
| cephfs_metadata | metadata | 2286  | 8451M |
|   cephfs_data   |   data   |   0   | 8451M |
+-----------------+----------+-------+-------+
+-------------+
| Standby MDS |
+-------------+
+-------------+
MDS version: ceph version 13.2.2 (02899bfda814146b021136e9d8e80eba494e1126) mimic (stable)
```

If the CephFS filesystem was not created, use the following command to create it:

```
sudo ceph fs create <Filesystem Name> <Metadata Pool> <Data Pool>
```

Now that the CephFS filesystem is active, it can be mounted to a client and used like any other Linux filesystem. When mounting a CephFS filesystem, the `cephx` user key needs to be passed via the mount command. This can be retrieved from the keyrings stored in the `/etc/ceph/` directory. In the following example, we will use the admin keyring; in production scenarios, it is recommended that a specific `cephx` user is created:

```
cat /etc/ceph/ceph.client.admin.keyring
```

```
vagrant@mon1:~$ sudo cat /etc/ceph/ceph.client.admin.keyring
[client.admin]
        key = AQC4Q85btsqTCRAAgzaNDpnLeo4q/c/q/0fEpw==
        caps mds = "allow *"
        caps mgr = "allow *"
        caps mon = "allow *"
        caps osd = "allow *"
```

The hashed key is what is required to mount the CephFS filesystem:

```
sudo mount -t ceph 192.168.0.41:6789:/ /mnt -o
name=admin,secret=AQC4Q85btsqTCRAAgzaNDpnLeo4q/c/q/0fEpw==
```

In this example, only a single monitor was specified; in production settings, it is recommended to supply all three monitor address in a comma-separated format to ensure failover.

Here is confirmation that the filesystem is mounted:

```
vagrant@mon1:~$ df -h
Filesystem                       Size  Used Avail Use% Mounted on
udev                             221M     0  221M   0% /dev
tmpfs                             48M  8.1M   40M  17% /run
/dev/mapper/vagrant--vg-root      62G  2.3G   57G   4% /
tmpfs                            240M     0  240M   0% /dev/shm
tmpfs                            5.0M     0  5.0M   0% /run/lock
tmpfs                            240M     0  240M   0% /sys/fs/cgroup
/dev/sda1                        472M   92M  356M  21% /boot
tmpfs                             48M     0   48M   0% /run/user/1000
192.168.0.41:6789:/              8.3G     0  8.3G   0% /mnt
```

How is data stored in CephFS?

To understand better how CephFS maps a POSIX-compatible filesystem over the top of an object store, we can look more closely at how Ceph maps file inodes to objects.

First, let's look at a file called `test`, which is stored on a CephFS filesystem mounted under `/mnt/tmp`. The following command uses the familiar Unix `ls` command, but with some extra parameters to show more details, including the file inode number:

```
ls -lhi /mnt/tmp/test
```

The following screenshot is the output of the preceding command:

```
1099511784612 -rw-r--r-- 1 root root 1.0G Dec 28 21:28 /mnt/tmp/test
```

The output shows that the file is 1 G in size and that the inode number is the long number at the far left.

Next, by listing the objects stored in the CephFS data pool and greping for that number, we can find the object responsible for holding the filesystem details for that file. Before we can proceed; however, we need to convert the inode number that is stored in decimal into hex, as that is how CephFS stores the inode numbers as object names:

```
printf "%x\n" 1099511784612
```

The following screenshot is the output of the preceding command:

```
$printf "%x\n" 1099511784612
100000264a4
```

Now we can find the object in the pool; note that this may take a long time on a CephFS pool with lots of data, as it will be listing every object in the background:

```
rados -p cephfs_data ls | grep 100000264a4 | wc -l
```

```
$sudo rados -p cephfs_data ls | grep 100000264a4 | wc -l
256
```

Note that 256 objects were found. By default, CephFS breaks larger files up into 4 MB objects, 256 of which would equal the size of the 1 G file.

The actual objects store the exact same data as the files viewable in the CephFS filesystem. If a text file is saved on a CephFS filesystem, its contents could be read by matching the underlying object to the inode number and using the `rados` command to download the object.

The `cephfs_metadata` pool stores all the metadata for the files stored on the CephFS filesystem; this includes values such as modified time, permissions, file names, and file locations in the directory tree. Without this metadata, the data objects stored in the data pool are literally just randomly-named objects; the data still exists but is fairly meaningless to human operators. The loss of CephFS metadata therefore does not lead to actual data loss, but still makes it more-or-less unreadable. Therefore, care should be taken to protect metadata pools just like any other RADOS pool in your Ceph cluster. There are some advanced recovery steps that may assist in metadata loss, which are covered in Chapter 12, *Disaster Recovery*.

File layouts

CephFS allows you to alter the way files are stored across the underlying objects by using settings that are known as file layouts. File layouts allow you to control the stripe size and width and also which RADOS pool the data objects will reside in. The file layouts are stored as extended attributes on files and directories. A new file or directory will inherit its parent's file layouts settings; however, further changes to a parent directory's layout will not affect existing files.

Adjusting the file striping will normally be done for performance reasons to increase the parallelism of reading larger files as a section of data will end up being spread across more OSDs. By default, there is no striping and a large file stored in CephFS will simply span across multiple objects of 4 MB in size.

File layouts can also be used to alter which data pool the objects for a file are stored in. This may be useful to allow different directories to be used for hot and cold data, where the hot files may reside on a 3x SSD pool and the cold files on an erasure-coded pool backed by spinning disks. A good example of this is possibly having a sub directory called Archive/, where users can copy files that are no longer expected to be in daily use. Any file copied into this directory would be stored on the erasure-coded pool.

File layouts can be viewed and edited by using the setfattr and getfattr tools:

```
getfattr -n ceph.file.layout /mnt/test
```

```
$getfattr -n ceph.file.layout /mnt/test
getfattr: Removing leading '/' from absolute path names
# file: mnt/test
ceph.file.layout="stripe_unit=4194304 stripe_count=1 object_size=4194304 pool=cephfs_data"
```

It can be seen that the default file layout is storing the data objects for the test file in the cephfs_data pool. It can also be seen that the file is split into 4 MB objects and, due to the stripe_unit also being 4 MB and stripe_count being equal to 1, that no striping is being used.

Snapshots

CephFS also supports snapshots down to a per-directory level; the snapshot doesn't need to include the whole CephFS filesystem. Each directory on a CephFS filesystem contains a hidden .snap directory; when a new sub directory is created inside, a snapshot is effectively taken and the view inside this new sub directory will represent the state of the original directory at the point when the snapshot was taken.

Multiple snapshots can be taken and browsed independently from each other, enabling the snapshots to be used as part of a short-term archiving scheme. One such use when CephFS is exported via Samba is to use the snapshot functionality to be exposed through the Windows Explorer previous versions tab.

In the following example, a test file is created, a snapshot taken, and then the file is modified. By examining the contents of the live and the file in the snapshot, we can see how CephFS snapshots present themselves:

```
root@mon1:~# echo "Before Snap" > /mnt/file
root@mon1:~# mkdir /mnt/.snap/mySnapshot
root@mon1:~# echo "After Snap" > /mnt/file
root@mon1:~# cat /mnt/file
After Snap
root@mon1:~# cat /mnt/.snap/mySnapshot/file
Before Snap
```

Multi-MDS

A new feature of CephFS is the support for multiple active MDSes. Previously, it was only recommended to have a single active MDS with one or more standby, which for smaller CephFS deployments was more than adequate. However, in larger deployments, a single MDS could possibly start to become a limitation, especially due to the single-threaded limitation of MDSes. It should be noted that multiple active MDSes are purely for increased performance and do not provide any failover or high availability themselves; therefore, sufficient standby MDSes should always be provisioned.

When multiple active MDSes are present, the CephFS filesystem is split across each MDS so that the metadata requests are hopefully not all being handled by a single MDS anymore. This splitting process is done at a per-directory level and is dynamically adjusted based on the metadata request load. This splitting process involves the creation of new CephFS ranks; each rank requires a working MDS to allow it to become active.

In the following example, three active MDS servers are in use in the Ceph cluster. The primary MDS running rank 0 always hosts the CephFS root. The second MDS is serving metadata for the vertically-striped pattern directories, as their metadata load is significantly high. All other directories are still getting their metadata served by the primary MDS as they have little-to-no activity, with the exception of the directory containing Cat Gifs; this directory experiences an extremely high metadata request load and so has a separate rank and MDS assigned all to itself, as shown by the horizontal pattern:

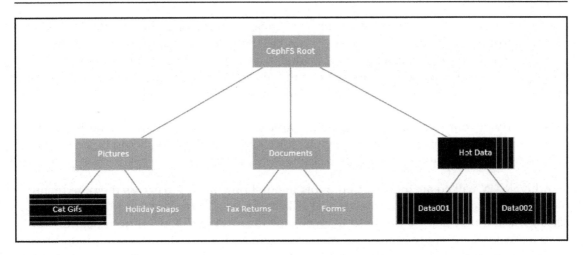

RGW

The **RADOS Gateway (RGW)** presents the Ceph native object store via a S3 or swift-compatible interface, which are the two most popular object APIs for accessing object storage, with S3 being the dominant one, mainly due to the success of Amazon's AWS S3. This section of the book will primarily focus on S3.

 RGW has recently been renamed to Ceph Object Gateway although both the previous names are still widely used.

The radosgw component of Ceph is responsible for turning S3 and swift API requests into RADOS requests. Although it can be installed alongside other components, for performance reasons, it's recommended to be installed on a separate server. The radosgw components are completely stateless and so lend themselves well to being placed behind a load balancer to allow for horizontal scaling.

Aside from storing user data, the RGW also requires a number of additional RADOS pools to store additional metadata. With the exception of the index pool, most of these pools are very lightly utilized and so can be created with a small amount of PGs, around 64 is normally sufficient. The index pools helps with the listing of bucket contents and so placing the index pool on SSDs is highly recommended. The data pool can reside on either spinning disks or SSDs, depending on the type of objects being stored, although object storage tends to be a fairly good match for spinning disks. Quite often, clients are remote and the latency of WAN connections offsets a lot of the gains to be had from SSDs. It should be noted that only the data pool should be placed on erasure-coded pools.

Handily, RGW will create the required pools the first time it tries to access them, reducing the complexity of installation somewhat. However, pools are created with their default settings, and it may be that you wish to create an erasure-coded pool for data-object storage. As long as no access has been made to the RGW service, the data pool should not exist after creation, and it can therefore be manually created as an erasure pool. As long as the name matches the intended pool name for the RGW zone, RGW will use this pool on first access, instead of trying to create a new one.

Deploying RGW

We will use the Ansible lab deployed in `Chapter 2`, *Deploying Ceph with Containers*, to deploy a RGW.

First, edit the `/etc/ansible/hosts` file and add the `rgws` role to the `mon3` VM:

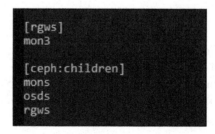

```
[rgws]
mon3

[ceph:children]
mons
osds
rgws
```

We also need to update the `/etc/ansible/group_vars/ceph` file to add the `radosgw_address` variable; it will be set to `[::]`, which means bind to all IPv4 and IPv6 interfaces:

```
ceph_origin: 'repository'
ceph_repository: 'community'
ceph_stable: true # use ceph stable branch
ceph_stable_key: https://download.ceph.com/keys/release.asc
ceph_stable_release: mimic # ceph stable release
ceph_stable_repo: "http://download.ceph.com/debian-{{ ceph_stable_release }}"
monitor_interface: eth1 #Check ifconfig
public_network: 192.168.0.0/24
radosgw_address: "[::]"
```

Now run the Ansible playbook again:

```
ansible-playbook -K site.yml
```

After running, you should see it has successfully deployed the RGW component:

```
INSTALLER STATUS ***********************************************************
Install Ceph Monitor       : Complete (0:01:46)
Install Ceph Manager       : Complete (0:00:17)
Install Ceph OSD           : Complete (0:00:49)
Install Ceph RGW           : Complete (0:00:16)
```

Viewing the Ceph status from a monitor node, we can check that the RGW service has registered with the Ceph cluster and is operational:

```
vagrant@mon3:~$ sudo ceph -s
  cluster:
    id:     66fd555c-7a6c-40e9-b775-9d712b4256e1
    health: HEALTH_WARN
            application not enabled on 1 pool(s)
            clock skew detected on mon.mon2, mon.mon3

  services:
    mon: 3 daemons, quorum mon1,mon2,mon3
    mgr: mon1(active)
    osd: 3 osds: 3 up, 3 in
    rgw: 1 daemon active
```

Now that the RGW is active, a user account is required to interact with the S3 API, and this can be created using the `radosgw-admin` tool shown as follows:

```
sudo radosgw-admin user create --uid=johnsmith --display-name="John Smith"
--email=john@smith.com
```

```
vagrant@mon1:~$ sudo radosgw-admin user create --uid=johnsmith --display-name="John Smith" --email=john@smith.com
{
    "user_id": "johnsmith",
    "display_name": "John Smith",
    "email": "john@smith.com",
    "suspended": 0,
    "max_buckets": 1000,
    "auid": 0,
    "subusers": [],
    "keys": [
        {
            "user": "johnsmith",
            "access_key": "F0ILEH0ZQW7RCCRB2XEY",
            "secret_key": "DR7s5xB4ymfwm6ImptvgyStoBRy9GseG7wsUnxKo"
        }
    ],
```

Note the output from the command, particularly the `access_key` and `secret_key`, these are used with S3 clients to authenticate with the RGW.

To upload objects to our S3-capable Ceph cluster, we first need to create an S3 bucket. We will use the `s3cmd` tool to do this, which is shown as follows:

```
sudo apt-get install s3cmd
```

```
vagrant@mon3:~$ sudo apt-get install s3cmd
Reading package lists... Done
Building dependency tree
Reading state information... Done
The following package was automatically installed and is no longer required:
  ceph-fuse
Use 'sudo apt autoremove' to remove it.
The following additional packages will be installed:
  python-dateutil python-magic
The following NEW packages will be installed:
  python-dateutil python-magic s3cmd
0 upgraded, 3 newly installed, 0 to remove and 93 not upgraded.
Need to get 141 kB of archives.
After this operation, 683 kB of additional disk space will be used.
Do you want to continue? [Y/n]
```

Now that `s3cmd` is installed, it needs to be configured to point at our RGW server; it has a built-in configuration tool that can be used to generate the initial configuration. During the configuration wizard, it will prompt for the access key and secret that was generated when the user account was created, which is shown as follows:

```
s3cmd --configure
```

```
vagrant@mon3:~$ s3cmd --configure

Enter new values or accept defaults in brackets with Enter.
Refer to user manual for detailed description of all options.

Access key and Secret key are your identifiers for Amazon S3. Leave them empty for using the env variables.
Access Key [F0ILEH0ZQW7RCCRB2XEY]:
Secret Key [DR7s5xB4ymfwm6ImptvgyStoBRy9GseG7wsUnxKo]:
Default Region [US]: default

Encryption password is used to protect your files from reading
by unauthorized persons while in transfer to S3
Encryption password:
Path to GPG program [/usr/bin/gpg]:

When using secure HTTPS protocol all communication with Amazon S3
servers is protected from 3rd party eavesdropping. This method is
slower than plain HTTP, and can only be proxied with Python 2.7 or newer
Use HTTPS protocol [Yes]: no

On some networks all internet access must go through a HTTP proxy.
Try setting it here if you can't connect to S3 directly
HTTP Proxy server name:

New settings:
  Access Key: F0ILEH0ZQW7RCCRB2XEY
  Secret Key: DR7s5xB4ymfwm6ImptvgyStoBRy9GseG7wsUnxKo
  Default Region: default
  Encryption password:
  Path to GPG program: /usr/bin/gpg
  Use HTTPS protocol: False
  HTTP Proxy server name:
  HTTP Proxy server port: 0

Test access with supplied credentials? [Y/n] n

Save settings? [y/N] y
Configuration saved to '/home/vagrant/.s3cfg'
```

The generated configuration will be pointing to Amazon's S3 service; the generated configuration file needs to be edited and a few options modified. Edit the `.s3cfg` file in your Linux user's home directory and make the following changes:

```
nano .s3cfg
```

Comment out the `bucket_location` variable:

```
[default]
access_key = F0ILEH0ZQW7RCCRB2XEY
access_token =
add_encoding_exts =
add_headers =
#bucket_location = default
```

Change the `host_base` and `host_buckets` to match the address of the RGW:

```
host_base = mon3:8080
host_bucket = mon3:8080
```

Save the file and quit back to the shell; `s3cmd` can now be used to manipulate your `s3` storage. The following example will create a `test` bucket where objects can be uploaded:

```
s3cmd mb s3://test
```

```
vagrant@mon3:~$ s3cmd mb s3://test
Bucket 's3://test/' created
```

You now have a fully functional S3-compatible storage platform ready to explore the world of object storage.

Summary

In this chapter, you learned about the differences between replicated and erasure-coded pools, and their strengths and weaknesses. Armed with this information, you should now be capable of making the best decision when it comes to deciding between replicated and erasure pools. You also have a more in-depth understanding of how erasure-coded pools function, which will aid planning and operations.

You should now feel confident in deploying Ceph clusters to provide block, file, and object storage, and be able to demonstrate regular administrative tasks.

In the next chapter, we will learn about librados and how to use it to make custom applications that talk directly to Ceph.

Questions

1. Name two different erasure-coding techniques.
2. What is the process called when an erasure-coded pool does a partial write to an object?
3. Why might you choose an erasure-coded profile with two parity shards?
4. What is the process called to turn a cloned snapshot into a full-fat RBD image?
5. What Ceph daemon is required to run a CephFS filesystem?
6. Why might you choose to run multiple active metadata servers over a single one in a CephFS filesystem?
7. What Ceph daemon is required to run a RGW?
8. What two APIs is Ceph's RGW capable of supporting?

Developing with Librados

6

Ceph provides block, file, and object storage via built-in interfaces that will meet the requirements of a large number of users. However, in scenarios where an application is developed internally, there may be benefits to directly interfacing it into Ceph via the use of librados. Librados is the Ceph library that allows applications to directly read and write objects to the RADOS layer in Ceph.

We will cover the following topics in this chapter:

- What is librados?
- Using librados and what languages it supports
- Writing an example librados application
- Writing a librados application that stores image files in Ceph using Python
- Writing a librados application using atomic operations with C++

What is librados?

Librados is a Ceph library that you can include in your applications to allow you to directly talk to a Ceph cluster using native protocols. As librados communicates with Ceph using its native communication protocols, it allows your application to harness the full power, speed, and flexibility of Ceph, instead of having to make use of high-level protocols, such as Amazon S3. A vast array of functions allows your application to read and write simple objects all the way to advanced operations, where you might want to wrap several operations in a transaction or run them asynchronously. Librados is available for several languages, including C, C++, Python, PHP, and Java.

How to use librados

To get started with librados, a development environment is needed. For the examples in this chapter, one of the monitor nodes can be used to act as both the development environment and the client to run the developed application. The examples in this book assume you are using a Debian-based distribution:

1. Install the base build tools for the operating system:

   $ sudo apt-get install build-essential

   The preceding command gives the following output:

```
vagrant@mon1:~$ sudo apt-get install build-essential
Reading package lists... Done
Building dependency tree
Reading state information... Done
The following additional packages will be installed:
  dpkg-dev g++ g++-5 libalgorithm-diff-perl libalgorithm-diff-xs-perl libalgorithm-merge-perl
  libstdc++-5-dev
Suggested packages:
  debian-keyring g++-multilib g++-5-multilib gcc-5-doc libstdc++6-5-dbg libstdc++-5-doc
The following NEW packages will be installed:
  build-essential dpkg-dev g++ g++-5 libalgorithm-diff-perl libalgorithm-diff-xs-perl
  libalgorithm-merge-perl libstdc++-5-dev
0 upgraded, 8 newly installed, 0 to remove and 93 not upgraded.
Need to get 10.4 MB of archives.
After this operation, 41.0 MB of additional disk space will be used.
Do you want to continue? [Y/n] 
```

2. Install the librados development library:

   $ sudo apt-get install librados-dev

   The preceding command gives the following output:

```
vagrant@mon1:~$ sudo apt-get install librados-dev
Reading package lists... Done
Building dependency tree
Reading state information... Done
The following NEW packages will be installed:
  librados-dev
0 upgraded, 1 newly installed, 0 to remove and 93 not upgraded.
Need to get 42.0 MB of archives.
After this operation, 358 MB of additional disk space will be used.
Get:1 http://download.ceph.com/debian-jewel xenial/main amd64 librados-dev amd64 10.2.5-1xenial [42.0 MB]
Fetched 42.0 MB in 30s (1,359 kB/s)
Selecting previously unselected package librados-dev.
(Reading database ... 40080 files and directories currently installed.)
Preparing to unpack .../librados-dev_10.2.5-1xenial_amd64.deb ...
Unpacking librados-dev (10.2.5-1xenial) ...
Processing triggers for man-db (2.7.5-1) ...
Setting up librados-dev (10.2.5-1xenial) ...
```

3. Create a quick application written in C to establish a connection to the test Ceph cluster:

```
$ mkdir test_app
$ cd test_app
```

4. Create a file called test_app.c with your favorite text editor and place the following in it:

```c
#include <rados/librados.h>
#include <stdio.h>
#include <stdlib.h>

rados_t rados = NULL;

int exit_func();


int main(int argc, const char **argv)
{
  int ret = 0;
  ret = rados_create(&rados, "admin"); // Use the
  client.admin keyring
  if (ret < 0) { // Check that the rados object was created
    printf("couldn't initialize rados! error %d\n", ret);
    ret = EXIT_FAILURE;
    exit_func;
  }
  else
    printf("RADOS initialized\n");

  ret = rados_conf_read_file(rados, "/etc/ceph/ceph.conf");
  if (ret < 0) { //Parse the ceph.conf to obtain cluster details
    printf("failed to parse config options! error %d\n", ret);
    ret = EXIT_FAILURE;
    exit_func();
  }
  else
    printf("Ceph config parsed\n");

  ret = rados_connect(rados); //Initiate connection to the
  Ceph cluster
  if (ret < 0) {
    printf("couldn't connect to cluster! error %d\n", ret);
    ret = EXIT_FAILURE;
    exit_func;
  } else {
    printf("Connected to the rados cluster\n");
```

```
    }

    exit_func(); //End of example, call exit_func to clean
    up and finish

}


int exit_func ()
{
    rados_shutdown(rados); //Destroy connection to the
    Ceph cluster
    printf("RADOS connection destroyed\n");
    printf("The END\n");
    exit(0);
}
```

5. Compile the test application by running the following command:

   $ gcc test_app.c −o test_app −lrados

It's important to note that you need to tell gcc to link to the librados library to make use of its functions.

6. Test that the app works by running it. Don't forget to run it as root or use sudo, otherwise you won't have access to the Ceph keyring:

   sudo ./test_app

   The preceding command gives the following output:

```
vagrant@mon1:~/test_app$ sudo ./test_app
RADOS initialised
Ceph config parsed
Connected to the rados cluster
RADOS connection destroyed
The END
```

The test application simply reads your ceph.conf configuration, uses it to establish a connection to your Ceph cluster, and then disconnects. It's hardly the most exciting of applications, but it tests that the basic infrastructure is in place and working, and establishes a foundation for the rest of the examples in this chapter.

Example librados application

We will now go through some example librados applications that use librados to get a better understanding of what you can accomplish with the library.

The following example will take you through the steps to create an application which, when given an image file as a parameter, will store the image as an object in a Ceph cluster and store various attributes about the image file as object attributes. The application will also allow you to retrieve the object and export it as an image file. This example will be written in Python, which is also supported by librados. The following example also uses the **Python Imaging Library (PIL)** to read an image's size and the argument parser library to read command-line parameters:

1. Install the librados Python bindings and image-manipulation libraries:

    ```
    $ sudo apt-get install python-rados python-imaging
    ```

    The preceding command gives the following output:

    ```
    Reading package lists... Done
    Building dependency tree
    Reading state information... Done
    python-rados is already the newest version (10.2.5-1xenial).
    python-rados set to manually installed.
    The following additional packages will be installed:
      libjbig0 libjpeg-turbo8 libjpeg8 liblcms2-2 libtiff5 libwebp5 libwebpmux1 python-pil
    Suggested packages:
      liblcms2-utils python-pil-doc python-pil-dbg
    The following NEW packages will be installed:
      libjbig0 libjpeg-turbo8 libjpeg8 liblcms2-2 libtiff5 libwebp5 libwebpmux1 python-imaging python-pil
    0 upgraded, 9 newly installed, 0 to remove and 93 not upgraded.
    Need to get 916 kB of archives.
    After this operation, 3,303 kB of additional disk space will be used.
    Do you want to continue? [Y/n] y
    ```

2. Create a new file for your Python application ending with the `.py` extension and enter the following into it:

    ```python
    import rados, sys, argparse
    from PIL import Image

    #Argument Parser used to read parameters and generate --help
    parser = argparse.ArgumentParser(description='Image to RADOS
    Object Utility')
    parser.add_argument('--action', dest='action', action='store',
    required=True, help='Either upload or download image to/from
    Ceph')
    parser.add_argument('--image-file', dest='imagefile',
    action='store', required=True, help='The image file to
    ```

```
         upload to RADOS')
parser.add_argument('--object-name', dest='objectname',
action='store', required=True, help='The name of the
RADOS object')
parser.add_argument('--pool', dest='pool', action='store',
required=True, help='The name of the RADOS pool to store
the object')
parser.add_argument('--comment', dest='comment', action=
'store', help='A comment to store with the object')


args = parser.parse_args()

try: #Read ceph.conf config file to obtain monitors
  cluster = rados.Rados(conffile='/etc/ceph/ceph.conf')
except:
  print "Error reading Ceph configuration"
  sys.exit(1)

try: #Connect to the Ceph cluster
  cluster.connect()
except:
  print "Error connecting to Ceph Cluster"
  sys.exit(1)

try: #Open specified RADOS pool
  ioctx = cluster.open_ioctx(args.pool)
except:
  print "Error opening pool: " + args.pool
  cluster.shutdown()
  sys.exit(1)

if args.action == 'upload': #If action is to upload
  try: #Open image file in read binary mode
    image=open(args.imagefile,'rb')
    im=Image.open(args.imagefile)
  except:
    print "Error opening image file"
    ioctx.close()
    cluster.shutdown()
    sys.exit(1)
  print "Image size is x=" + str(im.size[0]) + " y=" +
str(im.size[1])
  try: #Write the contents of image file to object and add
  attributes
    ioctx.write_full(args.objectname,image.read())
    ioctx.set_xattr(args.objectname,'xres',str(im.size[0])
    +"\n")
```

```
        ioctx.set_xattr(args.objectname,'yres',str(im.size[1])
        +"\n")
        im.close()
        if args.comment:
          ioctx.set_xattr(args.objectname,'comment',args.comment
          +"\n")
      except:
        print "Error writing object or attributes"
        ioctx.close()
        cluster.shutdown()
        sys.exit(1)
      image.close()
elif args.action == 'download':
    try: #Open image file in write binary mode
        image=open(args.imagefile,'wb')
    except:
      print "Error opening image file"
      ioctx.close()
      cluster.shutdown()
      sys.exit(1)
    try: #Write object to image file
        image.write(ioctx.read(args.objectname))
    except:
      print "Error writing object to image file"
      ioctx.close()
      cluster.shutdown()
      sys.exit(1)
    image.close()
else:
  print "Please specify --action as either upload or download"
ioctx.close() #Close connection to pool
cluster.shutdown() #Close connection to Ceph
#The End
```

3. Test the `help` functionality generated by the Argument Parser library:

```
$ sudo python app1.py --help
```

The preceding command gives the following output:

```
vagrant@mon1:~$ sudo python app1.py --help
usage: app1.py [-h] --action ACTION --image-file IMAGEFILE --object-name
               OBJECTNAME --pool POOL [--comment COMMENT]

Image to RADOS Object Utility

optional arguments:
  -h, --help            show this help message and exit
  --action ACTION       Either upload or download image to/from Ceph
  --image-file IMAGEFILE
                        The image file to upload to RADOS
  --object-name OBJECTNAME
                        The name of the RADOS object
  --pool POOL           The name of the RADOS pool to store the object
  --comment COMMENT     A comment to store with the object
```

4. Download the Ceph logo to use as a test image:

```
wget http://docs.ceph.com/docs/master/_static/logo.png
```

The preceding command gives the following output:

```
vagrant@mon1:~$ wget http://docs.ceph.com/docs/master/_static/logo.png
--2017-02-08 20:37:01--  http://docs.ceph.com/docs/master/_static/logo.png
Resolving docs.ceph.com (docs.ceph.com)... 158.69.67.53
Connecting to docs.ceph.com (docs.ceph.com)|158.69.67.53|:80... connected.
HTTP request sent, awaiting response... 200 OK
Length: 3898 (3.8K) [image/png]
Saving to: 'logo.png'

logo.png            100%[===================================>]   3.81K  --.-KB/s    in 0s

2017-02-08 20:37:01 (106 MB/s) - 'logo.png' saved [3898/3898]
```

5. Run our Python application to read an image file and upload it to Ceph as an object:

```
$ sudo python app1.py --action=upload --image-file=test1.png
        --object-name=image_test --pool=rbd --comment="Ceph Logo"
```

The preceding command gives the following output:

```
vagrant@mon1:~$ sudo python app1.py --action=upload --image-file=logo.png --object-name=image_test --pool
=rbd --comment="Ceph Logo"
Image size is x=140 y=38
```

6. Verify that the object has been created:

   ```
   $ sudo rados -p rbd ls
   ```

   The preceding command gives the following output:

   ```
   vagrant@mon1:~$ sudo rados -p rbd ls
   image_test
   ```

7. Use `rados` to verify that the attributes have been added to the object:

   ```
   $ sudo rados -p rbd listxattr image_test
   ```

   The preceding command gives the following output:

   ```
   vagrant@mon1:~$ sudo rados -p rbd ls
   image_test
   vagrant@mon1:~$ sudo rados -p rbd listxattr image_test
   comment
   xres
   yres
   ```

8. Use `rados` to verify the attributes' contents, as shown in the following screenshot:

   ```
   vagrant@mon1:~$ sudo rados -p rbd getxattr image_test comment
   Ceph Logo
   vagrant@mon1:~$ sudo rados -p rbd getxattr image_test xres
   140
   vagrant@mon1:~$ sudo rados -p rbd getxattr image_test yres
   38
   ```

Example of the librados application with atomic operations

In the previous librados application example, an object was created on the Ceph cluster and then the object's attributes were added. In most cases, this two-stage operation may be fine; however, some applications might require that the creation of the object and its attributes are atomic. That is to say, if service were interrupted, the object should only exist if it has all its attributes set, otherwise the Ceph cluster should roll back the transaction. The following example, written in C++, shows how to use librados atomic operations to ensure transaction consistency across multiple operations. The example will write an object and then ask the user whether they wish to abort the transaction. If they choose to abort then the object write operation will be rolled back. If they choose to continue, the attributes will be written and the whole transaction will be committed. Perform the following steps:

1. Create a new file with a `.cc` extension and place the following into it:

```cpp
#include <cctype>
#include <rados/librados.hpp>
#include <iostream>
#include <string>

void exit_func(int ret);

librados::Rados rados;

int main(int argc, const char **argv)
{
  int ret = 0;

  // Define variables
  const char *pool_name = "rbd";
  std::string object_string("I am an atomic object\n");
  std::string attribute_string("I am an atomic attribute\n");
  std::string object_name("atomic_object");
  librados::IoCtx io_ctx;

  // Create the Rados object and initialize it
  {
    ret = rados.init("admin"); // Use the default client.admin
    keyring
    if (ret < 0) {
      std::cerr << "Failed to initialize rados! error " << ret
      << std::endl;
      ret = EXIT_FAILURE;
    }
```

```
}

// Read the ceph config file in its default location
ret = rados.conf_read_file("/etc/ceph/ceph.conf");
if (ret < 0) {
  std::cerr << "Failed to parse config file "
            << "! Error" << ret << std::endl;
  ret = EXIT_FAILURE;
}

// Connect to the Ceph cluster
ret = rados.connect();
if (ret < 0) {
  std::cerr << "Failed to connect to cluster! Error " << ret
  << std::endl;
  ret = EXIT_FAILURE;
} else {
  std::cout << "Connected to the Ceph cluster" << std::endl;
}

// Create connection to the Rados pool
ret = rados.ioctx_create(pool_name, io_ctx);
if (ret < 0) {
  std::cerr << "Failed to connect to pool! Error: " << ret <<
  std::endl;
  ret = EXIT_FAILURE;
} else {
  std::cout << "Connected to pool: " << pool_name <<
  std::endl;
}

librados::bufferlist object_bl; // Initialize a bufferlist
object_bl.append(object_string); // Add our object text
string to the bufferlist
librados::ObjectWriteOperation write_op; // Create a write
transaction
write_op.write_full(object_bl); // Write our bufferlist to the
transaction
std::cout << "Object: " << object_name << " has been written
to transaction" << std::endl;
char c;
std::cout << "Would you like to abort transaction? (Y/N)? ";
std::cin >> c;
if (toupper( c ) == 'Y') {
  std::cout << "Transaction has been aborted, so object will
  not actually be written" << std::endl;
  exit_func(99);
}
```

```
librados::bufferlist attr_bl; // Initialize another bufferlist
attr_bl.append(attribute_string); // Add our attribute to the
bufferlist
write_op.setxattr("atomic_attribute", attr_bl); // Write our
attribute to our transaction
std::cout << "Attribute has been written to transaction" <<
std::endl;
ret = io_ctx.operate(object_name, &write_op); // Commit the
transaction
if (ret < 0) {
    std::cerr << "failed to do compound write! error " << ret <<
    std::endl;
    ret = EXIT_FAILURE;
} else {
    std::cout << "We wrote the transaction containing our object
    and attribute" << object_name << std::endl;
}

}

void exit_func(int ret)
{
    // Clean up and exit
    rados.shutdown();
    exit(ret);
}
```

2. Compile the source using g++:

```
g++ atomic.cc -o atomic -lrados -std=c++11
```

3. Let's run through the application and abort the transaction:

```
vagrant@mon1:~$ sudo ./atomic
Connected to the rados cluster
Connected to pool: rbd
Object: atomic_object has been written to transaction
Would you like to abort transaction? (Y/N)? y
Transaction has been aborted, so object will not actually be written
vagrant@mon1:~$ sudo rados -p rbd ls
```

The preceding screenshot shows that, even though we sent a write object command, as the transaction was not committed, the object was never actually written to the Ceph cluster.

4. Let's run the application again and, this time, let it continue the transaction:

```
vagrant@mon1:~$ sudo ./atomic
Connected to the rados cluster
Connected to pool: rbd
Object: atomic_object has been written to transaction
Would you like to abort transaction? (Y/N)? n
Attribute has been written to transaction
We wrote the transaction containing our object and attributeatomic_object
vagrant@mon1:~$ sudo rados -p rbd ls
atomic_object
vagrant@mon1:~$ sudo rados -p rbd getxattr atomic_object atomic_attribute
I am an atomic attribute
```

As you can see, this time the object was written along with its attribute.

Example of the librados application that uses watchers and notifiers

The following librados application is written in C and shows us how to use the watch or notify functionality in RADOS. Ceph enables a client to create a watcher on an object and receive notifications from a completely separate client connected to the same cluster.

The watcher functionality is implemented via callback functions. When you call the librados function to create the watcher, two of the arguments are for callback functions: one is for what to do when a notification is received and another is for what to do if the watcher loses contact or encounters an error with the object. These callback functions contain the code you want to run when a notification or error occurs.

This simple form of messaging is commonly used to instruct a client that has an RBD in use that a snapshot is wished to be taken. The client who wishes to take a snapshot sends a notification to all clients that may be watching the RBD object so that it can flush its cache and possibly make sure the filesystem is in a consistent state.

The following example creates a `watcher` instance on an object named `my_object` and then waits. When it receives a notification, it will display the payload and then send a received message back to the notifier:

1. Create a new file with a `.c` extension and place the following into it:

```
#include <stdio.h>
#include <stdlib.h>
#include <string.h>
#include <syslog.h>
```

```c
#include <rados/librados.h>
#include <rados/rados_types.h>

uint64_t cookie;
rados_ioctx_t io;
rados_t cluster;
char cluster_name[] = "ceph";
char user_name[] = "client.admin";
char object[] = "my_object";
char pool[] = "rbd";

/* Watcher callback function - called when watcher receives a
notification */
void watch_notify2_cb(void *arg, uint64_t notify_id, uint64_t
cookie, uint64_t notifier_gid, void *data, size_t data_len)
{
const char *notify_oid = 0;
char *temp = (char*)data+4;
int ret;
printf("Message from Notifier: %s\n",temp);
rados_notify_ack(io, object, notify_id, cookie, "Received", 8);
}

/* Watcher error callback function - called if watcher encounters
an error */
void watch_notify2_errcb(void *arg, uint64_t cookie, int err)
{
printf("Removing Watcher on object %s\n",object);
err = rados_unwatch2(io,cookie);
printf("Creating Watcher on object %s\n",object);
err = rados_watch2(io,object,&cookie,watch_notify2_cb,
watch_notify2_errcb,NULL);
if (err < 0) {
fprintf(stderr, "Cannot create watcher on %s/%s: %s\n", object,
pool, strerror(-err));
rados_ioctx_destroy(io);
rados_shutdown(cluster);
exit(1);
}
}

int main (int argc, char **argv)
{
int err;
uint64_t flags;

/* Create Rados object */
err = rados_create2(&cluster, cluster_name, user_name, flags);
```

```
if (err < 0) {
fprintf(stderr, "Couldn't create the cluster object!: %s\n",
strerror(-err));
exit(EXIT_FAILURE);
} else {
printf("Created the rados object.\n");
}


/* Read a Ceph configuration file to configure the cluster
handle. */
err = rados_conf_read_file(cluster, "/etc/ceph/ceph.conf");
if (err < 0) {
fprintf(stderr, "Cannot read config file: %s\n",
strerror(-err));
exit(EXIT_FAILURE);
} else {
printf("Read the config file.\n");
}
/* Connect to the cluster */
err = rados_connect(cluster);
if (err < 0) {
fprintf(stderr, "Cannot connect to cluster: %s\n",
strerror(-err));
exit(EXIT_FAILURE);
} else {
printf("\n Connected to the cluster.\n");
}

/* Create connection to the Rados pool */
err = rados_ioctx_create(cluster, pool, &io);
if (err < 0) {
fprintf(stderr, "Cannot open rados pool %s: %s\n", pool,
strerror( err));
rados_shutdown(cluster);
exit(1);
}

/* Create the Rados Watcher */
printf("Creating Watcher on object %s/%s\n",pool,object);
err = rados_watch2(io,object,&cookie,watch_notify2_cb,
watch_notify2_errcb,NULL);
if (err < 0) {
fprintf(stderr, "Cannot create watcher on object %s/%s: %s\n",
pool, object, strerror(-err));
rados_ioctx_destroy(io);
rados_shutdown(cluster);
exit(1);
```

```
}

/* Loop whilst waiting for notifier */
while(1){
sleep(1);
}
/* Clean up */
rados_ioctx_destroy(io);
rados_shutdown(cluster);
}
```

2. Compile the watcher example code:

```
$ gcc watcher.c -o watcher -lrados
```

3. Run the watcher example application:

```
vagrant@mon1:~$ sudo ./watcher
Created the rados object.
Read the config file.

Connected to the cluster.
Creating Watcher on object rbd/my_object
```

4. The watcher is now waiting for a notification. In another Terminal window, using rados, send a notification to the my_object object that is being watched:

```
vagrant@mon1:~$ sudo rados -p rbd notify my_object "Hello There!"
reply client.24135 cookie 29079312 : 8 bytes
00000000  52 65 63 69 65 76 65 64                            |Recieved|
00000008  _
```

5. You can see that the notification was sent and an acknowledgement notification has been received back. If we look at the first Terminal window again, we can see the message from the notifier:

```
vagrant@mon1:~$ sudo ./watcher
Created the rados object.
Read the config file.

Connected to the cluster.
Creating Watcher on object rbd/my_object
Message from Notifier: Hello There!
```

Summary

This concludes our chapter on developing applications with librados. You should now feel comfortable with the basic concepts of how to include librados functionality in your application and how to read and write objects to your Ceph cluster. It would be recommended to read the official librados documentation if you intend to develop an application with librados, so that you can gain a better understanding of the full range of functions that are available.

In the next chapter, we will learn about RADOS classes and how they can be used to speed up processing for larger applications.

Questions

1. Name a reason you might want to write an application that uses the native librados API.
2. What does a RADOS `watcher` do?
3. Name the five languages that librados is available in.

Distributed Computation with Ceph RADOS Classes

An often-overlooked feature of Ceph is the ability to load custom code directly into OSD, which can then be executed from within a librados application. This allows you to take advantage of the large distributed scale of Ceph to not only provide high-performance scale-out storage, but also to distribute computational tasks over OSDs to achieve mass parallel computing. This ability is realized by dynamically loading in RADOS classes to each OSD.

In this chapter, we will cover the following topics:

- Example applications and the benefits of using RADOS classes
- Writing a simple RADOS class in Lua
- Writing a RADOS class that simulates distributed computing

Example applications and the benefits of using RADOS classes

As mentioned earlier, with RADOS classes, code is executed directly inside the OSD code base and so can harness the combined power of all of the OSD nodes. With a typical client application approach, where the client would have to read the object from the Ceph cluster, run computations on it, and then write it back, there is a large amount of round-trip overhead. Using RADOS classes dramatically reduces the amount of round trips to and from OSDs, and also the available compute power is much higher than that single client could provide. Offloading operations directly to the OSDs therefore enables a single client to dramatically increase its processing rate.

A simple example of where RADOS classes could be used is where you need to calculate a hash of every object in a RADOS pool and store each object's hash as an attribute. Having a client perform this would highlight the bottlenecks and extra latency introduced by having the client perform these operations remotely from the cluster. With a RADOS class that contains the required code to read the object, calculate the hash, and store it as an attribute, all that the client would need to do is send the command to OSD to execute the RADOS class.

Writing a simple RADOS class in Lua

One of the default RADOS classes in Ceph from the Kraken release onward is one that can run Lua scripts. The Lua script is dynamically passed to the Lua RADOS object class, which then executes the contents of the script. The scripts are typically passed in a JSON-formatted string to the object class. Although this brings advantages over the traditional RADOS object classes, which need to be compiled before they can be used, it also limits the complexity of what the Lua scripts can accomplish. As such, thought should be given as to what method is appropriate for the task you wish to accomplish.

The following Python code example demonstrates how to create and pass a Lua script to be executed on an OSD. The Lua script reads the contents of the specified object and returns the string of text back in uppercase—all processing is done on the remote OSD, which holds the object; the original object contents are never sent to the client.

Place the following into a file named `rados_lua.py`:

```
import rados, json, sys

try: #Read ceph.conf config file to obtain monitors
  cluster = rados.Rados(conffile='/etc/ceph/ceph.conf')
except:
  print "Error reading Ceph configuration"
  exit(1)

try: #Connect to the Ceph cluster
  cluster.connect()
except:
  print "Error connecting to Ceph Cluster"
  exit(1)

try: #Open specified RADOS pool
  ioctx = cluster.open_ioctx("rbd")
except:
  print "Error opening pool"
```

```
    cluster.shutdown()
    exit(1)

cmd = {
  "script": """
      function upper(input, output)
        size = objclass.stat()
        data = objclass.read(0, size)
        upper_str = string.upper(data:str())
        output:append(upper_str)
      end
      objclass.register(upper)
  """,
  "handler": "upper",
}

ret, data = ioctx.execute(str(sys.argv[1]), 'lua', 'eval_json',
json.dumps(cmd))
print data[:ret]

ioctx.close() #Close connection to pool
cluster.shutdown() #Close connection to Ceph
```

Let's now create a test object with all lowercase characters:

echo this string was in lowercase | sudo rados -p rbd put LowerObject -

The Lua object class, by default, is not allowed to be called by OSDs; we need to add the following to all the OSDs in their `ceph.conf`:

```
[osd]
osd class load list = *
osd class default list = *
```

And now, run our Python librados application:

sudo python rados_lua.py LowerObject

The preceding command gives the following output:

```
vagrant@mon1:~$ sudo python rados_lua.py LowerObject
THIS STRING WAS IN LOWERCASE
```

You should see that the text from our object has been converted all into uppercase. You can see from the Python code earlier that we are not doing any of the conversion in the local Python code and it's all being done remotely on OSD.

Writing a RADOS class that simulates distributed computing

As mentioned in the example given earlier, although using the Lua object class reduces the complexity to use RADOS object classes, there is a limit to what you can currently achieve. In order to write a class that is capable of performing more advanced processing, we need to fall back to writing the class in C. We will then need to compile the new class in the Ceph source.

To demonstrate this, we will write a new RADOS object class that will calculate the MD5 hash of the specified object and then store it as an attribute of the object. This process will be repeated 1,000 times to simulate a busy environment and also to make the runtime easier to measure. We will then compare the operating speed of doing this via the object class versus calculating the MD5 hash on the client. Although this is still a fairly basic task, it will allow us to produce a controlled repeatable scenario and to compare the speed of completing a task client-side, versus doing it directly on the OSD via a RADOS class. It will also serve as a good foundation to enable understanding on how to build more advanced applications.

Preparing the build environment

Use the following command to clone the Ceph Git repository:

```
git clone https://github.com/ceph/ceph.git
```

The preceding command will give the following output:

```
vagrant@ansible:~$ git clone https://github.com/ceph/ceph.git
Cloning into 'ceph'...
remote: Counting objects: 500133, done.
remote: Compressing objects: 100% (21/21), done.
remote: Total 500133 (delta 12), reused 2 (delta 2), pack-reused 500110
Receiving objects: 100% (500133/500133), 203.37 MiB | 2.38 MiB/s, done.
Resolving deltas: 100% (394234/394234), done.
Checking connectivity... done.
```

Once we have cloned the Ceph Git repository, we need to edit the `CMakeLists.txt` file and add in a section for our new class that we are going to write.

Edit the following file in the source tree:

~/ceph/src/cls/CMakeLists.txt

Also, place the following in the file:

```
# cls_md5
set(cls_md5_srcs md5/cls_md5.cc)
add_library(cls_md5 SHARED ${cls_md5_srcs})
set_target_properties(cls_md5 PROPERTIES
   VERSION "1.0.0"
   SOVERSION "1"
   INSTALL_RPATH "")
install(TARGETS cls_md5 DESTINATION ${cls_dir})
target_link_libraries(cls_md5 crypto)
list(APPEND cls_embedded_srcs ${cls_md5_srcs})
```

Once the `cmakelist.txt` file is updated, we can get `cmake` to make the build environment by running the following command:

do_cmake.sh

The preceding command will give the following output:

```
-- Configuring done
-- Generating done
-- Build files have been written to: /home/vagrant/ceph/build
+ cat
+ echo 40000
+ echo done.
done.
```

This will create a `build` directory in the source tree.

In order for us to build the RADOS class, we need to install the required packages that contain the `make` command:

sudo apt-get install build-essentials

There is also an `install-deps.sh` file in the Ceph source tree, which will install the remaining packages required when run.

RADOS classes

The following code sample is a RADOS class which, when executed, reads the object, calculates the MD5 hash, and then writes it as an attribute to the object without any client involvement. Each time this class is called, it repeats this operation 1,000 times locally to OSD and only notifies the client at the end of this processing. We have the following steps to perform:

1. Create the directory for our new RADOS class:

   ```
   mkdir ~/ceph/src/cls/md5
   ```

2. Create the C++ source file:

   ```
   ~/ceph/src/cls/md5/cls_md5.cc
   ```

3. Place the following code in it:

   ```cpp
   #include "objclass/objclass.h"
   #include <openssl/md5.h>

   CLS_VER(1,0)
   CLS_NAME(md5)

   cls_handle_t h_class;
   cls_method_handle_t h_calc_md5;

   static int calc_md5(cls_method_context_t hctx, bufferlist *in,
   bufferlist *out)
   {
     char md5string[33];

     for(int i = 0; i < 1000; ++i)
     {
       size_t size;
       int ret = cls_cxx_stat(hctx, &size, NULL);
       if (ret < 0)
         return ret;

       bufferlist data;
       ret = cls_cxx_read(hctx, 0, size, &data);
       if (ret < 0)
         return ret;
       unsigned char md5out[16];
       MD5((unsigned char*)data.c_str(), data.length(), md5out);
       for(int i = 0; i < 16; ++i)
         sprintf(&md5string[i*2], "%02x", (unsigned int)md5out[i]);
   ```

```
      CLS_LOG(0,"Loop:%d - %s",i,md5string);
      bufferlist attrbl;
      attrbl.append(md5string);
      ret = cls_cxx_setxattr(hctx, "MD5", &attrbl);
      if (ret < 0)
      {
        CLS_LOG(0, "Error setting attribute");
        return ret;
      }
    }
    out->append((const char*)md5string, sizeof(md5string));
    return 0;
  }

  void __cls_init()
  {
    CLS_LOG(0, "loading cls_md5");
    cls_register("md5", &h_class);
    cls_register_cxx_method(h_class, "calc_md5", CLS_METHOD_RD |
    CLS_METHOD_WR, calc_md5, &h_calc_md5)
  }
```

4. Change into the `build` directory created previously and create our new RADOS class using `make`:

```
cd ~/ceph/build
make cls_md5
```

The preceding commands will give the following output:

```
vagrant@ansible:~/ceph/build$ make cls_md5
Scanning dependencies of target cls_md5
[  0%] Building CXX object src/cls/CMakeFiles/cls_md5.dir/md5/cls_md5.cc.o
[100%] Linking CXX shared library ../../lib/libcls_md5.so
[100%] Built target cls_md5
```

5. Copy our new class to the OSDs in our cluster:

```
sudo scp vagrant@ansible:/home/vagrant/ceph/build/lib/libcls_md5.so*
/usr/lib/rados-classes/
```

The preceding command will give the following output:

```
vagrant@osd2:~$ sudo scp vagrant@ansible:/home/vagrant/ceph/build/lib/libcls_md5.so* /usr/lib/rados-classes/
vagrant@ansible's password:
libcls_md5.so                                             100%   155KB  155.0KB/s   00:00
libcls_md5.so.1                                           100%   155KB  155.0KB/s   00:00
libcls_md5.so.1.0.0                                       100%   155KB  155.0KB/s   00:00
```

Also, restart the OSD for it to load the class. You will now see in the Ceph OSD log that it is loading our new class:

```
2017-05-10 19:47:57.251739 7fdb99ca2700  1 leveldb: Compacting 400 + 401 files
2017-05-10 19:47:57.260570 7fdba409fa40  1 journal _open /var/lib/ceph/osd/ceph-1/journal fd 28: 1073741824 bytes,
ock size 4096 bytes, directio = 1, aio = 1
2017-05-10 19:47:57.280605 7fdba409fa40  1 journal _open /var/lib/ceph/osd/ceph-1/journal fd 28: 1073741824 bytes,
ock size 4096 bytes, directio = 1, aio = 1
2017-05-10 19:47:57.283291 7fdba409fa40  1 filestore(/var/lib/ceph/osd/ceph-1) upgrade
2017-05-10 19:47:57.300701 7fdba409fa40  0 <cls> /home/vagrant/ceph/src/cls/md5/cls_md5.cc:46: loading cls_md5
2017-05-10 19:47:57.301246 7fdba409fa40  0 <cls> /tmp/buildd/ceph-11.2.0/src/cls/cephfs/cls_cephfs.cc:198: loading
phfs
2017-05-10 19:47:57.308766 7fdba409fa40  0 <cls> /tmp/buildd/ceph-11.2.0/src/cls/hello/cls_hello.cc:296: loading
hello
2017-05-10 19:47:57.318132 7fdba409fa40  0 osd.1 279 crush map has features 2200130813952, adjusting msgr requires
r clients
2017-05-10 19:47:57.318940 7fdba409fa40  0 osd.1 279 crush map has features 2200130813952 was 8705, adjusting msgr
quires for mons
2017-05-10 19:47:57.318966 7fdba409fa40  0 osd.1 279 crush map has features 2200130813952, adjusting msgr requires
r osds
```

This needs to be repeated for all OSD nodes in the cluster.

Client librados applications

As mentioned earlier, we will use two librados applications, one to calculate the MD5 hash directly on the client, and another to call our RADOS class and have it calculate the MD5 hash. The applications both need to be run from the monitor nodes in the test cluster, but can be compiled on any node and copied across if desired. For the purpose of this example, we will compile the applications directly on the monitor nodes.

Before we start, let's make sure that the build environment is present on the monitor node:

```
apt-get install build-essential librados-dev
```

Calculating MD5 on the client

The following code sample is the librados client-side application, which will read the object from the OSD, calculate the MD5 hash of the object on the client, and write it back as an attribute to the object. This is doing the calculation and storage in the same way as the RADOS class, with the only difference being the location of the processing.

Create a new file named `rados_md5.cc` and incorporate the following in it:

```cpp
#include <cctype>
#include <rados/librados.hpp>
#include <iostream>
#include <string>
#include <openssl/md5.h>

void exit_func(int ret);

librados::Rados rados;

int main(int argc, const char **argv)
{
  int ret = 0;

  // Define variables
  const char *pool_name = "rbd";
  std::string object_name("LowerObject");
  librados::IoCtx io_ctx;

  // Create the Rados object and initialize it
  {
    ret = rados.init("admin"); // Use the default client.admin keyring
    if (ret < 0) {
      std::cerr << "Failed to initialize rados! error " << ret <<
      std::endl;
      ret = EXIT_FAILURE;
    }
  }

  // Read the ceph config file in its default location
  ret = rados.conf_read_file("/etc/ceph/ceph.conf");
  if (ret < 0) {
    std::cerr << "Failed to parse config file "
              << "! Error" << ret << std::endl;
    ret = EXIT_FAILURE;
  }

  // Connect to the Ceph cluster
  ret = rados.connect();
  if (ret < 0) {
    std::cerr << "Failed to connect to cluster! Error " << ret <<
    std::endl;
    ret = EXIT_FAILURE;
  } else {
    std::cout << "Connected to the Ceph cluster" << std::endl;
  }
```

```cpp
      // Create connection to the Rados pool
      ret = rados.ioctx_create(pool_name, io_ctx);
      if (ret < 0) {
        std::cerr << "Failed to connect to pool! Error: " << ret <<
        std::endl;
        ret = EXIT_FAILURE;
      } else {
        std::cout << "Connected to pool: " << pool_name << std::endl;
      }
      for(int i = 0; i < 1000; ++i)
      {
        size_t size;
        int ret = io_ctx.stat(object_name, &size, NULL);
        if (ret < 0)
          return ret;

        librados::bufferlist data;
        ret = io_ctx.read(object_name, data, size, 0);
        if (ret < 0)
          return ret;
        unsigned char md5out[16];
        MD5((unsigned char*)data.c_str(), data.length(), md5out);
        char md5string[33];
        for(int i = 0; i < 16; ++i)
          sprintf(&md5string[i*2], "%02x", (unsigned int)md5out[i]);
        librados::bufferlist attrbl;
        attrbl.append(md5string);
        ret = io_ctx.setxattr(object_name, "MD5", attrbl);
        if (ret < 0)
        {
          exit_func(1);
        }
      }
      exit_func(0);
}

void exit_func(int ret)
{
    // Clean up and exit
    rados.shutdown();
    exit(ret);
}
```

Calculating MD5 on the OSD via the RADOS class

Finally, the last code sample is the librados application, which instructs OSD to calculate the MD5 hash locally without transferring any data to or from the client. You will note that the code given later has no librados read or write statements and relies purely on the `exec` function to trigger the MD5 hash creation.

Create a new file named `rados_class_md5.cc` and place the following in it:

```
#include <cctype>
#include <rados/librados.hpp>
#include <iostream>
#include <string>

void exit_func(int ret);

librados::Rados rados;

int main(int argc, const char **argv)
{
 int ret = 0;

 // Define variables
 const char *pool_name = "rbd";
 std::string object_name("LowerObject");
 librados::IoCtx io_ctx;
 // Create the Rados object and initialize it
 {
 ret = rados.init("admin"); // Use the default client.admin keyring
 if (ret < 0) {
 std::cerr << "Failed to initialize rados! error " << ret <<
 std::endl;
 ret = EXIT_FAILURE;
 }
 }

 // Read the ceph config file in its default location
 ret = rados.conf_read_file("/etc/ceph/ceph.conf");
 if (ret < 0) {
 std::cerr << "Failed to parse config file "
 << "! Error" << ret << std::endl;
 ret = EXIT_FAILURE;
 }

 // Connect to the Ceph cluster
 ret = rados.connect();
 if (ret < 0) {
```

```
std::cerr << "Failed to connect to cluster! Error " << ret <<
std::endl;
ret = EXIT_FAILURE;
} else {
std::cout << "Connected to the Ceph cluster" << std::endl;
}

// Create connection to the Rados pool
ret = rados.ioctx_create(pool_name, io_ctx);
if (ret < 0) {
std::cerr << "Failed to connect to pool! Error: " << ret <<
std::endl;
ret = EXIT_FAILURE;
} else {
std::cout << "Connected to pool: " << pool_name <<
std::endl;
}
librados::bufferlist in, out;
io_ctx.exec(object_name, "md5", "calc_md5", in, out);
exit_func(0);

}
void exit_func(int ret)
{
// Clean up and exit
rados.shutdown();
exit(ret);
}
```

We can now compile both applications:

```
vagrant@mon1:~$ g++ rados_class_md5.cc -o rados_class_md5 -lrados -std=c++11
vagrant@mon1:~$ g++ rados_md5.cc -o rados_md5 -lrados -lcrypto -std=c++11
```

If the applications compile successfully, there will be no output.

Testing

We will run the two librados applications using the standard Linux `time` utility to measure how long each run takes:

```
time sudo ./rados_md5
```

The preceding command will give the following output:

```
vagrant@mon1:~$ time sudo ./rados_md5
Connected to the Ceph cluster
Connected to pool: rbd

real    0m4.708s
user    0m0.084s
sys     0m1.008s
```

Let's make sure that the attribute was actually created:

```
sudo rados -p rbd getxattr LowerObject MD5
```

The preceding command will give the following output:

```
vagrant@mon1:~$ sudo rados -p rbd getxattr LowerObject MD5
9d40bae4ff2032c9eff59806298a95bdvagrant@mon1:~$
```

Let's delete the object attribute, so we can be certain that the RADOS class correctly creates it when it runs:

```
sudo rados -p rbd rmxattr LowerObject MD5
```

And now, run the application that performs the MD5 calculation via the RADOS class:

```
time sudo ./rados_class_md5
```

The preceding command will give the following output:

```
vagrant@mon1:~$ time sudo ./rados_class_md5
Connected to the Ceph cluster
Connected to pool: rbd

real    0m0.038s
user    0m0.004s
sys     0m0.012s
```

As you can see, using the RADOS class method is a lot faster, in fact, almost two orders of magnitude faster.

However, let's also confirm that the attribute was created and that the code ran 1,000 times:

```
sudo rados -p rbd getxattr LowerObject MD5
```

The preceding command will give the following output:

```
vagrant@mon1:~$ sudo rados -p rbd getxattr LowerObject MD5
9d40bae4ff2032c9eff59806298a95bdvagrant@mon1:~$
```

Due to the logging we inserted in the RADOS class, we can also check the OSD logs to confirm that the RADOS class did indeed run 1,000 times:

```
0 <cls> /home/vagrant/ceph/src/cls/md5/cls_md5.cc:30: Loop:984 - 9d40bae4ff2032c9eff59806298a95bd
0 <cls> /home/vagrant/ceph/src/cls/md5/cls_md5.cc:30: Loop:985 - 9d40bae4ff2032c9eff59806298a95bd
0 <cls> /home/vagrant/ceph/src/cls/md5/cls_md5.cc:30: Loop:986 - 9d40bae4ff2032c9eff59806298a95bd
0 <cls> /home/vagrant/ceph/src/cls/md5/cls_md5.cc:30: Loop:987 - 9d40bae4ff2032c9eff59806298a95bd
0 <cls> /home/vagrant/ceph/src/cls/md5/cls_md5.cc:30: Loop:988 - 9d40bae4ff2032c9eff59806298a95bd
0 <cls> /home/vagrant/ceph/src/cls/md5/cls_md5.cc:30: Loop:989 - 9d40bae4ff2032c9eff59806298a95bd
0 <cls> /home/vagrant/ceph/src/cls/md5/cls_md5.cc:30: Loop:990 - 9d40bae4ff2032c9eff59806298a95bd
0 <cls> /home/vagrant/ceph/src/cls/md5/cls_md5.cc:30: Loop:991 - 9d40bae4ff2032c9eff59806298a95bd
0 <cls> /home/vagrant/ceph/src/cls/md5/cls_md5.cc:30: Loop:992 - 9d40bae4ff2032c9eff59806298a95bd
0 <cls> /home/vagrant/ceph/src/cls/md5/cls_md5.cc:30: Loop:993 - 9d40bae4ff2032c9eff59806298a95bd
0 <cls> /home/vagrant/ceph/src/cls/md5/cls_md5.cc:30: Loop:994 - 9d40bae4ff2032c9eff59806298a95bd
0 <cls> /home/vagrant/ceph/src/cls/md5/cls_md5.cc:30: Loop:995 - 9d40bae4ff2032c9eff59806298a95bd
0 <cls> /home/vagrant/ceph/src/cls/md5/cls_md5.cc:30: Loop:996 - 9d40bae4ff2032c9eff59806298a95bd
0 <cls> /home/vagrant/ceph/src/cls/md5/cls_md5.cc:30: Loop:997 - 9d40bae4ff2032c9eff59806298a95bd
0 <cls> /home/vagrant/ceph/src/cls/md5/cls_md5.cc:30: Loop:998 - 9d40bae4ff2032c9eff59806298a95bd
0 <cls> /home/vagrant/ceph/src/cls/md5/cls_md5.cc:30: Loop:999 - 9d40bae4ff2032c9eff59806298a95bd
```

When repeating small tasks, the overhead of communication between the client and OSDs really adds up. By moving processing directly to OSD, we can eliminate this.

RADOS class caveats

Although we have seen the power that can be harnessed using Ceph's RADOS classes, it's important to note that this is achieved by calling your own customized code from deep inside OSDs. As a consequence, great care needs to be taken that your RADOS class is bug free. A RADOS class has the ability to modify any data on your Ceph cluster, and so accidental data corruption is easily possible. It is also possible for the RADOS class to crash the OSD process. If the class is used in large-scale cluster operations, this has the ability to affect all OSDs in the cluster, so great care should be taken to ensure that error handling is done properly to avoid errors.

Summary

You should now have an understanding of what RADOS classes are and how they can be used to speed up processing by moving tasks directly to OSD. From building simple classes via Lua to developing classes in the Ceph source tree via C++, you should now have the knowledge to build a RADOS class for whatever problem you are trying to solve. By building on this concept, there is nothing stopping you from creating a larger application that can take advantage of the scale-out nature of a Ceph cluster to provide large amounts of storage and compute resources.

In the next chapter, we will use some examples to explore the importance of monitoring in Ceph.

Questions

1. What Ceph component are RADOS classes executed in?
2. What languages can RADOS classes be written in?
3. What advantages do RADOS classes bring?
4. What disadvantages do RADOS classes bring?

8
Monitoring Ceph

When you are operating a Ceph cluster, it's important to monitor its health and performance. By monitoring Ceph, you can be sure that your cluster is running at full health and also be able to quickly react to any issues that may arise. By capturing and graphing performance counters, you will also have the data that's required to tune Ceph and observe the impact of your tuning on your cluster.

In this chapter, you will learn about the following topics:

- Why it is important to monitor Ceph
- How to monitor Ceph's health by using the new built-in dashboard
- What should be monitored
- The states of PGs and what they mean
- How to capture Ceph's performance counters with collectd
- Example graphs using Graphite

Why it is important to monitor Ceph

The most important reason to monitor Ceph is to ensure that the cluster is running in a healthy state. If Ceph is not running in a healthy state, be it because of a failed disk or for some other reason, the chances of a loss of service or data increase. Although Ceph is highly automated in recovering from a variety of scenarios, being aware of what is going on and when manual intervention is required is essential.

Monitoring isn't just about detecting failures; monitoring other metrics such as used disk space is just as essential as knowing when a disk has failed. If your Ceph cluster fills up, it will stop accepting I/O requests and will not be able to recover from future OSD failures.

Finally, monitoring both the operating systems and Ceph's performance metrics can help you spot performance issues or identify tuning opportunities.

What should be monitored

The simple answer is everything, or, as much as you can. You can never predict what scenario may be forced upon you and your cluster, and having the correct monitoring and alerting in place can mean the difference between handing a situation gracefully or having a full-scale outage. A list of things that should be monitored in decreasing order of importance is as follows.

Ceph health

The most important thing to capture is the health status of Ceph. The main reporting item is the overall health status of the cluster, either HEALTH_OK, HEALTH_WARN, or HEALTH_ERR. By monitoring this state, you will be alerted any time Ceph itself thinks that something is not right. In addition to this, you may also want to capture the status of the PGs and number of degraded objects, as they can provide additional information as to what might be wrong without having to actually log on to a Ceph server and use the Ceph toolset to check the status.

Operating system and hardware

It's also highly recommended that you capture the current status of the operating system running the Ceph software and also the status of the underlying hardware. Capturing things such as CPU and RAM usage will alert you to possible resource starvation before it potentially becomes critical. Also, long-term trending on this data can help to plan hardware choices for Ceph. Monitoring the hardware to capture hardware failures, such as disks, PSUs, and fans, is also highly recommended. Most server hardware is redundant and it may not be obvious that it is running in a degraded state unless it is monitored. In addition, monitoring network connections so that you can be sure that both NICs are available in bonded configuration are working is also a good idea.

Smart stats

Using your operating system's smart monitoring tool suite to probe the health of the disks is also a good idea. They may help to highlight failing disks or ones with abnormal error rates. For SSDs, you can also measure the wear rate of the flash cells, which is a good indication of when the SSD is likely to fail. Finally, being able to capture the temperature of the disks will allow you to make sure that your servers are not overheating.

Network

As Ceph relies on the network it runs over to be reliable, it can be beneficial to monitor network devices for errors and performance issues. Most network devices can be polled via SNMP to obtain this data. Since the Mimic release of Ceph, it automatically sends jumbo-sized frames in its heartbeats to try and catch scenarios where jumbo frames are not correctly configured across the network. However, it is also worth considering deploying your own jumbo-frame-checking monitoring to catch misconfigurations, as misconfigured jumbo frames can easily bring a Ceph cluster to its knees.

Performance counters

By monitoring performance counters from both the operating system and Ceph, you are arming yourself with a wealth of knowledge to gain a better understanding of how your Ceph cluster is performing. If storage permits, it's worth trying to capture as many of these metrics as possible; you never know when the metrics will come in handy. It's quite often the case when diagnosing a problem that a metric that was previously thought to have no connection to the issue suddenly sheds light on the actual cause. The traditional approach of only monitoring key metrics is very limiting in this regard.

Most monitoring agents that run on Linux will allow you to capture a large array of metrics, from resource consumption to filesystem usage. It's worth spending time analyzing what metric you can collect and configuring them appropriately. Some of these monitoring agents will also have plugins for Ceph, which can pull out all of the performance counters from Ceph's various components, such as osd and mon nodes.

The Ceph dashboard

Introduced in the Mimic release, Ceph now has an extremely useful dashboard based on the open ATTIC project. The dashboard in the initial Mimic release gives the Ceph operator the ability to monitor many aspects of their Ceph cluster that are needed on a daily basis. With preceding releases of Ceph, the dashboard has had further refinements and can now be used to manage some common tasks; over time, it is expected that the dashboard will continue to gain new features.

The dashboard is provided as a Ceph Mgr module and is included along with any dependencies in the standard Ceph installation. That means that all that is required to start using the Ceph dashboard is to simply enable the `mgr` module:

```
sudo ceph mgr module enable dashboard
```

SSL either needs to be disabled or a SSL certificate needs to be configured. Luckily, Ceph has a simple one-liner to get you started with a self-signed certificate:

```
sudo ceph dashboard create-self-signed-cert
```

It's recommended that you use a proper certificate in production deployments.

Lastly, a username and password are required to log in to the dashboard. Again, Ceph has a simple command to carry out this action:

```
sudo ceph dashboard set-login-credentials <user> <password>
```

Now you should be able to browse to `https://<active mgr>:8443` and log in with the credentials you have just created. In this is case, `<active mgr>` is the Ceph node that is currently running the active mgr daemon; this can be seen via the `ceph -s` Ceph status screen:

The first screen that's presented when you log into the dashboard gives an overview of the Ceph cluster's health and utilization.

Across the top of the page are a number of menus that allow you to view more detailed information about the Ceph cluster, such as details on the OSDs and PGs. The block menu allows you to view details on created RBD images and likewise the filesystems menu shows information about any CephFS filesystems.

The Object Gateway will show information about the RADOS Gateway, but requires configuration with a valid RGW user; please consult the official Ceph documentation for more information if required.

With the development future of the Ceph dashboard looking bright, it is highly recommended to deploy it for any Ceph cluster you manage. With future releases set to bring further enhancements around being able to manage your Ceph cluster from it, the dashboard will certainly become more and more useful over time. However, even in its current state, the ability for less knowledgeable administrators to easily be able to explore the current status of a running Ceph cluster is extremely useful.

PG states – the good, the bad, and the ugly

Each placement group in Ceph has one or more statuses assigned to it; normally, you want to see all your PGs with `active+clean` against them. Understanding what each state means can help us identify what is happening to PG and whether you need to take action.

The good ones

The following states are indications of a healthy operating cluster, for which no action needs to be taken.

The active state

The `active` state means that the PG is in full health, and it is capable of accepting client requests.

The clean state

The `clean` state means that the PG's objects are being replicated the correct number of times and are all in a consistent state.

Scrubbing and deep scrubbing

Scrubbing means that Ceph checks the consistency of your data and is a normal background process. Scrubbing on its own is where Ceph checks that the objects and relevant metadata exists. When Ceph performs a deep scrub, it compares the contents of the objects and their replicas for consistency.

The bad ones

The following states indicate that Ceph is not in full health, but shouldn't cause any immediate problems.

The inconsistent state

The `inconsistent` state means that during the scrub process, Ceph has found one or more objects that are inconsistent with its replicas. See `Chapter 11`, *Troubleshooting*, later in this book on how to deal with these errors.

The backfilling, backfill_wait, recovering, and recovery_wait states

These states mean that Ceph is copying or migrating data from one OSD to another. This may possibly mean that this PG has less than the desired number of copies. If it's in the `wait` state, it means that due to throttles on each OSD, Ceph is limiting the number of concurrent operations to reduce the impact on client operations.

The degraded state

The `degraded` state means that the PG is missing or has out-of-date copies of one or more objects. These will normally be corrected by the recovery/backfill process.

Remapped

In order to become active, the PG is currently mapped to a different OSD or set of OSDs. This is likely to occur when OSD is down but has not been recovered to the remaining OSDs.

Peering

The peering state is part of the normal process of a PG becoming active and it should only be in this state briefly. It is listed in the bad section as a PG that remains in the peering state will block I/O.

The ugly ones

These states are not ones you want to see. If you see any of these states, it's quite likely that client access to the cluster will be affected, and unless the situation can be fixed, data loss may occur.

The incomplete state

An `incomplete` state means that Ceph is unable to find any valid copies of objects within the PG across any of the OSDs that are currently up in the cluster. This can either be that the objects are simply not there or the available objects are missing newer writes that may have occurred on now unavailable OSDs.

The down state

This will accompany the `incomplete` state. The PG is missing objects that are known to possibly be on unavailable OSDs and the PG cannot be started.

The backfill_toofull and recovery_toofull state

Ceph has tried to recover your data, but your OSD disks are too full and it cannot continue. Extra OSDs are needed to fix this situation.

Monitoring Ceph with collectd

Previously in this chapter, we covered what monitoring should be done around your entire Ceph infrastructure and also looked at the new, builtin Ceph dashboard. To gain further insights into the operation of your Ceph cluster and associated infrastructure, a more detailed monitoring setup is required. Although alert monitoring is out of scope of this book, we will now look at capturing the Ceph performance metrics with collectd, storing them in Graphite, and then finally creating a dashboard with graphs using Grafana. These captured metrics can then be used in the following chapter to help tune your Ceph cluster.

We will build this monitoring infrastructure on one of our monitor nodes in our test cluster. In a production cluster, it is highly recommended that it gets its own dedicated server.

Graphite

Graphite is a time series database that excels in storing large amounts of metrics and has a mature query language, which can be used by applications to manipulate data.

We first need to install the required Graphite packages:

```
sudo apt-get install graphite-api graphite-carbon graphite-web
```

The preceding command gives the following output:

```
vagrant@ansible:~$ sudo apt-get install graphite-api graphite-carbon graphite-web
Reading package lists... Done
Building dependency tree
Reading state information... Done
The following additional packages will be installed:
  fontconfig-config fonts-dejavu-core javascript-common libcairo2 libfontconfig1 libgdk-pixbuf2.0-0
  libgdk-pixbuf2.0-common libjbig0 libjpeg-turbo8 libjpeg8 libjs-jquery libjs-prototype libjs-scriptaculous
  libpixman-1-0 libtiff5 libx11-6 libx11-data libxau6 libxcb-render0 libxcb-shm0 libxcb1 libxdmcp6 libxext6
  libxrender1 python-attr python-cairo python-cffi-backend python-cryptography python-django python-django-common
  python-django-tagging python-enum34 python-idna python-ipaddress python-openssl python-pam python-pyasn1
  python-pyasn1-modules python-pyparsing python-serial python-service-identity python-simplejson python-sqlparse
  python-twisted-bin python-twisted-core python-tz python-whisper python-zope.interface python3-cairocffi python3-cffi
  python3-cffi-backend python3-cryptography python3-flask python3-idna python3-itsdangerous python3-jinja2
  python3-markupsafe python3-openssl python3-ply python3-pyasn1 python3-pycparser python3-pyinotify python3-pyparsing
  python3-structlog python3-tz python3-tzlocal python3-werkzeug python3-xcffib python3-yaml
```

Edit the `/etc/graphite/storage-schemas.conf` storage schemas file and place the following into it:

```
[carbon]
pattern = ^carbon\.
retentions = 60:90d
[default_1min_for_1day]
pattern = .*
retentions = 60s:1d
```

Now, we can create the graphite database by running the following command:

```
sudo graphite-manage syncdb
```

The preceding command will give the following output:

```
You have installed Django's auth system, and don't have any superusers defined.
Would you like to create one now? (yes/no): yes
Username (leave blank to use 'root'):
Email address:
Password:
Password (again):
Superuser created successfully.
```

Set the password for the root user when prompted:

```
sudo apt-get install apache2 libapache2-mod-wsgi
```

The preceding command gives the following output:

```
vagrant@ansible:~$ sudo apt-get install apache2 libapache2-mod-wsgi
Reading package lists... Done
Building dependency tree
Reading state information... Done
The following additional packages will be installed:
  apache2-bin apache2-data apache2-utils libaprutil1-dbd-sqlite3 libaprutil1-ldap liblua5.1-0 libpython2.7 ssl-cert
Suggested packages:
  www-browser apache2-doc apache2-suexec-pristine | apache2-suexec-custom openssl-blacklist
The following NEW packages will be installed:
  apache2 apache2-bin apache2-data apache2-utils libapache2-mod-wsgi libaprutil1-dbd-sqlite3 libaprutil1-ldap
  liblua5.1-0 libpython2.7 ssl-cert
0 upgraded, 10 newly installed, 0 to remove and 122 not upgraded.
Need to get 2,538 kB of archives.
After this operation, 9,814 kB of additional disk space will be used.
Do you want to continue? [Y/n]
```

To stop the default Apache site from conflicting with the Graphite web service, we need to disable it by running the following command:

```
sudo a2dissite 000-default
```

The preceding command gives the following output:

```
vagrant@ansible:~$ sudo a2dissite 000-default
Site 000-default disabled.
To activate the new configuration, you need to run:
  service apache2 reload
vagrant@ansible:~$
```

We can now copy the Apache Graphite configuration into the Apache environment:

```
sudo cp /usr/share/graphite-web/apache2-graphite.conf
/etc/apache2/sites-available
sudo a2ensite apache2-graphite
```

The preceding commands give the following output:

```
vagrant@ansible:~$ sudo a2ensite apache2-graphite
Enabling site apache2-graphite.
To activate the new configuration, you need to run:
  service apache2 reload
vagrant@ansible:~$
```

Restart the Apache service:

```
sudo service apache2 reload
```

Grafana

We will edit the apt repository file and add the repository for Grafana:

```
sudo nano /etc/apt/sources.list.d/grafana.list
```

Place the following line into the file and save it:

```
deb https://packagecloud.io/grafana/stable/debian/ jessie main
```

Now run the following commands to retrieve the gpg key and update the package lists:

```
curl https://packagecloud.io/gpg.key | sudo apt-key add -
sudo apt-get update
```

Install Grafana using the following command:

```
sudo apt-get install grafana
```

The preceding command gives the following output:

```
vagrant@ansible:~$ sudo apt-get install grafana
Reading package lists... Done
Building dependency tree
Reading state information... Done
The following additional packages will be installed:
  build-essential dpkg-dev fonts-font-awesome g++ g++-5 golang-1.6-go golang-1.6-race-detector-runtime golang-1.6-src
  golang-go golang-race-detector-runtime golang-src grafana-data libalgorithm-diff-perl libalgorithm-diff-xs-perl
  libalgorithm-merge-perl libjs-angularjs libjs-jquery-metadata libjs-jquery-tablesorter libjs-twitter-bootstrap
  libstdc++-5-dev pkg-config
Suggested packages:
  debian-keyring g++-multilib g++-5-multilib gcc-5-doc libstdc++6-5-dbg bzr mercurial libjs-bootstrap libstdc++-5-doc
The following NEW packages will be installed:
  build-essential dpkg-dev fonts-font-awesome g++ g++-5 golang-1.6-go golang-1.6-race-detector-runtime golang-1.6-src
  golang-go golang-race-detector-runtime golang-src grafana grafana-data libalgorithm-diff-perl
  libalgorithm-diff-xs-perl libalgorithm-merge-perl libjs-angularjs libjs-jquery-metadata libjs-jquery-tablesorter
  libjs-twitter-bootstrap libstdc++-5-dev pkg-config
0 upgraded, 22 newly installed, 0 to remove and 122 not upgraded.
Need to get 43.1 MB of archives.
After this operation, 268 MB of additional disk space will be used.
Do you want to continue? [Y/n]
```

With the standard Vagrant configuration, you will not be able to connect to the HTTP port provided by Grafana. To access Grafana, we will need to port forward via `ssh port 3000` to our local machine.

An example of using PuTTY is shown in the following screenshot:

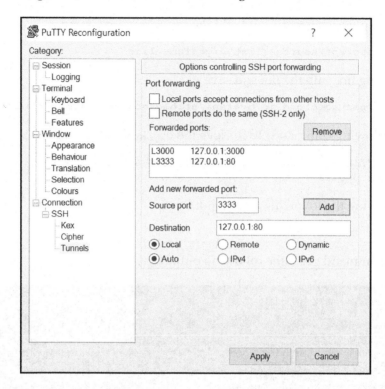

Now, use `http://localhost:3000` in the URL. You should be taken to the Grafana home page. Navigate to data sources and then configure Grafana to poll our newly installed Graphite installation:

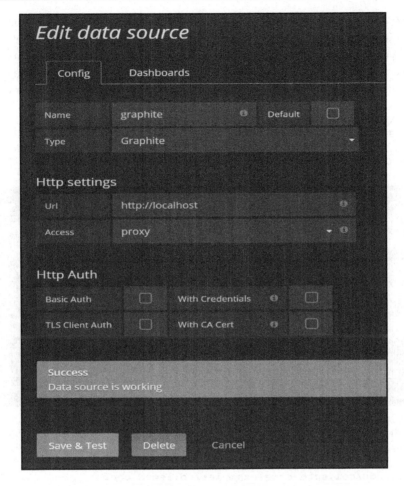

If you get the green success bar when you click on the **Save & Test** button, then you have successfully installed and configured Graphite and Grafana.

collectd

Now that we have a shiny installation of Graphite and Grafana to look at, we need to put some data into it to be able to generate some graphs. collectd is a well-respected metric collection tool, which can output metrics to Graphite. The core collectd application is very minimal, and it relies on a series of plugins to collect metrics and forwards them onto applications such as Graphite for storage.

Before we start collecting metrics from our Ceph nodes, let's install collectd on the same VM where we installed Graphite and Grafana. We will do this to gain a better understanding of collectd and the process required to configure it. We will then use Ansible to install and configure collectd on all of our Ceph nodes, which would be the recommended approach if this was being rolled out in a production environment. We have the following code:

```
sudo apt-get install collectd-core
```

The preceding command will give the following output:

```
vagrant@ansible:~$ sudo apt-get install collectd-core
Reading package lists... Done
Building dependency tree
Reading state information... Done
The following additional packages will be installed:
  fontconfig libdatrie1 libdbi1 libgraphite2-3 libharfbuzz0b libltdl7 libpango-1.0-0 libpangocairo-1.0-0
  libpangoft2-1.0-0 librrd4 libthai-data libthai0 rrdtool
Suggested packages:
  collectd-dev librrds-perl liburi-perl libhtml-parser-perl libregexp-common-perl libconfig-general-perl
  apcupsd bind9 ceph hddtemp ipvsadm lm-sensors mbmon memcached mysql-server | virtual-mysql-server nginx
  notification-daemon nut openvpn olsrd pdns-server postgresql redis-server slapd time-daemon varnish
  zookeeper libatasmart4 libesmtp6 libganglia1 libhiredis0.13 libmemcached11 libmodbus5 libmysqlclient20
  libnotify4 libopenipmi0 liboping0 libowcapi-3.1-1 libpq5 libprotobuf-c1 librabbitmq4 librdkafka1
  libsensors4 libsigrok2 libsnmp30 libtokyotyrant3 libupsclient4 libvarnishapi1 libvirt0 libyajl2
  default-jre-headless
The following NEW packages will be installed:
  collectd-core fontconfig libdatrie1 libdbi1 libgraphite2-3 libharfbuzz0b libltdl7 libpango-1.0-0
  libpangocairo-1.0-0 libpangoft2-1.0-0 librrd4 libthai-data libthai0 rrdtool
0 upgraded, 14 newly installed, 0 to remove and 122 not upgraded.
Need to get 2,193 kB of archives.
After this operation, 8,419 kB of additional disk space will be used.
Do you want to continue? [Y/n]
```

This will install collectd and a basic set of plugins for querying standard operating system resources. There is a sample configuration stored in the following location:

/usr/share/doc/collectd-core/examples/collectd.conf

It lists all of the core plugins and sample configuration options. It is worth reviewing this file to learn about the various plugins and their configuration options. For this example, however, we will start with an empty configuration file and configure a few basic resources:

1. Create a new `collectd` configuration file using the following command:

   ```
   sudo nano /etc/collectd/collectd.conf
   ```

2. Add the following to it:

   ```
   Hostname "ansible"

   LoadPlugin cpu
   ```

```
LoadPlugin df
LoadPlugin load
LoadPlugin memory
LoadPlugin write_graphite

<Plugin write_graphite>
   <Node "graphing">
       Host "localhost"
       Port "2003"
       Protocol "tcp"
       LogSendErrors true
       Prefix "collectd."
       StoreRates true
       AlwaysAppendDS false
       EscapeCharacter "_"
   </Node>
</Plugin>

<Plugin "df">
   FSType "ext4"
</Plugin>
```

3. Restart the `collectd` service using the following command:

   ```
   sudo service collectd restart
   ```

4. Now, navigate back to Grafana and browse the dashboard's menu item. Click on the button in the middle of the screen to create a new dashboard:

5. Select **Graph** to add a new graph to the dashboard. An example graph will now appear, which we will want to edit to replace with our own graphs. To do this, click on the graph title and a floating menu will appear:

6. Click on **Edit** to go to the graph widget editing screen. From here, we can delete the fake graph data by selecting the *dustbin* icon, as shown in the following three-button menu box:

7. Now, from the drop-down menu, change the panel data source to the Graphite source we have just added and click on the `Add query` button:

8. A query box will appear at the top of the editing panel. It will also have the three-button menu box, like before. From here, we can toggle the edit mode of the query editor by clicking on the button with the three horizontal lines:

The **Toggle Edit Mode** option switches the query editor between click and select mode, where you can explore the available metrics and build up basic queries and the text editor mode. The click and select mode is useful if you do not know the names of the metrics and only want to create basic queries. For more advanced queries, the text editor is required.

We will first make a query for our graph using the basic editor mode and then switch to the text mode for the rest of this chapter to make it easier to copy the queries from this book.

Let's first graph the system load of VM where we have installed **collectd**:

This will now produce a graph, showing the system load.

By further clicking on the + symbol, you can expand the query by applying different functions against the data. These could be used to add multiple data sources together or to find the average. We will cover this further in this chapter as we begin to craft some queries to analyze Ceph performance. Before we continue, let's switch the query editor mode to text mode to see what the query looks like:

You can see that each leaf of the tree of metrics is separated by a dot. This is how the Graphite query language works.

Deploying collectd with Ansible

Now that we have confirmed that our monitoring stack is installed and working correctly, let's use Ansible to deploy collectd to all our Ceph nodes, so we can start monitoring it.

Switch to the `ansible` directory:

```
cd /etc/ansible/roles
git clone https://github.com/fiskn/Stouts.collectd
```

Edit your Ansible `site.yml` file and add the `collectd` role to the plays for your `mon` and `osd` nodes so that they look like the following:

```
- hosts: mons
  gather_facts: false
  become: True
  roles:
    - ceph-mon
    - Stouts.collectd
```

Edit `group_vars/all` and enter the following:

```
collectd_use_ppa: yes
collectd_use_ppa_latest: yes
collectd_ppa_source: 'deb http://pkg.ci.collectd.org/deb xenial collectd-5.7'

collectd_write_graphite: yes
collectd_write_graphite_options:
  Host: "ansible"
  Port: 2003
  Prefix: collectd.
  # Postfix: .collectd
  Protocol: tcp
  AlwaysAppendDS: false
  EscapeCharacter: _
  LogSendErrors: true
  StoreRates: true
  SeparateInstances: true
  PreserveSeparator: true

collectd_ceph: yes
```

Now, run your `site.yml` playbook:

```
ansible-playbook -K site.yml
```

The preceding command gives the following output:

```
RUNNING HANDLER [Stouts.collectd : collectd restart] ****************************
changed: [osd2]
changed: [osd3]
changed: [osd1]

PLAY RECAP ***********************************************************************
mon1                       : ok=67    changed=8    unreachable=0    failed=0
mon2                       : ok=61    changed=6    unreachable=0    failed=0
mon3                       : ok=61    changed=6    unreachable=0    failed=0
osd1                       : ok=65    changed=6    unreachable=0    failed=0
osd2                       : ok=63    changed=6    unreachable=0    failed=0
osd3                       : ok=63    changed=6    unreachable=0    failed=0
```

You should see from the status at the end that Ansible has deployed `collectd` to all your Ceph nodes, and it has configured the `collectd` Ceph plugin. In Grafana, you should now be able to see your Ceph nodes showing up as available metrics. The following is one of our monitor nodes:

For example, we can now create a graph showing the number objects stored in the Ceph cluster. Create a new graph in Grafana and enter the following query:

```
collectd.mon1.ceph.mon.mon1.ceph_bytes.Cluster.numObject
```

This will produce a graph like the following one:

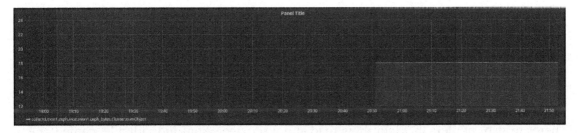

It's advised that you spend some time browsing through the available metrics so that you are familiar with them before proceeding to the next section.

Sample Graphite queries for Ceph

Although you can generate some very useful graphs by simply selecting individual metrics, by harnessing the power of Graphite's functions to manipulate the metrics, graphs can be created, which offer a much more detailed insight into your Ceph cluster. The following Graphite queries are useful for generating common graphs and are also a good starting point so that you can create your own custom queries.

Number of Up and In OSDs

It's very handy to be able to quickly glance at a dashboard and see how many OSDs are Up and In. The following two queries show these values:

```
maxSeries(collectd.mon*.ceph.mon.mon*.ceph_bytes.Cluster.numOsdIn)
```

```
maxSeries(collectd.mon*.ceph.mon.mon*.ceph_bytes.Cluster.numOsdUp)
```

Note the use of the maxSeries function, which allows data to be pulled from all the mon nodes and will take the highest value.

Showing the most deviant OSD usage

Due to the way CRUSH places PGs on each OSD, there will never be a perfect balance of PGs per OSD. The following query will create a graph that will show the ten most deviant OSDs, so you can see if PG balancing would be beneficial. We have the following code:

```
mostDeviant(10,collectd.osd*.df.var-lib-ceph-osd-ceph-
*.df_complex.used)
```

Total number of IOPs across all OSDs

This uses the sumSeries function and wildcards to add all the op metrics from every OSD together:

```
sumSeries(collectd.osd*.ceph.osd.*.ceph_rate.Osd.op)
```

There are also counters that will show read and write operations individually, named opR and opW, respectively.

Total MBps across all OSDs

Similarly, there are also counters that show MBps for each OSD, such as the op counters; the sumSeries function can also be used. We have the following code:

```
sumSeries(collectd.osd*.ceph.osd.*.ceph_rate.Osd.{opInBytes,opOutBytes})
```

Cluster capacity and usage

The following two queries show the total capacity of bytes in the cluster and the number of bytes used. They can be used to generate a pie chart in Grafana to show the percentage of used space. Note that these counters show the raw capacity before replication:

```
maxSeries(collectd.mon*.ceph.mon.mon*.ceph_bytes.Cluster.osdBytes)
```

```
maxSeries(collectd.mon*.ceph.mon.mon*.ceph_bytes.Cluster.osdBytesUsed)
```

Average latency

The following two queries can be used to graph the average latency of the cluster. Larger I/O sizes per operation will increase the average latency, as larger I/Os take longer to process. As such, these graphs will not give a clear picture of your cluster's latency if the average I/O size changes over time. We have the following code:

```
averageSeries(collectd.osd*.ceph.osd.*.ceph_latency.Osd.opWLatency)
```

```
averageSeries(collectd.osd*.ceph.osd.*.ceph_latency.Osd.opRLatency)
```

Custom Ceph collectd plugins

Although the standard collectd Ceph plugin does a good job of collecting all of Ceph's performance counters, it falls short of collecting all the required data to allow you to get a complete view of your cluster health and performance. This section will demonstrate how to use additional custom collectd plugins to collect the PG states, per pool performance stats, and more realistic latency figures:

1. Jump on to one of your mon nodes via SSH and clone the following Git repository:

```
git clone https://github.com/grinapo/collectd-ceph
```

2. Create a `ceph` directory under the `collectd/plugins` directory:

```
sudo mkdir -p /usr/lib/collectd/plugins/ceph
```

3. Copy the `plugins` directory to `/usr/lib/collectd/plugins/ceph` using the following command:

```
sudo cp -a collectd-ceph/plugins/*
/usr/lib/collectd/plugins/ceph/
```

4. Now, create a new `collectd` configuration file to enable the plugins:

```
sudo nano /etc/collectd/collectd.conf.d/ceph2.conf
```

5. Place the following configuration inside it and save the new file:

```
<LoadPlugin "python">
Globals true
</LoadPlugin>

<Plugin "python">
ModulePath "/usr/lib/collectd/plugins/ceph"

Import "ceph_pool_plugin"
Import "ceph_pg_plugin"
Import "ceph_latency_plugin"

<Module "ceph_pool_plugin">
Verbose "True"
Cluster "ceph"
Interval "60"
</Module>
<Module "ceph_pg_plugin">
Verbose "True"
Cluster "ceph"
Interval "60"
</Module>
<Module "ceph_latency_plugin">
Verbose "True"
Cluster "ceph"
Interval "60"
TestPool "rbd"
</Module>
</Plugin>
```

The latency plugin uses a RADOS bench to determine the cluster latency; this means that it is actually running RADOS bench and will write data to your cluster. The `TestPool` parameter determines the target for the RADOS bench command. It is therefore recommended that on a production cluster, a separate small pool is created for this use.

 If you are trying to use these extra plugins on Kraken+ releases of Ceph, you will need to edit the `ceph_pg_plugin.py` file and modify the variable name on line 71 from `fs_perf_stat` to `perf_stat`.

6. Restart the `collectd` service:

```
service collectd restart
```

The average cluster latency can now be obtained with the following query:

```
collectd.mon1.ceph-ceph.cluster.gauge.avg_latency
```

This figure is based on doing 64 KB writes, and so, unlike the OSD metrics, it will not change depending on the average client I/O size.

Summary

In this chapter, you learned the importance of monitoring your Ceph cluster and its supporting infrastructure. You should also have a good understanding of the various components that you should monitor and some example tools that can be used. We covered some of the PG states that, in conjunction with a monitoring solution will allow you to understand the current status of your Ceph cluster. Finally, we deployed a highly scalable monitoring system comprising collectd, Graphite, and Grafana, which will enable you to create professional looking dashboards to show the status and performance of your Ceph cluster.

In the next chapter, we will look at ways to tune the performance of you Ceph cluster, this leans heavily on being able to capture performance stats, which you should now be able to do following this chapter.

Questions

1. What port does the Ceph Dashboard run on?
2. What Ceph daemon is the Ceph Dashboard controlled by?
3. What does the inconsistent PG state mean?
4. What does the backfilling PG state mean?
5. What should you aim to monitor in your Ceph infrastructure?

9
Tuning Ceph

While the default configuration of Linux and Ceph will likely provide reasonable performance due to many years of research and tweaking by developers, it is likely that a Ceph administrator may want to try to squeeze more performance out of the hardware. By tuning both the operating system and Ceph, performance gains may be realized. In Chapter 1, *Planning for Ceph*, you learned about how to choose hardware for a Ceph cluster; now, let's learn how to make the most of it.

In this chapter, you will learn about the following topics:

- Latency and why it matters
- The importance of being able to observe the results of your tuning
- Key tuning options that you should look at

Latency

When running benchmarks to test the performance of a Ceph cluster, you are ultimately measuring the result of latency. All other forms of benchmarking metrics, including IOPS, MBps, or even higher-level application metrics, are derived from the latency of that request.

IOPS are the number of I/O requests done in a second; the latency of each request directly effects the possible IOPS and can be calculated using this formula:

$$IOP = \frac{1\ Second}{Latency}\ (in\ seconds)$$

An average latency of 2 milliseconds per request will result in roughly 500 IOPS, assuming each request is submitted in a synchronous fashion:

$$1/0.002 = 500$$

MBps is simply the number of IOPS multiplied by the I/O size:

$$500\ IOPS * 64\ KB = 32,000\ KBps$$

When you are carrying out benchmarks, you are actually measuring the end result of a latency. Therefore, any tuning that you are carrying out should be done to reduce end-to-end latency for each I/O request.

Before moving on to learning how to benchmark various components of your Ceph cluster and the various tuning options available, we first need to understand the various sources of latency from a typical I/O request. Once we can break down each source of latency into its own category, it will be possible to perform benchmarking on each one so that we can reliably track both negative and positive tuning outcomes at each stage.

The following diagram shows an example Ceph write request with the main sources of latency:

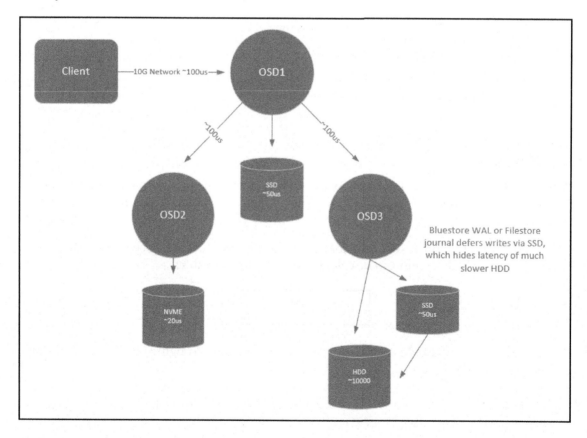

Client to Primary OSD

Starting with the client, we can see that, on average, there is probably around 100 microseconds of latency for it to talk to the primary OSD. With 1 G networking, this latency figure could be nearer to 1 millisecond. We can confirm this figure by either using `ping` or `iperf` to measure the round-trip delay between two nodes.

From the previous formula, we can see that with 1 G networking, even if there were no other sources of latency, the maximum synchronous write IOPS would be around 1,000.

Although the client introduces some latency of its own, it is minimal compared to the other sources, and so it is not included in the diagram.

Primary OSD to Replica OSD(s)

Next, the OSD that runs the Ceph code introduces latency as it processes the request. It is hard to put an exact figure on this, but it is affected by the speed of the CPU. A faster CPU with a higher frequency will run through the code path faster, reducing latency. Early on in this book, the primary OSD would send the request to the other two OSDs in the replica set. These are both processed in parallel so that there is minimal increase in latency going from 2x to 3x replicas, assuming the backend disks can cope with the load.

There is also an extra network hop between the primary and the replicated OSDs, which introduces latency into each request.

Primary OSD to Client

Once the primary OSD has committed the request to its journal and has had an acknowledgement back from all the replica OSDs that they have also done so, it can then send an acknowledgment back to the client and submit the next I/O request.

Regarding the journal, depending on the type of media being used, the commit latency can vary. NVMe SSDs will tend to service requests in the 10-20 microseconds range, whereas SATA/SAS-based SSDs will typical service requests in the 50-100 microseconds range. NVMe devices also tend to have a more consistent latency profile with an increase in the queue depth, making them ideal for cases where multiple disks might use a single SSD as the same journal. Way ahead are the hard drives that are measured in tens of milliseconds, although they are fairly consistent in terms of latency as the I/O size increases.

It should be obvious that for small, high-performance workloads, hard drive latency would dominate the total latency figures, and so, SSDs, preferably NVMe, should be used for it.

Overall, in a well-designed and well-tuned Ceph cluster, all of these parts combined should allow an average write 4 KB request to be serviced in around 500-750 microseconds.

Benchmarking

Benchmarking is an important tool to quickly be able to see the effects of your tuning efforts and to determine the limits of what your cluster is capable of. However, it's important that your benchmarks reflect the type of workload that you would be running normally on your Ceph cluster. It is pointless to tune your Ceph cluster to excel in large-block sequential reads and writes if your final intention is to run highly-latency sensitive **Online Transaction Processing (OLTP)** databases on it. If possible, you should try to include some benchmarks that actually use the same software as your real-life workload. Again, in the example of the OLTP database, look to see whether there are benchmarks for your database software, which will give the most accurate results.

Benchmarking tools

The following list of tools is the recommended set of tools to get you started with benchmarking:

- **Fio**: Fio, the flexible I/O testing tool, allows you to simulate a variety of complex I/O patterns through its extensive configuration options. It has plugins for both local block devices and RBD, meaning that you can test RBDs from your Ceph cluster either directly or by mounting them via the Linux RBD kernel driver.
- **Sysbench**: Sysbench has a MySQL OLTP test suite that simulates an OLTP application.
- **Ping**: Don't underestimate the humble ping tool; along with being able to diagnose many network problems, its round-trip time is helpful in determining the latency of a network link.
- **iPerf**: iPerf allows you to conduct a series of network tests to determine the bandwidth between two servers.

Network benchmarking

There are a number of areas that we need to benchmark on the network to be able to understand any limitation and make sure there are no misconfigurations.

A standard Ethernet frame is 1,500 bytes, while a **jumbo frame** is typically 9,000 bytes. This increased frame size reduces the overheads for sending data. If you have configured your network with a jumbo frame, the first thing to check is that they are configured correctly across all your servers and networking devices. If jumbo frames are configured incorrectly, Ceph will exhibit strange, random behavior that is very hard to trace; therefore, it is essential that jumbo frames are configured correctly and confirmed to be working before deploying Ceph over the top of your network.

To confirm whether jumbo frames are working correctly, you can use `ping` to send large packets with the **don't fragment** flag set:

```
ping -M do -s 8972 <destination IP>
```

This command should be run across all your nodes to make sure they can ping each other using jumbo frames. If it fails, investigate the issue and resolve it before deploying Ceph.

The next test to undertake is to measure the round-trip time, also with the ping tool. Using the packet size parameter again but with the don't fragment flag, it is possible to test the round-trip time of certain packet sizes up to 64 KB, which is the maximum IP packet size.

Here are some example readings between two hosts on a **10GBase-T** network:

- 32 B = 85 microseconds
- 4 KB = 112 microseconds
- 16 KB = 158 microseconds
- 64 KB = 248 microseconds

As you can see, larger packet sizes impact the round-trip time; this is one reason why larger I/O sizes will see a decrease in IOPS in Ceph.

Finally, let's test the bandwidth between two hosts to determine whether we get the expected performance.

Run `iperf -s` on the server that will run the iPerf server role:

```
Server listening on TCP port 5001
TCP window size: 85.3 KByte (default)
```

Then, run the `iperf -c <address of iperf server>` command:

```
Client connecting to 10.1.111.1, TCP port 5001
TCP window size:  325 KByte (default)

[  3] local 10.1.111.5 port 59172 connected with 10.1.111.1 port 5001
[ ID] Interval        Transfer      Bandwidth
[  3]  0.0-10.0 sec  11.1 GBytes  9.51 Gbits/sec
```

In this example, the two hosts are connected via a 10 G network and obtain near the maximum theoretical throughput. If you do not see the correct throughput, an investigation into the network, including host configuration, needs to be done.

Disk benchmarking

It is a good idea to understand the underlying performance of the hard disks and SSDs in your Ceph cluster, as this will enable you to predict the overall performance of your Ceph cluster. To benchmark the disks in your cluster, the fio tool will be used.

 Use fio carefully if you're operating in write mode. If you specify a block device, fio will happily write over any data that exists on that disk.

Fio is a complex tool with many configuration options. For the purpose of this chapter, we will concentrate on using it to perform basic read and write benchmarks:

1. Install the fio tool on a Ceph OSD node:

    ```
    apt-get install fio
    ```

The preceding command gives the following output:

```
The following NEW packages will be installed
  fio
0 to upgrade, 1 to newly install, 0 to remove and 121 not to upgrade.
Need to get 368 kB of archives.
After this operation, 1,572 kB of additional disk space will be used.
Get:1 http://gb.archive.ubuntu.com/ubuntu xenial/universe amd64 fio amd64 2.2.10-1ubuntu1 [368 kB]
Fetched 368 kB in 5s (69.7 kB/s)
Selecting previously unselected package fio.
(Reading database ... 579847 files and directories currently installed.)
Preparing to unpack .../fio_2.2.10-1ubuntu1_amd64.deb ...
Unpacking fio (2.2.10-1ubuntu1) ...
Processing triggers for man-db (2.7.5-1) ...
Setting up fio (2.2.10-1ubuntu1) ...
```

2. Create a new file and place the following fio configuration into it:

```
[global]
ioengine=libaio
randrepeat=0
invalidate=0
rw=randwrite
bs=4k
direct=1
time_based=1
runtime=30
numjobs=1
iodepth=1
filename=/test.fio
size=1G
```

The previous fio configuration will run a single-threaded 4 KB random write test for 30 seconds. It will create a 1G test.fio file in the root of the filesystem. If you wish to target a block device directly, simply set the filename to the block device. However note that with the preceding warning, fio will overwrite any data on that block device.

Notice that the job is set to use direction, so the page cache will not accelerate any I/O operations.

To run the fio job, simply call fio with the name of the file to which you saved the previous configuration:

```
fio <filename>
```

The preceding command gives the following output:

```
file1: (g=0): rw=read, bs=4M-4M/4M-4M/4M-4M, ioengine=libaio, iodepth=1
fio-2.2.10
Starting 1 process
Jobs: 1 (f=1): [R(1)] [100.0% done] [100.0MB/0KB/0KB /s] [25/0/0 iops] [eta 00m:00s]
file1: (groupid=0, jobs=1): err= 0: pid=26999: Sun Mar 12 22:20:33 2017
  read : io=9496.0MB, bw=162052KB/s, iops=39, runt= 60005msec
    slat (usec): min=174, max=31852, avg=244.48, stdev=649.33
    clat (msec): min=15, max=338, avg=25.03, stdev=12.58
     lat (msec): min=15, max=338, avg=25.27, stdev=12.61
    clat percentiles (msec):
     |  1.00th=[    22],  5.00th=[    22], 10.00th=[    22], 20.00th=[    23],
     | 30.00th=[    23], 40.00th=[    23], 50.00th=[    24], 60.00th=[    24],
     | 70.00th=[    24], 80.00th=[    24], 90.00th=[    25], 95.00th=[    26],
     | 99.00th=[    80], 99.50th=[   102], 99.90th=[   182], 99.95th=[   223],
     | 99.99th=[   338]
    bw (KB  /s): min=77722, max=183641, per=100.00%, avg=163013.63, stdev=21774.82
    lat (msec) : 20=0.25%, 50=97.60%, 100=1.64%, 250=0.46%, 500=0.04%
  cpu          : usr=0.04%, sys=0.97%, ctx=2382, majf=0, minf=1036
  IO depths    : 1=100.0%, 2=0.0%, 4=0.0%, 8=0.0%, 16=0.0%, 32=0.0%, >=64=0.0%
     submit    : 0=0.0%, 4=100.0%, 8=0.0%, 16=0.0%, 32=0.0%, 64=0.0%, >=64=0.0%
     complete  : 0=0.0%, 4=100.0%, 8=0.0%, 16=0.0%, 32=0.0%, 64=0.0%, >=64=0.0%
     issued    : total=r=2374/w=0/d=0, short=r=0/w=0/d=0, drop=r=0/w=0/d=0
     latency   : target=0, window=0, percentile=100.00%, depth=1

Run status group 0 (all jobs):
   READ: io=9496.0MB, aggrb=162051KB/s, minb=162051KB/s, maxb=162051KB/s, mint=60005msec, maxt=60005msec
```

Once the job is done, fio will produce an output similar to what's shown in the previous screenshot. You can see that the fio job runs 39 IOPS and 162 MBps on an average, and that the average latency was 25 milliseconds.

There is also a breakdown of latency percentiles, which can be useful for understanding the spread of the request latency.

RADOS benchmarking

The next step is to benchmark the RADOS layer. This will give you a combined figure, including the performance of the disks, networking—along with the overheads of the Ceph code—and extra replicated copies of data.

The RADOS command-line tool has a built-in benchmarking command, which by default initiates 16 threads, all writing 4 MB objects. To run the RADOS benchmark, run the following command:

```
rados -p rbd bench 10 write
```

This will run the write benchmark for 10 seconds:

```
Maintaining 16 concurrent writes of 4194304 bytes to objects of size 4194304 for up to 10 seconds or 0 objects
Object prefix: benchmark_data_ms-r1-c1-osd1_25645
  sec Cur ops   started  finished  avg MB/s  cur MB/s last lat(s)  avg lat(s)
    0       0         0         0         0         0          -           0
    1      16       121       105   419.977       420  0.0683843    0.138681
    2      15       254       239   477.947       536   0.139127    0.128909
    3      16       370       354   471.939       460  0.0906016    0.131449
    4      16       491       475   474.937       484  0.0822003    0.132115
    5      16       611       595   475.935       480   0.142927    0.132402
    6      16       731       715   476.602       480   0.110139    0.131169
    7      16       859       843    481.65       512  0.0932729    0.131419
    8      15       984       969   484.435       504   0.214752    0.131099
    9      16      1115      1099    488.38       520   0.131412    0.129911
   10      15      1229      1214   485.536       460    0.13085    0.130238
Total time run:          10.120543
Total writes made:       1230
Write size:              4194304
Object size:             4194304
Bandwidth (MB/sec):      486.14
Stddev Bandwidth:        34.0562
Max bandwidth (MB/sec):  536
Min bandwidth (MB/sec):  420
Average IOPS:            121
Stddev IOPS:             8
Max IOPS:                134
Min IOPS:                105
Average Latency(s):      0.13146
Stddev Latency(s):       0.0673788
Max latency(s):          0.703673
Min latency(s):          0.0400385
Cleaning up (deleting benchmark objects)
Clean up completed and total clean up time :0.701427
```

In the previous example, it can be seen that the cluster was able to sustain a write bandwidth of around 480 MBps. The output also gives you latency and other useful figures. Notice that at the end of the test, it deletes the objects that were created as part of the benchmark automatically. If you wish to use the RADOS tool to carry out read benchmarks, you need to specify the `--no-cleanup` option to leave the objects in place, and then run the benchmark again with the benchmark type specified as `seq` instead of `write`. You will manually need to clear the bench objects afterward.

RBD benchmarking

Finally, we will test the performance of RBDs using our favorite tool, fio. This will test the entire software and hardware stack, and the results will be very close to what clients would expect to observe. By configuring fio to emulate certain client applications, we can also get a feel for the expected performance of these applications.

To test the performance of an RBD, we will use the fio RBD engine, which allows fio to talk directly to the RBD image. Create a new fio configuration and place the following into it:

```
[global]
ioengine=rbd
randrepeat=0
clientname=admin
pool=rbd
rbdname=test
invalidate=0
rw=write
bs=1M
direct=1
time_based=1
runtime=30
numjobs=1
iodepth=1
```

You can see that, unlike the disk benchmarking configuration, instead of using the `libaio` engine, this configuration file now uses the `rbd` engine. When using the `rbd` engine, you also need to specify the RADOS pool and the `cephx` user. Finally, instead of specifying a filename or block device, you simply need to specify an RBD image that exists in the RADOS pool that you configured.

Then, run the fio job to test the performance of your RBD:

```
Starting 1 process
rbd engine: RBD version: 0.1.10
Jobs: 1 (f=1): [W(1)] [100.0% done] [0KB/69632KB/0KB /s] [0/68/0 iops] [eta 00m:00s]
rbd_iodepth32: (groupid=0, jobs=1): err= 0: pid=5021: Sun Mar 12 22:29:13 2017
  write: io=2020.0MB, bw=68947KB/s, iops=67, runt= 30001msec
    slat (usec): min=11, max=1741, avg=36.49, stdev=39.93
    clat (msec): min=4, max=612, avg=14.81, stdev=37.84
     lat (msec): min=4, max=612, avg=14.85, stdev=37.84
    clat percentiles (msec):
     |  1.00th=[    5],  5.00th=[    5], 10.00th=[    5], 20.00th=[    5],
     | 30.00th=[    5], 40.00th=[    5], 50.00th=[    5], 60.00th=[    6],
     | 70.00th=[    6], 80.00th=[    9], 90.00th=[   30], 95.00th=[   60],
     | 99.00th=[  186], 99.50th=[  265], 99.90th=[  420], 99.95th=[  437],
     | 99.99th=[  611]
    bw (KB  /s): min= 7231, max=174080, per=100.00%, avg=71772.68, stdev=35752.42
    lat (msec) : 10=82.13%, 20=4.95%, 50=6.73%, 100=3.66%, 250=1.93%
    lat (msec) : 500=0.54%, 750=0.05%
  cpu          : usr=0.29%, sys=0.01%, ctx=2026, majf=0, minf=0
  IO depths    : 1=100.0%, 2=0.0%, 4=0.0%, 8=0.0%, 16=0.0%, 32=0.0%, >=64=0.0%
     submit    : 0=0.0%, 4=100.0%, 8=0.0%, 16=0.0%, 32=0.0%, 64=0.0%, >=64=0.0%
     complete  : 0=0.0%, 4=100.0%, 8=0.0%, 16=0.0%, 32=0.0%, 64=0.0%, >=64=0.0%
     issued    : total=r=0/w=2020/d=0, short=r=0/w=0/d=0, drop=r=0/w=0/d=0
     latency   : target=0, window=0, percentile=100.00%, depth=1

Run status group 0 (all jobs):
  WRITE: io=2020.0MB, aggrb=68947KB/s, minb=68947KB/s, maxb=68947KB/s, mint=30001msec, maxt=30001msec
```

As can be seen in the preceding output, the fio tool is using the RBD engine directly, bypassing the requirement for an RBD to be mounted to the Linux operating system before it can be tested.

Recommended tunings

Tuning your Ceph cluster will enable you to get the best performance and the most benefits from your hardware. In this section, we will look at recommended Ceph tuning options. It's important to understand that by tuning, all you are doing is reducing bottlenecks. If you manage to reduce enough bottlenecks in one area, the bottleneck will simply shift to another area. You will always have a bottleneck somewhere, and eventually, you will reach a point where you are simply over the limit of what a particular hardware can provide. Therefore, the goal should be to reduce bottlenecks in the software and operating system to unlock the entire potential of your hardware.

CPU

As Ceph is software-defined for storage, its performance is heavily affected by the speed of the CPUs in the OSD nodes. Faster CPUs mean that the Ceph code can run faster and will spend less time processing each I/O request. The result is a lower latency per I/O, which, if the underlying storage can cope, will reduce the CPU as a bottleneck and give a higher overall performance. Chapter 1, *Planning for Ceph*, stated a preference for high Ghz processors rather than high core count, for performance reasons; however, there are additional concerns with high-core-count CPUs when they are over-specified for the job.

To understand these concerns, we will need to cover a brief history on CPU design. During the early 2000s, CPUs were all single-core designs, which ran constantly at the same frequency and didn't support many low-power modes. As they moved to higher frequencies and core counts started, it became apparent that not every core would be able to run at its maximum frequency all the time. The amount of heat generated from the CPU package was simply too great. Fast forward to today, and this still holds true: there is no such thing as a 4 GHz 20-core CPU; it would simply generate too much heat to be feasible.

However, the clever people who designed CPUs came up with a solution, which allowed each core to run at a different frequency and also allowed them to power themselves down into deep sleep states. Both approaches lowered the power and cooling requirements of the CPU down to single-digit watts.

The CPUs have much lower clock speeds, but with the ability for a certain total number of cores to engage turbo mode, higher GHz are possible. There is normally a gradual decrease in the top turbo frequency as the number of active cores increases to keep the heat output below a certain threshold. If a low-threaded process is started, the CPU wakes up a couple of cores and speeds them up to a much higher frequency to get better single-threaded performance. In Intel CPUs, the different frequency levels are called **P-states** and sleep levels are called **C-states**.

This all sounds like the perfect package: a CPU that, when idle, consumes hardly any power, and yet when needed, it can turbo boost a handful of cores to achieve high clock speed. Unfortunately, there is no such thing as a free lunch. There are some overheads with this approach that have a detrimental effect on the latency of sensitive applications, with Ceph being one of them.

There are two main problems with this approach that impact the latency of sensitive applications, the first being that it takes time for a core to wake up from a sleep state. The deeper the sleep, the longer it takes to wake up. The core has to reinitialize certain internal components before it is ready to be used. Here is a list from an Intel E3-1200v5 CPU; older CPUs may fare slightly worse:

- POLL = 0 microsecond
- C1-SKL = 2 microseconds
- C1E-SKL = 10 microseconds
- C3-SKL = 70 microseconds
- C6-SKL = 85 microseconds
- C7s-SKL = 124 microseconds
- C8-SKL = 200 microseconds

We can see that in the worst case, it may take a core up to 200 microseconds to wake up from its deepest sleep. When you consider that a single Ceph I/O may require several threads across several nodes to wake up a CPU core, these exit latencies can start to really add up. While P-states that effect the core frequency don't impact performance quite as much as the C-state exit latencies, the core's frequency doesn't immediately increase in a speed to maximum as soon as its in use. This means that under low utilization, the CPU cores may only be operating at a low GHz. This leads us to the second problem, which lies with the Linux scheduler.

Linux is aware of what core is active and which C-state and P-state each core is running at. It can fully control each core's behavior. Unfortunately, Linux's scheduler doesn't take any of this information into account; instead, it prefers to try to balance threads across cores evenly. This means that at low utilization, all the CPU cores will spend the bulk on their time in their lowest C-state and will operate at a low frequency. During a low utilization, this can impact the latency for small I/Os by 4-5x, which is a significant impact.

Until Linux has a power-aware scheduler that will take into account which cores are already active and schedules threads on them to reduce latency, the best approach is to force the CPU to only sleep down to a certain C-state and force it to run at the highest frequency all the time. This does increase the power draw, but in the newest models of CPU, this has somewhat been reduced. For this reason, it should be clear why it is recommended to size your CPU to your workload. Running a 40-core server at a high C-state and high frequency will consume a lot of power.

To force Linux to only drop-down to the C1 C-state, add this to your GRUB configuration:

```
intel_idle.max_cstate=1
```

Some Linux distributions have a performance mode where this runs the CPUs at a maximum frequency. However, the manual way to achieve this is to echo values via `sysfs`. Sticking the following in `/etc/rc.local` will set all your cores to run at their maximum frequency on the boot:

```
/sys/devices/system/cpu/intel_pstate/min_perf_pct
```

After you restart your OSD node, these changes should be in effect. Confirm this by running these commands:

```
sudo cpupower monitor
```

As mentioned earlier in this chapter, before making these changes, run a reference benchmark, and then do it again afterward so that you can understand the gains made by this change.

BlueStore

The latest versions of Ceph contain an auto-tuning functionality for BlueStore OSDs. The auto-tuning works by analyzing the cache utilization of the OSDs and adjusting the caching thresholds for the OSD, RocksDB, and data caches, depending on the current hit rate. It also limits the sum of these caches to try to limit the total OSD memory usage to the limit set by the `osd_memory_target` variable, which is set to 4 GB by default.

Obviously, if you have less RAM in the Ceph node and therefore it unable to provide 4 GB for each OSD, this figure would need to be reduced to avoid the node running out of memory. However, if the Ceph node has sufficient memory, it would be recommended to increase the `osd_memory_target` variable to allow Ceph to make as much use of the installed memory as possible. Once enough RAM has been assigned to the OSD and RocksDB, any additional RAM will be used as a data cache and will help to service the top-percentile read IOs much more effectively. The current auto-tuning algorithm is fairly slow and takes a while to ramp up, so at least 24-48 hours should be given to see the full effect of a change to the `osd_memory_target` variable.

WAL deferred writes

BlueStore can journal writes in the RocksDB WAL and flush them at a later date, allowing for write coalescing and ordering. This can bring large performance improvements for clusters that use spinning disks with flash-based devices for RocksDB.

By default, if the OSD is identified as a spinning HDD, writes less or equal to 32 KB are written into the WAL of the OSD and are then acknowledged and sent back to the client. This is controlled by the `bluestore_prefer_deferred_size_hdd` variable; this value can be adjusted if it is determined that your workload would benefit from also deferring larger writes via the WAL to achieve lower latency and higher IOPS. Thought should also be given to the write load of the flash device holding the WAL, both for bandwidth and endurance reasons.

The BlueStore configuration also limits how many writes can be queued up before the OSD is forced to flush them down to the disk; this can be controlled via the `bluestore_deferred_batch_ops` variable and is set by default to `64`. Increasing this value may increase total throughput, but also runs the risk of the HDD spending large amounts of time being saturated and raising the average latency.

Filestore

In nearly all cases, BlueStore outperforms filestore and solves several limitations, and therefore it is recommended that your cluster be upgraded to BlueStore. However, for completeness, the following are the items you can tune to improve the performance of filestore, should your cluster still be running it.

VFS cache pressure

As the name suggests, the filestore object store works by storing RADOS objects as files on a standard Linux filesystem. In most cases, this will be XFS. As each object is stored as a file, there will likely be hundreds of thousands, if not millions, of files per disk. A Ceph cluster is composed of 8 TB disks and is used for an RBD workload. Assuming that the RBD is made up of the standard 4 MB objects, there would be nearly 2,000,000 objects per disk.

When an application asks Linux to read or write to a file on a filesystem, it needs to know where that file actually exists on the disk. To find this location, it needs to follow the structure of directory entries and inodes. Each one of these lookups will require disk access if it's not already cached in memory. This can lead to poor performance in some cases if the Ceph objects, which are required to be read or written to, haven't been accessed in a while and are hence not cached. This penalty is a lot higher in spinning disk clusters as opposed to SSD-based clusters, due to the impact of the random reads.

By default, Linux favors the caching of data in the page cache versus the caching of inodes and directory entries. In many cases in Ceph, this is the opposite of what you want to happen. Luckily, there is a tuneable kernel that allows you to tell Linux to prefer directory entries and inodes over page caches; this can be controlled with the following `sysctl` setting:

        `vm.vfs_cache_pressure`

Where a lower number sets a preference to cache inodes and directory entries, do not set this to zero. A zero setting tells the kernel not to flush old entries, even in the event of a low-memory condition, and can have adverse effects. A value of 1 is recommended.

WBThrottle and/or nr_requests

Filestore uses buffered I/O to write; this brings a number of advantages if the filestore journal is on a faster media. Client requests are acknowledged as soon as they are written to the journal, and are then flushed to the data disk at a later date by the standard writeback functionality in Linux. This allows the spinning-disk OSDs to provide write latency similar to SSDs when writing in small bursts. The delayed writeback also allows the kernel to rearrange I/O requests to the disk to hopefully either coalesce them, or allow the disk heads to take a more optimal path across the platters. The end effect is that you can squeeze some more I/O out of each disk than what would be possible with a direct or sync I/O.

However, the problem occurs when the amount of incoming writes to the Ceph cluster outstrips the capabilities of the underlying disks. In this scenario, the number of pending I/Os waiting to be written on disk can increase uncontrollably, and the resulting queue of I/Os can saturate the disk and Ceph queues. Read requests are particularly poorly effected, as they get stuck behind potentially thousands of write requests, which may take several seconds to flush to the disk.

To combat this problem, Ceph has a writeback throttle mechanism built into filestore called **WBThrottle**. It is designed to limit the amount of writeback I/Os that can queue up and start the flushing process earlier than what would be naturally triggered by the kernel. Unfortunately, testing has shown that the defaults may still not curtail the behavior that can reduce the impact on the read latency.

Tuning can alter this behavior to reduce the write queue lengths and allow reads not to get too impacted. However, there is a trade-off; by reducing the maximum number of writes allowed to be queued up, you can reduce the kernel's opportunity to maximize the efficiency of reordering the requests. Some thought needs to be given to what is important for your given use case, workloads, and tune to match it.

To control the writeback queue depth, you can either reduce the maximum amount of outstanding I/Os using Ceph's WBThrottle settings, or lower the maximum outstanding requests at the block layer in the kernel. Both can effectively control the same behavior, and it's really a preference of how you want to implement the configuration.

It should also be noted that the operation priorities in Ceph are more effective with a shorter queue at the disk level. By shortening the queue at the disk, the main queuing location moves up into Ceph, where it has more control over what I/O has priority. Consider the following example:

```
echo 8 > /sys/block/sda/queue/nr_requests
```

With the release of the Linux 4.10 kernel, a new feature was introduced, which deprioritizes writeback I/O; this greatly reduces the impact of write-starvation with Ceph and is worth investigating if running the 4.10 kernel is feasible.

Throttling filestore queues

In the default configuration, when a disk becomes saturated, its disk queue will gradually fill up. Then, the filestore queue will start to fill up. Until this point, I/O would have been accepted as fast as the journal could accept it. As soon as the filestore queue fills up and/or the WBThrottle kicks in, I/O will suddenly be stopped until the queues fall back below the thresholds. This behavior will lead to large spikes and, most likely, periods of low performance, where other client requests will experience high latency.

To reduce the spikiness of filestore when the disks become saturated, there are some additional configuration options that can be set to gradually throttle back operations as the filestore queue fills up, instead of bouncing around the hard limit.

filestore_queue_low_threshhold

This is expressed as a percentage between 0.0 and 1.0. Below this threshold, no throttling is performed.

filestore_queue_high_threshhold

This is expressed as a percentage between 0.0 and 1.0. Between the low and high threshold, throttling is carried out by introducing a per-I/O delay, which is linearly increased from 0 to `filestore_queue_high_delay_multiple/filestore_expected_throughput_ops`.

From the high threshold to the maximum, it will throttle at the rate determined by `filestore_queue_max_delay_multiple/filestore_expected_throughput_ops`.

Both of these throttle rates use the configured one, which is the expected throughput of the disk to calculate the correct delay to introduce. The `delay_multiple` variables are there to allow an increase of this delay if the queue goes over the high threshold.

filestore_expected_throughput_ops

This should be set to the expected IOPS's performance of the underlying disk where the OSD is running.

filestore_queue_high_delay_multiple

Between the low and high thresholds, this multiple is used to calculate the correct amount of delay to introduce.

filestore_queue_max_delay_multiple

Above the maximum queue size, this multiplier is used to calculate an even greater delay to hopefully stop the queue from ever filling up.

Splitting PGs

A filesystem has a limit on the number of files that can be stored in a directory before performance starts to degrade when asked to list the contents:

- As Ceph is storing millions of objects per disk—which are just files. It splits the files across a nested directory structure to limit the number of files placed in each directory.
- As the number of objects in the cluster increases, so does the number of files per directory.
- When the number of files in these directories exceeds these limits, Ceph splits the directory into further subdirectories and migrates the objects to them.

This operation can have a significant performance penalty when it occurs. Furthermore, XFS tries to place its files in the same directory close together on the disk. When PG splitting occurs, fragmentation of the XFS filesystem can occur, leading to further performance degradation.

By default, Ceph will split a PG when it contains 320 objects. An 8 TB disk in a Ceph cluster configured with the recommended number of PGs per OSD will likely have over 5,000 objects per PG. This PG would have gone through several PG split operations in its lifetime, resulting in a deeper and more complex directory structure.

As mentioned in the *VFS cache pressure* section, to avoid costly dentry lookups, the kernel tries to cache them. The result of PG splitting means that there is a higher number of directories to cache, and there may not be enough memory to cache them all, leading to poorer performance.

A common approach to this problem is to increase the allowed number of files in each directory by setting the OSD configuration options, as follows:

```
filestore_split_multiple
```

Also, use the following setting:

```
filestore_merge_threshold
```

With the following formula, you can set at what threshold Ceph will split a PG:

$$\text{filestore\_split\_multiple} * \text{abs(filestore\_merge\_threshold)}*16$$

Care should be taken, however. Although increasing the threshold will reduce the occurrences of PG splitting and also reduce the complexity of the directory structure, when a PG split does occur, it will have to split far more objects. The greater the number of objects that need to be split, the greater the impact on performance, which may even lead to OSDs timing out. There is a trade-off of split frequency to split time; the defaults may be slightly on the conservative side, especially with larger disks.

Doubling or tripling the split threshold can probably be done safely without too much concern; greater values should be tested with the cluster under I/O load before putting it into production.

Scrubbing

Scrubbing is Ceph's way of verifying that the objects stored in RADOS are consistent, and to protect against bit rot or other corruptions. Scrubbing can either be normal or deep, depending on the set schedule. During a normal scrub operation, Ceph reads all objects for a certain PG and compares the copies to make sure that their size and attributes match.

A deep scrub operation goes one step further and compares the actual data contents of the objects. This generates a lot more I/O than the simpler standard scrubbing routine. Normal scrubbing is carried out daily, whereas deep scrubbing should be carried out weekly due to the extra I/O load.

Despite being deprioritized, scrubbing does have an impact on client IO, and so, there are a number of OSD settings that can be tweaked to guide Ceph as to when it should carry out the scrubbing.

The osd _scrub_begin_hour and osd _scrub_end_hour OSD configuration options determine the window Ceph will try to schedule scrubs in. By default, these are set to allow scrubbing to occur throughout a 24-hour period. If your workload only runs during the day, you might want to adjust the scrub start and end times to tell Ceph that you want it to scrub during off-peak times only. The osd_scrub_sleep configuration option controls the amount of time in seconds that a scrub operation waits between each chunk—this can help to allow the client IO to be serviced in-between the reading of each object. The chunk size is determined by the two variables osd_scrub_chunk_min and osd_scrub_chunk_max.

It should be noted that this time, a window is only honored if the PG has not fallen outside its maximum scrub interval. If it has, it will be scrubbed, regardless of the time window settings. The default maximum intervals for both normal and deep scrubs are set to one week.

OP priorities

Ceph has the ability to prioritize certain operations over others, with the idea that the client I/Os should have precedence over the recovery, scrubbing, and snapshot trimming IO. These priorities are controlled by the following configuration options:

```
osd client op priority
osd recovery op priority
osd scrub priority
osd snap trim priority
```

Here, the higher the value, the higher priority. The default values work fairly well, and there shouldn't be much requirement to change them. But there can be some benefit in lowering the priority of scrub and recovery operations to limit their impact on the client I/O. It's important to understand that Ceph can only prioritize the I/O in the sections of the I/O path that it controls. Therefore, tuning the disk queue lengths in the previous section may be needed to get the maximum benefits.

The network

The network is a core component of a Ceph cluster, and its performance will greatly affect the overall performance of the cluster. 10 GB should be treated as a minimum; 1 GB networking will not provide the required latency for a high performance Ceph cluster. There are a number of tunings that can help to improve network performance which is done by decreasing latency and increasing throughput.

The first thing to consider if you wish to use jumbo frames is using an MTU of 9,000 instead of 1,500; each I/O request can be sent using fewer Ethernet frames. As each Ethernet frame has a small overhead, increasing the maximum Ethernet frame to 9,000 can help. In practice, gains are normally less than 5% and should be weighed against the disadvantages of having to make sure every device is configured correctly.

The following network options set in your `sysctl.conf` file are recommended to maximize network performance:

```
#Network buffers
net.core.rmem_max = 56623104
net.core.wmem_max = 56623104
net.core.rmem_default = 56623104
net.core.wmem_default = 56623104
net.core.optmem_max = 40960
net.ipv4.tcp_rmem = 4096 87380 56623104
net.ipv4.tcp_wmem = 4096 65536 56623104

#Maximum connections and backlog
net.core.somaxconn = 1024
net.core.netdev_max_backlog = 50000

#TCP tuning options
net.ipv4.tcp_max_syn_backlog = 30000
net.ipv4.tcp_max_tw_buckets = 2000000
net.ipv4.tcp_tw_reuse = 1
net.ipv4.tcp_tw_recycle = 1
net.ipv4.tcp_fin_timeout = 10

#Don't use slow start on idle TCP connections
net.ipv4.tcp_slow_start_after_idle = 0
```

 If you are using IPv6 for your Ceph cluster, make sure you use the appropriate IPv6 `sysctl` options.

General system tuning

There are a number of general system parameters that are recommended to be tuned to best suit Ceph's performance requirements. The following settings can be added to your `/etc/sysctl.conf` file.

Make sure that the system has sufficient memory free at all times:

```
vm/min_free_kbytes = 524288
```

Increase the maximum number of allowed processes:

```
kernel.pid_max=4194303
```

Use the following to set the maximum number of file handles:

```
fs.file-max=26234859
```

Kernel RBD

The Linux kernel RBD driver allows you to directly map Ceph RBDs as standard Linux block devices and use them in the same way as any other device. Generally, kernel-mapped RBDs need minimum configuration, but in some special cases, some tuning may be necessary.

Firstly, it is recommended to use a kernel that is as new as possible because newer kernels will have better RBD support, and in some cases, improved performance.

Queue depth

Since kernel 4.0, the RBD driver uses `blk-mq`, which is designed to offer higher performance than the older queuing system. By default, the maximum outstanding requests possible with RBD when using `blk-mq` are 128. For most use cases, this is more than enough; however, if your workload needs to utilize the full power of a large Ceph cluster, you may find that only having 128 outstanding requests is not enough. There is an option that can be specified when mapping the RBD to increase this value, which can be set next.

readahead

By default, RBD will be configured with a 128 KB `readahead`. If your workload mainly involves large sequential reading, you can get a significant boost in performance by increasing the `readahead` value. In kernels before 4.4, there was a limitation where `readahead` values larger than 2 MB were ignored. In most storage systems, this was not an issue, as the stripe sizes would have been smaller than 2 MB. As long as `readahead` is bigger than the stripe size, all the disks will be involved and performance will increase.

By default, a Ceph RBD is striped across 4 MB objects, and so an RBD has a chunk size of 4 MB and *a stripe size of 4 MB * number of OSDS in the cluster*. Therefore, with a `readahead` size smaller than 4 MB, most of the time, `readahead` will be doing very little to improve performance, and you will likely see that read's performance is struggling to exceed that of a single OSD.

In kernel 4.4 and above, you can set the `readahead` value much higher and experience read performance in the range of hundreds of MBs in a second.

Tuning CephFS

There are two main performance characteristics that determine CephFS performance—the speed of metadata access and the speed of data access, although in the majority of cases, both of these contribute to access requests.

It is important to understand that in CephFS, once the metadata has been retrieved for a file, reads to the actual file data do not require any further metadata operations until the file is closed by the client. Similarly, when writing files, only when dirty data is flushed by the client is the metadata updated. Thus, for a large, sequential buffered IO, metadata operations will likely only make up a small proportion of the total cluster IO.

Similarly, for CephFS filesystems that are dealing with a large number of clients constantly opening and closing lots of smaller files, metadata operations will have a much bigger role to play in determining overall performance. Additionally, metadata is used to supply client information surrounding the filesystem, such as providing directory listings.

Dealing with CephFS's data pool performance should be handled like any other Ceph performance requirements that were covered in this chapter, so for the purpose of this section, metadata performance will be the focus.

Metadata performance is determined by two factors: the speed of reading/writing metadata via the RADOS metadata pool, and the speed at which the MDS can handle client requests. First, make sure that the metadata pool is residing on flash storage, as this will reduce the latency of metadata requests by at least and order of magnitude, if not more. However, as was discussed earlier in the *Latency* section of this chapter, the latency introduced by a distributed network-storage platform can also have an impact on metadata performance.

To work around some of this latency, the MDS has the concept of a local cache to serve hot metadata requests from. By default, an MDS reserves 1 GB of RAM to use as a cache and, generally speaking, the more ram you can allocate, the better. The reservation is controlled by the `mds_cache_memory_limit` variable. By increasing the amount of memory the MDS can use as a cache, the number of requests having to go to the RADOS pool are reduced, and the locality of the RAM will reduce metadata access latency.

There will come a point when adding additional RAM brings very little benefit. This may either be due to the cache being sufficiently sized that the majority of requests are being served from cache, or that the number of requests the actual MDS can handle has been reached.

Regarding the later point, the MDS process is single-threaded and so there will come a point where the number of metadata requests is causing an MDS to consume 100% of a single CPU core and no additional caching or SSDs will help. The current recommendations are to try and run the MDS on a high clocked CPU as possible. The quad core Xeon E3s are ideal for this use and can often be obtained with frequencies nearing 4 GHz for a reasonable price. Compared to some of the lower-clocked Xeon CPUs, often with high core counts, the performance gain could almost be double by ensuring a fast CPU is used.

If you have purchased the fastest CPU possible and are finding that a single MDS process is still the bottleneck, the last option should be to start deploying multiple active MDSes, so that the metadata requests are sharded across multiple MDSes.

RBDs and erasure-coded pools

When using RBDs stored in erasure-coded pools, to maintain the best performance, you should try to generate full stripe writes wherever possible. When an erasure-coded pool performs a full stripe write, the operation can be done via a single IO and not have the penalties associated with the read-modify-write cycle with partial writes.

The RBD clients have some intelligence where they will issue RADOS, thus writing full commands if they detect that the higher-level client IO is overwriting an entire object. Making sure that the filesystem on top of the RBD is formatted with the correct stripe alignment is important to ensure that as many write fulls are generated as possible.

An example of formatting an XFS filesystem on an RBD on a 4 + 2 EC pool is as follows:

```
mkfs.xfs /dev/rbd0 -d su=1m,sw=4
```

This would instruct XFS to align allocations that are best suited for the 4x1 MB shards that make up a 4 MB object stored on a 4 + 2 erasure pool.

Additionally, if the use case requires the direct mounting of RBDs to a Linux server rather than through a QEMU/KVM virtual machine, it is also worth considering using `rbd-nbd`. The userspace RBD client makes use of librbd, whereas the kernel RBD client relies fully on the Ceph code present in the running kernel.

Not only does librbd mean that you can use the latest features, which may not be present in the running kernel, but it also has the additional feature of a writeback cache. The writeback cache performs a much better job of coalescing writes into full-sized object writes than the kernel client is capable of and so less performance overhead is incurred. Keep in mind that the writeback cache in librbd is not persistent, so any synchronous writes will not benefit.

PG distributions

While not strictly a performance-tuning option, ensuring even PG distribution across your Ceph cluster is an essential task that should be undertaken during the early stages of the deployment of your cluster. As Ceph uses CRUSH to pseudo-randomly determine where to place data, it will not always balance PG equally across every OSD. A Ceph cluster that is not balanced will be unable to take full advantage of the raw capacity, as the most oversubscribed OSD will effectively become the limit to the capacity.

An unevenly balanced cluster will mean that a higher number of requests will be targeted at the OSDs holding the most PGs. These OSDs will then place an artificial performance ceiling on the cluster, especially if the cluster is composed of spinning-disk OSDs.

To rebalance PGs across a Ceph cluster, you simply have to reweight the OSD so that CRUSH adjusts how many PGs will be stored on it. It's important to note that, by default, the weight of every OSD is 1, and you cannot weight an underutilized OSD above 1 to increase its utilization. The only option is to decrease the reweight value of over-utilized OSDs, which should move PGs to the less-utilized OSDs.

It is also important to understand that there is a difference between the CRUSH weight of an OSD and the reweight value. The reweight value is used as an override to correct the misplacement from the CRUSH algorithm. The reweight command only affects the OSD and will not affect the weight of the bucket (for example, host) that it is a member of. It is also reset to 1.0 on restart of the OSD. While this can be frustrating, it's important to understand that any future modification to the cluster, be it increasing the number of PGs or adding additional OSDs, would have likely made any reweight value incorrect. Therefore, reweighting OSDs should not be looked at as a one-time operation, but something that is being continuously done and will adjust to the changes in the cluster.

To reweight an OSD, use this simple command:

```
Ceph osd reweight <osd number> <weight value 0.0-1.0>
```

Once executed, Ceph will start backfilling to move PGs to their newly-assigned OSDs.

Of course, searching through all your OSDs and trying to find the OSD that needs weighting and then running this command for every one would be a very lengthy process. Luckily, there is another Ceph tool that can automate a large part of this process:

```
ceph osd reweight-by-utilization <threshold> <max change>
<number of OSDs>
```

This command will compare all the OSDs in your cluster and change the override weighting of the top N OSDs, where N is controlled by the last parameter, which is over the threshold value. You can also limit the maximum change applied to each OSD by specifying the second parameter: 0.05 or 5% is normally a recommended figure.

There is also a test-reweight-by-utilization command, which will allow you to see what the command will do before running it.

While this command is safe to use, there are a number of things that should be taken into consideration before running it:

- It has no concept of different pools on different OSDs. If, for example, you have an SSD tier and an HDD tier, the reweight-by-utilization command will still try to balance data across all OSDs. If your SSD tier is not as full as the HDD tier, the command will not work as expected. If you wish to balance OSDs confined to a single bucket, look into the script version of this command that was created by CERN.
- It is possible to reweight the cluster to the point that CRUSH is unable to determine placement for some PGs. If recovery halts and one or more PGs are left in a remapped state, this is likely what happened. Simply increase or reset the reweight values to fix it.

Once you are confident with the operation of the command, it is possible to schedule it via `cron` so that your cluster is kept in a more balanced state automatically.

Since the Luminous release, a new manager module has been included, called **Ceph balancer**. This new module works continuously in the background to optimize PG distribution and ensure that the maximum amount of capacity is available on your Ceph cluster.

The Ceph balancer module can use one of two methods to balance data distribution. The first is crush-compat; this method uses an additional weight field to adjust the weights of each OSD. The main benefit of crush-compat is that it's backward-compatible with older clients. The other method is called upmap; upmap can achieve much more fine-grained PG mapping than is possible with crush-compat as it uses new capabilities in the OSD map to influence PG mapping. The downside is that due to these new capabilities, Ceph clients need to be running Luminous or a newer release.

To enable ceph balancer, simply run these two commands:

```
ceph mgr module enable balancer
ceph balancer on
```

You will see Ceph start to backfill as PGs are remapped to new OSDs to balance out the space utilization; this will continue to occur until the Ceph balancer has reduced deviation of OSD utilization.

Summary

You should now have extensive knowledge on how to tune a Ceph cluster to maximize performance and achieve lower latency. Through the use of benchmarks, you should now be able to perform before and after tests to confirm whether your tunings have had the desired effect. It is worth reviewing the official Ceph documentation to get a better understanding of some of the other configuration options that may be beneficial to your cluster.

You have also learned about some of the key factors that effect Ceph performance and how to tune them, such as CPU clock speed and sleep states. Ensuring that the infrastructure your Ceph cluster is running on is running at peak performance will ensure that Ceph can perform at its very best.

In the next chapter we will discuss tiering and how it can be used to increase performance by combining different disk technologies together.

Questions

1. Is PG distribution uniform by default?
2. Why is a full stripe write on an EC pool preferred?
3. For low latency, what type of CPU should be preferred?
4. What three factors largely impact latency?
5. What automated tool can be used to balance space utilization in your cluster?

Tiering with Ceph 10

The tiering functionality in Ceph allows you to overlay one RADOS pool over another and let Ceph intelligently promote and evict objects between them. In most configurations, the top-level pool will be comprised of fast storage devices such as **Solid State Drives (SSDs)** and the base pool will be comprised of slower storage devices such as **Serial ATA (SATA)** or **Serial Attached SCSI (SAS)** disks. If the working set of your data is of a comparatively small percentage, then this allows you to use Ceph to provide high capacity storage but still maintain a good level of performance of frequently accessed data.

In this chapter, we will cover the following topics:

- How Ceph's tiering functionality works
- What good use cases for tiering are
- How to configure two pools into a tier
- Various tuning options available for tiering

 It's recommended that you should be running at least the Jewel release of Ceph if you wish to use the tiering functionality. Previous releases were lacking a lot of features that made tiering usable.

Tiering versus caching

Although often described as **cache tiering**, it's better to think of the functionality in Ceph as a tiering technology rather than a cache. It's important that you take this into consideration before reading any further, as it's vital to understand the difference between the two.

A cache is typically designed to accelerate access to a set of data unless it's a writeback cache; it will not hold the only copy of the data, and normally there is little overhead to promoting data to cache. The cache tends to operate over a shorter time frame and quite often everything that is accessed is promoted into the cache.

A tiering solution is also designed to accelerate access to a set of data; however, its promotion strategy normally works over a longer period of time and is more selective about what data is promoted, mainly due to the promotion action having a small impact on overall storage performance. Also, it is quite common with tiering technologies that only a single tier may hold the valid state of the data, and so all tiers in the system need equal protection against data loss.

How Ceph's tiering functionality works

Once you have configured a RADOS pool to be an overlay of another RADOS pool, Ceph's tiering functionality works on the basic principal that if an object does not exist in the top-level tier, then it must exist in the base tier. All object requests from clients are sent to the top tier; if the OSD does not have the requested object, then, depending on the tiering mode, it may either proxy the read or write request down to the base tier or force a promotion. The base tier then proxies the request back through the top tier to the client. It's important to note that the tiering functionality is transparent to clients, and there is no specific client configuration needed.

There are three main actions in tiering that move objects between tiers. **Promotions** copy objects from the base tier up to the top tier. If tiering is configured in writeback mode, the **flushing** action is used to update the contents of the base tier object from the top tier. Finally, when the top-tier pool reaches capacity, objects are evicted by the **eviction** action.

In order to be able to make decisions on what objects to move between the two tiers, Ceph uses HitSets to track access to objects. A **HitSet** is a collection of all object access requests and is consulted to determine if an object has had either a read or write request since that HitSet was created. The HitSets use a **bloom filter** to statistically track object access rather than storing every access to every object, which would generate large overheads. The bloom filter only stores binary states, an object can only be marked as accessed or not, and there is no concept of storing the number of accesses to an object in a single HitSet. If an object appears in a number of the most recent HitSets and is in the base pool, then it will be promoted.

Likewise, objects that no longer appear in recent HitSets will become candidates for flushing or eviction if the top tier comes under pressure. The number of HitSets and how often a new one gets created can be configured, along with the required number of recent HitSets a write or read I/O must appear in, in order for a promotion to take place. The size of the top-level tier can also be configured and is disconnected from the available capacity of the RADOS pool it sits on.

There are a number of configuration and tuning options that define how Ceph reacts to the generated HitSets and the thresholds at which promotions, flushes, and evictions occur. These will be covered in more detail later in the chapter.

What is a bloom filter?

A bloom filter is used in Ceph to provide an efficient way of tracking whether an object is a member of a HitSet without having to individually store the access status of each object. It is probabilistic in nature, and although it can return **false positives**, it will never return a **false negative**. This means that when querying a bloom filter, it may report that an item is present when it is not, but it will never report that an item is not present when it is.

Ceph's use of bloom filters allows it to efficiently track the access to millions of objects without the overhead of storing every single access. In the event of a false positive, it could mean that an object is incorrectly promoted; however, the probability of this happening combined with the minimal impact is of little concern.

Tiering modes

There are a number of tiering modes that determine the precise actions of how Ceph reacts to the contents of the HitSets. However, in most cases, the writeback mode will be used. The available modes for use in tiering are **writeback**, **forward**, **read-forward**, **proxy**, and **read-proxy**. The following sections provide brief descriptions of the available modes and how they act.

Writeback

In writeback mode, data is promoted to the top-level tier by both reads and writes depending on how frequently accessed the object is. Objects in the top-level tier can be modified, and dirty objects will be flushed to the pool at a later date. If an object needs to be read or written to in the bottom tier and the bottom pool supports it, then Ceph will try and directly proxy the operation that has a minimal impact on latency.

Forward

The forward mode simply forwards all requests from the top tier to the base tier without doing any promotions. It should be noted that a forward causes the OSD to tell the client to resend the request to the correct OSD and so has a greater impact on latency than just simply proxying it.

Read-forward

Read-forward mode forces a promotion on every write and, like the forward mode earlier, redirects the client for all reads to the base pool. This can be useful if you wish to only use the top-tier pool for write acceleration. Using write-intensive SSDs overlayed over read-intensive SSDs is one such example.

Proxy

This is similar to forward mode, except it proxies all reads and writes without promoting anything. By proxying the request, OSD itself retrieves data from the base-tier OSD and then passes it back to the client. This reduces the overhead compared with using forwarding.

Read-proxy

Similar to read-forward mode, except that it proxies reads and always promotes write requests. It should be noted that the writeback and read-proxy modes are the only modes that receive rigorous testing, and so care should be taken when using the other modes. Also, there is probably little gain from using the other modes, and they will likely be phased out in future releases.

Uses cases

As mentioned at the start of the chapter, the tiering functionality should be thought of as tiering and not a cache. The reason behind this statement is that the act of promotions has a detrimental effect to cluster performance when compared with most caching solutions, which do not normally degrade performance if enabled on non-cacheable workloads. The performance impact of promotions are caused for two main reasons. First, the promotion happens in the I/O path; the entire object to be promoted needs to be read from the base tier and then written into the top tier before the I/O is returned to the client.

Second, this promotion action will likely also cause a flush and an eviction, which causes even more reads and writes to both tiers. If both tiers are using 3x replication, this starts to cause a large amount of write amplification for even just a single promotion. In the worse-case scenario, a single 4 KB access that causes a promotion could cause 8 MB of read I/O and 24 MB of write I/O across the two tiers. This increased I/O will cause an increase in latency; for this reason, promotions should be considered expensive, and tuning should be done to minimize them.

With that in mind, Ceph tiering should only be used where the hot or active part of the data will fit into the top tier. Workloads that are uniformly random will likely see no benefit and in many cases may actually cause performance degradation, either due to no suitable objects being available to promote, or too many promotions occurring.

Most workloads that involve providing storage for generic virtual machines tend to be good candidates as normally only a small percentage of a VM tends to be accessed.

Online transaction processing (OLTP) databases will normally show improvements when used with either caching or tiering as their hot set of data is relatively small and data patterns are reasonably consistent. However, reporting or batch processing databases are generally not a good fit as they can quite often require a large range of the data to be accessed without any prior warm-up period.

RADOS Block Devices (RBD) workloads that involve random access with no specific pattern or workloads that involve large read or write streaming should be avoided and will likely suffer from the addition of a cache tier.

Creating tiers in Ceph

To test Ceph's tiering functionality, two RADOS pools are required. If you are running these examples on a laptop or desktop hardware, although spinning disk-based OSDs can be used to create the pools, SSDs are highly recommended if there is any intention to read and write data. If you have multiple disk types available in your testing hardware, then the base tier can exist on spinning disks and the top tier can be placed on SSDs.

Let's create tiers using the following commands, all of which make use of the Ceph `tier` command:

1. Create two RADOS pools:

   ```
   ceph osd pool create base 64 64 replicated

   ceph osd pool create top 64 64 replicated
   ```

The preceding commands give the following output:

```
root@mon1:/home/vagrant# ceph osd pool create base 64 64 replicated
pool 'base' created
root@mon1:/home/vagrant# ceph osd pool create top 64 64 replicated
pool 'top' created
```

2. Create a tier consisting of the two pools:

```
ceph osd tier add base top
```

The preceding command gives the following output:

```
root@mon1:/home/vagrant# ceph osd tier add base top
pool 'top' is now (or already was) a tier of 'base'
```

3. Configure the cache mode:

```
ceph osd tier cache-mode top writeback
```

The preceding command gives the following output:

```
root@mon1:/home/vagrant# ceph osd tier cache-mode top writeback
set cache-mode for pool 'top' to writeback
```

4. Make the top tier and overlay of the base tier:

```
ceph osd tier set-overlay base top
```

The preceding command gives the following output:

```
root@mon1:/home/vagrant# ceph osd tier set-overlay base top
overlay for 'base' is now (or already was) 'top'
```

5. Now that the tiering is configured, we need to set some simple values to make sure that the tiering agent can function. Without these, the tiering mechanism will not work properly. Note that these commands are just setting variables on the pool:

```
ceph osd pool set top hit_set_type bloom

ceph osd pool set top hit_set_count 10

ceph osd pool set top hit_set_period 60

ceph osd pool set top target_max_bytes 100000000
```

The preceding commands give the following output:

```
root@mon1:/home/vagrant# ceph osd pool set top hit_set_type bloom
set pool 5 hit_set_type to bloom
root@mon1:/home/vagrant# ceph osd pool set top hit_set_count 10
set pool 5 hit_set_count to 10
root@mon1:/home/vagrant# ceph osd pool set top hit_set_period 60
set pool 5 hit_set_period to 60
root@mon1:/home/vagrant# ceph osd pool set top target_max_bytes 100000000
set pool 5 target_max_bytes to 100000000
```

The previously mentioned commands are simply telling Ceph that the HitSets should be created using the bloom filter. It should create a new HitSet every 60 seconds and that it should keep ten of them before discarding the oldest one. Finally, the top tier pool should hold no more than 100 MB; if it reaches this limit, I/O operations will block. More detailed explanations of these settings will follow in the next section.

6. Next, we need to configure the various options that control how Ceph flushes and evicts objects from the top to the base tier:

```
ceph osd pool set top cache_target_dirty_ratio 0.4

ceph osd pool set top cache_target_full_ratio 0.8
```

The preceding commands give the following output:

```
root@mon1:/home/vagrant# ceph osd pool set top cache_target_dirty_ratio 0.4
set pool 5 cache_target_dirty_ratio to 0.4
root@mon1:/home/vagrant# ceph osd pool set top cache_target_full_ratio 0.8
set pool 5 cache_target_full_ratio to 0.8
```

The earlier example tells Ceph that it should start flushing dirty objects in the top tier down to the base tier when the top tier is 40% full. And that objects should be evicted from the top tier when the top tier is 80% full.

7. And, finally, the last two commands instruct Ceph that any object should have been in the top tier for at least 60 seconds before it can be considered for flushing or eviction:

```
ceph osd pool set top cache_min_flush_age 60

ceph osd pool set top cache_min_evict_age 60
```

The preceding commands give the following output:

```
root@mon1:/home/vagrant# ceph osd pool set top cache_min_flush_age 60
set pool 5 cache_min_flush_age to 60
root@mon1:/home/vagrant# ceph osd pool set top cache_min_evict_age 60
set pool 5 cache_min_evict_age to 60
```

Tuning tiering

Unlike the majority of Ceph's features, which by default perform well for a large number of workloads, Ceph's tiering functionality requires careful configuration of its various parameters to ensure good performance. You should also have a basic understanding of your workload's I/O profile; tiering will only work well if your data has a small percentage of hot data. Workloads that are uniformly random or involve lots of sequential access patterns will either show no improvement or in some cases may actually be slower.

Flushing and eviction

The main tuning options that should be looked at first are the ones that define the size limit to the top tier, when it should flush and when it should evict.

The following two configuration options configure the maximum size of the data to be stored in the top-tier pool:

```
target_max_bytes

target_max_objects
```

The size is either specified in bytes or the number of objects and does not have to be the same size as the actual pool – but it cannot be larger. The size is also based on the available capacity after replication of the RADOS pool, so for a 3x replica pool, this will be one-third of your raw capacity. If the number of bytes or objects in this pool goes above this limit, I/O will block; therefore, it's important that thought is given to the other config options later so that this limit is not reached. It's also important that this value is set, as without it, no flushing or evictions will occur and the pool will simply fill up OSDs to their full limit and then block I/O.

The reason that this setting exists instead of Ceph just using the size of the underlying capacity of the disks in the RADOS pool is that by specifying the size, you could have multiple top-level tier pools on the same set of disks if you desire.

As you have learned earlier, `target_max_bytes` sets the maximum size of the tiered data on the pool and if this limit is reached, I/O will block. In order to make sure that the RADOS pool does not reach this limit, `cache_target_full_ratio` instructs Ceph to try and keep the pool at a percentage of `target_max_bytes` by evicting objects when this target is breached. Unlike promotions and flushes, evictions are fairly low-cost operations:

```
cache_target_full_ratio
```

The value is specified as a value between 0 and 1 and works like a percentage. It should be noted that although `target_max_bytes` and `cache_target_full_ratio` are set against the pool, internally Ceph uses these values to calculate per PG limits instead. This can mean that in certain circumstances, some PGs may reach the calculated maximum limit before others and can sometimes lead to unexpected results. For this reason, it is recommended not to set `cache_target_full_ratio` to high and leave some headroom; a value of 0.8 normally works well. We have the following code:

```
cache_target_dirty_ratio
```

```
cache_target_dirty_high_ratio
```

These two configuration options control when Ceph flushes dirty objects from the top tier to the base tier if the tiering has been configured in writeback mode. An object is considered dirty if it has been modified while being in the top tier; objects modified in the base tier do not get marked as dirty. Flushing involves copying the object out of the top tier and into the base tier; as this is a full object write, the base tier can be an erasure-coded pool. The behavior is asynchronous, and aside from increasing I/O on the RADOS pools, is not directly linked to any impact on client I/O. Objects are typically flushed at a lower speed than what they can be evicted at. As flushing is an expensive operation compared with eviction, this means that if required, large amounts of objects can be evicted quickly if needed.

The two ratios control what speed of flushing OSD allows, by restricting the number of parallel flushing threads that are allowed to run at once. These can be controlled by the osd_agent_max_ops and osd_agent_max_high_ops OSD configuration options, respectively. By default, these are set to 2 and 4 parallel threads.

In theory, the percentage of dirty objects should hover around the low dirty ratio during normal cluster usage. This will mean that objects are flushed with a low parallelism of flushing to minimize the impact on cluster latency. As normal bursts of writes hit the cluster, the number of dirty objects may rise, but over time, these writes are flushed down to the base tier.

However, if there are periods of sustained writes that outstrip the low speed flushing's capability, then the number of dirty objects will start to rise. Hopefully, this period of high write I/O will not go on for long enough to fill the tier with dirty objects and thus will gradually reduce back down to the low threshold. However, if the number of dirty objects continues to increase and reaches the high ratio, then the flushing parallelism gets increased and will hopefully be able to stop the number of dirty objects from increasing any further. Once the write traffic reduces, the number of dirty objects will be brought back down the low ratio again. This sequence of events is illustrated in the following graph:

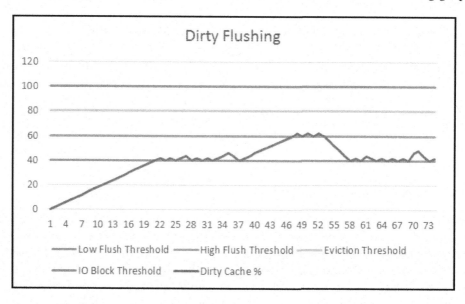

The two dirty ratios should have sufficient difference between them that normal bursts of writes can be absorbed, without the high ratio kicking in. The high ratio should be thought of as an emergency limit. A good value to start with is 0.4 for the low ratio and 0.6 for the high ratio.

The `osd_agent_max_ops` configuration settings should be adjusted so that in normal operating conditions, the number of dirty objects hovers around or just over the low dirty ratio. It's not easy to recommend a value for these settings as they will largely depend on the ratio of the size and performance of the top tier to the base tier. However, start with setting `osd_agent_max_ops` to 1 and increase as necessary, and set `osd_agent_max_high_ops` to at least double.

If you see status messages in the Ceph status screen indicating that high-speed flushing is occurring, then you will want to increase `osd_agent_max_ops`. If you ever see the top tier getting full and blocking I/O, then you either need to consider lowering the `cache_target_dirty_high_ratio` variable or increasing the `osd_agent_max_high_ops` setting to stop the tier filling up with dirty objects.

Promotions

The next tuning options that should be looked at are the ones that define the HitSets and the required recency to trigger a promotion:

> **hitset_count**

> **hitset_period**

The `hitset_count` setting controls how many HitSets can exist before the oldest one starts getting trimmed. The `hitset_period` setting controls how often a HitSet should be created. If you are testing tiering in a laboratory environment, it should be noted that I/O to the PG needs to be occurring in order for a HitSet to be created; on an idle cluster, no HitSets will be created or trimmed.

Having the correct number and controlling how often HitSets are created is key to being able to reliably control when objects get promoted. Remember that HitSets only contain data about whether an object has been accessed or not; they don't contain a count of the number of times an object was accessed. If `hitset_period` is too large, then even relatively low-accessed objects will appear in the majority of the HitSets. For example, if `hitset_period` is two minutes, an RBD object containing the disk block where a log file is updated once a minute would be in all the same HitSets as an object getting access 100 times a second.

Conversely, if the period is too low, then even hot objects may fail to appear in enough HitSets to make them candidates for promotion and your top tier will likely not be fully used. By finding the correct HitSet period, you should be able to capture the right view of your I/O that a suitable sized proportion of hot objects are candidates for promotion:

```
min_read_recency_for_promote
```

```
min_write_recency_for_promote
```

These two settings define how many of the last recent HitSets an object must appear in to be promoted. Due to the effect of probability, the relationship between semi-hot objects and recency setting is not linear. Once the recency settings are set past about 3 or 4, the number of eligible objects for promotion drops off in a logarithmic fashion. It should be noted that while promotion decisions can be made on reads or writes separately, they both reference the same HitSet data, which has no way of determining an access from being either a read or a write. As a handy feature, if you set the recency higher than the `hitset_count` setting, then it will never promote. This can be used for example to make sure that a write I/O will never cause an object to be promoted, by setting the write recency higher than the `hitset_count` setting.

Promotion throttling

As has been covered earlier, promotions are very expensive operations in tiering and care should be taken to make sure that they only happen when necessary. A large part of this is done by carefully tuning the HitSet and recency settings. However, in order to limit the impact of promotions, there is an additional throttle that restricts the number of promotions to a certain speed. This limit can either be specified as number of bytes or objects per second via two OSD configuration options:

```
osd_tier_promote_max_bytes_sec
```

```
osd_tier_promote_max_objects_sec
```

The default limits are 4 MBps or five objects a second. While these figures may sound low, especially when compared with the performance of the latest SSDs, their primary goal is to minimize the impact of promotions on latency. Careful tuning should be done to find a good balance on your cluster. It should be noted that this value is configured per OSD, and so the total promotion speed will be a sum across all OSDs.

Finally, the following configuration options allow tuning of the selection process for flushing objects:

```
hit_set_grade_search_last_n
```

This controls how may HitSets are queried in order to determine object temperature, where the the temperature of an object reflects how often it is accessed. A cold object is rarely accessed, while hot objects being accessed far more frequently are candidates for eviction. Setting this to a similar figure as the recency settings is recommended. We have the following code:

```
hit_set_grade_decay_rate
```

This works in combination with the `hit_set_grade_search_last_n` setting and decays the HitSet results the older they become. Objects that have been accessed more frequently than others have a hotter rating and will make sure that objects that are more frequently accessed are not incorrectly flushed. It should be noted that the `min_flush` and `evict_age` settings may override the temperature of an object when it comes to being flushed or evicted:

```
cache_min_flush_age
```

```
cache_min_evict_age
```

The `cache_min_evict_age` and `cache_min_flush_age` settings simply define how long an object must have not been modified for before it is allowed to be flushed or evicted. These can be used to stop objects that are only just below the threshold to be promoted from continually being stuck in a cycle of moving between tiers. Setting them between 10 and 30 minutes is probably a good approach, although care needs to be taken that the top tier does not fill up in the case where there are no eligible objects to be flushed or evicted.

Monitoring parameters

In order to monitor the performance and characteristics of a cache tier in a Ceph cluster, there are a number of performance counters you can monitor. We will assume for the moment that you are already collecting the Ceph performance counters from the admin socket as discussed in the next chapter.

The most important thing to remember when looking at the performance counters is that once you configure a tier in Ceph, all client requests go through the top-level tier. Therefore, only read and write operation counters on OSDs that make up your top-level tier will show any requests, assuming that the base-tier OSDs are not used for any other pools. To understand the number of requests handled by the base tier, there are proxy operation counters, which will show this number. These proxy operation counters are also calculated on the top-level OSDs, and so to monitor the throughput of a Ceph cluster with tiering, only the top-level OSDs need to be included in the calculations.

The following counters can be used to monitor tiering in Ceph; all are to be monitored on the top-level OSDs:

Counter	Description
op_r	Read operations handled by the OSD
op_w	Write operations handled by the OSD
tier_proxy_read	Read operations that were proxied to the base tier
tier_proxy_write	Write operations that were proxied to the base tier
tier_promote	The number of promotions from base to the top-level tier
tier_try_flush	The number of flushes from the top level to the base tier
tier_evict	The number of evictions from the top level to the base tier

Alternative caching mechanisms

The native RADOS tiering functionality provides numerous benefits around flexibility and allows management by the same Ceph toolset. However, it cannot be denied that for pure performance, RADOS tiering lags behind other caching technologies that typically function at the block-device level.

 Bcache is a block device cache in the Linux kernel that can use a SSD to cache a slower block device such as a spinning disk.

Bcache is one example of a popular way of increasing the performance of Ceph with SSDs. Unlike RADOS tiering, where you can choose which pool you wish to cache, with bcache the entire OSD is cached. This method of caching brings a number of advantages around performance. The first is that the OSD itself has a much more consistent latency response due to the SSD caching. The filestore adds an increased amount of random I/O to every Ceph request regardless of whether the Ceph request is random of sequential in nature. Bcache can absorb these random I/Os and allow the spinning disk to perform a larger amount of sequential I/O. This can be very helpful during high periods of utilization where normal spinning disk OSDs would start to exhibit high latency. Second, RADOS tiering operates at the size of the object stored in the pool, which is 4 MB by default for RBD workloads. Bcache caches data in much smaller blocks; this allows it to make better use of available SSD space and also suffer less from promotion overheads.

The SSD capacity assigned to bcache will also be used as a read cache for hot data; this will improve read performance as well as writes. Since bcache will only be using this capacity for read caching, it will only store one copy of the data and so will have three times more read cache capacity than compared with using the same SSD in a RADOS-tiered pool.

However, there are a number of disadvantages to using bcache that make using RADOS cache pools still look attractive. As mentioned earlier, bcache will cache the entire OSD. In some cases where multiple pools may reside on the same OSDs, this behavior may be undesirable. Also, once bcache has been configured with SSD and HDD, it is harder to expand the amount of cache if needed in the future. This also applies if your cluster does not currently have any form of caching; in this scenario, introducing bcache would be very disruptive. With RADOS tiering, you can simply add additional SSDs or specifically designed SSD nodes to add or expand the top tier as and when needed.

dm-cache is another Linux block caching solution that is built into Linux's **Logical Volume Manager (LVM)**. Although its caching algorithms are not quite as advanced as bcache's, the fact that it is very easy to enable in LVM, even post volume creation, means that it is ideally suited to working with BlueStore OSD's. BlueStore OSD's are now created using ceph-volume, which creates logical volumes on top of block devices, thus only requiring a few steps to enable caching of an existing OSD.

Another approach is to place the spinning disk OSDs behind a RAID controller with a battery-backed writeback cache. The RAID controller performs a similar role to bcache and absorbs a lot of the random write I/O relating to the OSD's extra metadata. Both latency and sequential write performance will increase as a result. Read performance is unlikely to increase, however, due to the relatively small size of the RAID controllers cache.

By using a RAID controller with filestore OSDs, the OSDs journal can also be placed directly on the disk instead of using a separate SSD. By doing this, journal writes are absorbed by the RAID controllers cache and will improve the random performance of the journal, as likely most of the time, the journals contents will just be sitting in the controllers cache. Care does need to be taken though, as if the incoming write traffic exceeds the capacity of the controllers cache, journal contents will start being flushed to disk, and performance will degrade. For best performance, a separate SSD or NVMe should be used for the filestore journal, although attention should be paid to the cost of using both a RAID controller with sufficient performance and cache, in addition to the cost of the SSDs.

With BlueStore OSDs, a writeback cache on a RAID controller greatly benefits write latency; however, BlueStore's metadata is still required to be stored on flash media for good performance. Thus, separate SSDs are still highly recommended when using writeback RAID controllers.

Both methods have their merits and should be considered before implementing caching in your cluster.

Summary

In this chapter, we have covered the theory behind Ceph's RADOS tiering functionality and looked at the configuration and tuning operations available to make it work best for your workload. It should not be forgotten that the most important aspect is to understand your workload and be confident that its I/O pattern and distribution is cache-friendly. By following the examples in this chapter, you should also now understand the required steps to implement tiered pools and how to apply the configuration options.

In the next chapter, we will see what problems occur in maintaining a healthy Ceph cluster and how can we handle them.

Questions

1. Name two reasons you might want to use tiering technologies.
2. Name a tiering technology that exists outside of Ceph.
3. What method does RADOS tiering use to track hit requests?
4. What pool variable controls the amount of recent hits before a read request promotes an object?
5. What is a good use case for RADOS tiering?

Section 3: Troubleshooting and Recovery

This section of the book covers the darker moments of a Ceph administrator's day. By the end of this section, the reader will be more confident in recovering Ceph clusters and fixing problems, should they occur.

The following chapters are in this section:

- Chapter 11, *Troubleshooting*
- Chapter 12, *Disaster Recovery*

11
Troubleshooting

Ceph is largely autonomous in taking care of itself and recovering from failure scenarios, but in some cases human intervention is required. This chapter will look at common errors and failure scenarios and how to bring Ceph back to working order by troubleshooting them.

In this chapter we will cover the following topics:

- How to correctly repair inconsistent objects
- How to solve problems with the help of peering
- How to deal with `near_full` and `too_full` OSDs
- How to investigate errors via Ceph logging
- How to investigate poor performance
- How to investigate PGs in a down state

Repairing inconsistent objects

With BlueStore, all data is checksumed by default, so the steps in this section to safely determine the correct copy of the object no longer apply.

We will now see how we can correctly repair inconsistent objects:

1. To be able to recreate an inconsistent scenario, create an RBD, and later we'll make a filesystem on it:

```
vagrant@mon1:~$ sudo rbd create test --size=1G
vagrant@mon1:~$ sudo rbd feature disable test exclusive-lock object-map fast-diff deep-flatten
vagrant@mon1:~$ sudo rbd map test
/dev/rbd0
vagrant@mon1:~$ sudo mkfs.ext4 /dev/rbd0
mke2fs 1.42.13 (17-May-2015)
Discarding device blocks: done
Creating filesystem with 262144 4k blocks and 65536 inodes
Filesystem UUID: a95d7f60-3be3-4c15-bafd-9d37559174db
Superblock backups stored on blocks:
        32768, 98304, 163840, 229376

Allocating group tables: done
Writing inode tables: done
Creating journal (8192 blocks): done
Writing superblocks and filesystem accounting information: done
```

2. Check to see which objects have been created by formatting the RBD with a filesystem:

```
root@mon1:/home/vagrant# rados -p rbd ls
rbd_data.1e502238e1f29.0000000000000086
rbd_data.1e502238e1f29.0000000000000000
rbd_data.1e502238e1f29.0000000000000083
rbd_data.1e502238e1f29.0000000000000060
rbd_data.1e502238e1f29.0000000000000004
```

3. Pick one object at random and use the `osd map` command to find out which PG the object is stored in:

```
root@mon1:/home/vagrant# ceph osd map rbd rbd_data.1e502238e1f29.0000000000000086
osdmap e234 pool 'rbd' (0) object 'rbd_data.1e502238e1f29.0000000000000086' -> pg 0.5ee4eb42 (0.2)
> up ([1,0,2], p1) acting_([1,0,2], p1)
```

4. Find this object on the disk on one of the OSD nodes; in this case, it is `OSD.0` on `OSD1`:

```
vagrant@osd1:~$ sudo ls -l /var/lib/ceph/osd/ceph-0/current/0.5_head/
total 4096
-rw-r--r-- 1 ceph ceph        0 Feb  7 22:07 __head_00000005__0
-rw-r--r-- 1 ceph ceph 4194304 Mar 17 21:28 rbd\udata.1e502238e1f29.0000000000000083__head_327C8305__0
```

5. Corrupt it by echoing garbage over the top of it:

```
root@osd1:/home/vagrant# echo blah > /var/lib/ceph/osd/ceph-0/current/0.5_head/rbd\udata.1e502238e1f29.
0000000000000083__head_327C8305__0
```

6. Tell Ceph to do a scrub on the PG that contains the object we corrupted:

```
root@mon1:/home/vagrant# ceph pg deep-scrub 0.5
instructing pg 0.5 on osd.2 to deep-scrub
```

7. If you check the Ceph status, you will see that Ceph has detected the corrupted object and marked the PG as inconsistent. From this point onward, forget that we corrupted the object manually and work through the process as if it were for real:

```
root@mon1:/home/vagrant# ceph -s
    cluster d9f58afd-3e62-4493-ba80-0356290b3d9f
     health HEALTH_ERR
            1 pgs inconsistent
            3 scrub errors
            too many PGs per OSD (320 > max 300)
            all OSDs are running kraken or later but the 'require_kraken_osds' osdmap flag is not set
     monmap e2: 3 mons at {mon1=192.168.0.41:6789/0,mon2=192.168.0.42:6789/0,mon3=192.168.0.43:6789/0}
            election epoch 158, quorum 0,1,2 mon1,mon2,mon3
        mgr active: mon2 standbys: mon3, mon1
     osdmap e234: 3 osds: 3 up, 3 in
            flags sortbitwise,require_jewel_osds
      pgmap v3879: 320 pgs, 4 pools, 37575 kB data, 23 objects
            229 MB used, 26665 MB / 26894 MB avail
                319 active+clean
                  1 active+clean+inconsistent
```

By looking at the detailed health report, we can find the PG that contains the corrupted object. We could just tell Ceph to repair the PG now; however, if the primary OSD is the one that holds the corrupted object, it will overwrite the remaining good copies. This would be bad, so in order to make sure this doesn't happen, before running the `repair` command, we will confirm which OSD holds the corrupt object.

```
root@mon1:/home/vagrant# ceph health detail
HEALTH_ERR 1 pgs inconsistent; 3 scrub errors; too many PGs per OSD (320 > max 300); all OSDs are running kr
aken or later but the 'require_kraken_osds' osdmap flag is not set
pg 0.5 is active+clean+inconsistent, acting [2,0,1]
3 scrub errors
```

By looking at the health report, we can see the three OSDs that hold a copy of the object; the first OSD is the primary.

8. Log onto the primary OSD node and open the log file for the primary OSD. You should be able to find the log entry that indicates what object was flagged by the PG scrub.

9. Navigate through the PG structure, find the object mentioned in the log file, and calculate a md5sum of each copy:

```
root@osd1:/var/lib/ceph/osd/ceph-0/current/0.5_head# md5sum rbd\\udata.1e502238e1f29.0000000000000083__head_327C8305__0
\0d599f0ec05c3bda8c3b8a68c32a1b47  rbd\\udata.1e502238e1f29.0000000000000083__head_327C8305__0
```

md5sum of object on osd node one.

```
root@osd2:/home/vagrant# cd /var/lib/ceph/osd/ceph-2/current/0.5_head/
root@osd2:/var/lib/ceph/osd/ceph-2/current/0.5_head# md5sum rbd\\udata.1e502238e1f29.0000000000000083__
head_327C8305__0
\b5cfa9d6c8febd618f91ac2843d50a1c  rbd\\udata.1e502238e1f29.0000000000000083__head_327C8305__0
```

md5sum of object on osd node two.

```
root@osd3:/home/vagrant# cd /var/lib/ceph/osd/ceph-1/current/0.5_head/
root@osd3:/var/lib/ceph/osd/ceph-1/current/0.5_head# md5sum rbd\\udata.1e502238e1f29.0000000000000083__
head_327C8305__0
\b5cfa9d6c8febd618f91ac2843d50a1c  rbd\\udata.1e502238e1f29.0000000000000083__head_327C8305__0
```

md5sum of object on osd node three.

We can see that the object on OSD.0 has a different md5sum, and so we know that it is the corrupt object.

```
OSD.0 = \0d599f0ec05c3bda8c3b8a68c32a1b47
OSD.2 = \b5cfa9d6c8febd618f91ac2843d50a1c
OSD.3 = \b5cfa9d6c8febd618f91ac2843d50a1c
```

Although we already know which copy of the object was corrupted as we manually corrupted the object on OSD.0, let's pretend we hadn't done it, and that this corruption was caused by some random cosmic ray. We now have the md5sum of the three replica copies and can clearly see that the copy on OSD.0 is wrong. This is a big reason why a 2x replication scheme is bad; if a PG becomes inconsistent, you can't figure out which one is the bad one. As the primary OSD for this PG is 2, as can be seen in both the Ceph health details and the Ceph OSD map commands, we can safely run the ceph pg repair command without the fear of copying the bad object over the top of the remaining good copies:

```
root@mon1:/home/vagrant# ceph pg repair 0.5
instructing pg 0.5 on osd.2 to repair
```

We can see that the inconsistent PG has repaired itself:

```
root@mon1:/home/vagrant# ceph -s
    cluster d9f58afd-3e62-4493-ba80-0356290b3d9f
     health HEALTH_WARN
            too many PGs per OSD (320 > max 300)
            all OSDs are running kraken or later but the 'require_kraken_osds' osdmap flag is not
     monmap e2: 3 mons at {mon1=192.168.0.41:6789/0,mon2=192.168.0.42:6789/0,mon3=192.168.0.43:67
            election epoch 158, quorum 0,1,2 mon1,mon2,mon3
        mgr active: mon2 standbys: mon3, mon1
     osdmap e234: 3 osds: 3 up, 3 in
            flags sortbitwise,require_jewel_osds
      pgmap v3900: 320 pgs, 4 pools, 37575 kB data, 23 objects
            229 MB used, 26665 MB / 26894 MB avail
                 320 active+clean
```

In the event that the copy is corrupt on the primary OSD, then the following steps should be taken:

1. Stop the primary OSD.
2. Delete the object from the PG directory.
3. Restart the OSD.
4. Instruct Ceph to repair the PG.

Full OSDs

By default, Ceph will warn us when OSD utilization approaches 85%, and it will stop writing I/O to the OSD when it reaches 95%. If, for some reason, the OSD completely fills up to 100%, the OSD is likely to crash and will refuse to come back online. An OSD that is above the 85% warning level will also refuse to participate in backfilling, so the recovery of the cluster may be impacted when OSDs are in a near-full state.

Before covering the troubleshooting steps around full OSDs, it is highly recommended that you monitor the capacity utilization of your OSDs, as described in Chapter 8, *Monitoring Ceph*. This will give you advanced warning as OSDs approach the near_full warning threshold.

If you find yourself in a situation where your cluster is above the near-full warning state, you have two options:

- Add some more OSDs
- Delete some data

However, in the real world, both of these are either impossible or will take time, in which case the situation can deteriorate. If the OSD is only at the `near_full` threshold, you can probably get things back on track by checking whether your OSD utilization is balanced, and then perform PG balancing if not. This was covered in more detail in Chapter 9, *Tuning Ceph*. The same applies to the `too_full` OSDs as; although you are unlikely going to get them back below 85%, at least you can resume write operations.

If your OSDs have completely filled up, they are in an offline state and will refuse to start. Now you have an additional problem. If the OSDs will not start, no matter what rebalancing or deletion of data you carry out, it will not be reflected on the full OSDs as they are offline. The only way to recover from this situation is to manually delete some PGs from the disk's filesystem to let the OSD start.

The following steps should be undertaken for this:

1. Make sure the OSD process is not running.
2. Set `nobackfill` on the cluster, to stop the recovery from happening when the OSD comes back online.
3. Find a PG that is in an active, clean, and remapped state and exists on the offline OSD.
4. Delete this PG from the offline OSD using ceph-objectstore-tool.
5. Restart the OSD.
6. Delete data from the Ceph cluster or rebalance the PGs.
7. Remove `nobackfill`.
8. Run a scrub and repair the PG you just deleted.

Ceph logging

When investigating errors, it is very handy to be able to look through the Ceph log files to get a better idea of what is going on. By default, the logging levels are set so that only the important events are logged. During troubleshooting, the logging levels may need to be increased in order to reveal the cause of the error. To increase the logging level, you can either edit `ceph.conf`, add the new logging level, and then restart the component, or, if you don't wish to restart the Ceph daemons, you can inject the new configuration parameter into the live running daemon. To inject parameters, use the `ceph tell` command:

```
ceph tell osd.0 injectargs --debug-osd 0/5
```

Then, set the logging level for the OSD log on `osd.0` to `0/5`. The number `0` is the disk logging level, and the number `5` is the in-memory logging level.

> At a logging level of `20`, the logs are extremely verbose and will grow quickly. Do not keep high-verbosity logging enabled for too long. Higher logging levels will also have an impact on performance.

Slow performance

Slow performance is defined as when the cluster is actively processing I/O requests, but it appears to be operating at a lower performance level than what is expected. Generally, slow performance is caused by a component of your Ceph cluster reaching saturation and becoming a bottleneck. This maybe due to an increased number of client requests or a component failure that is causing Ceph to perform recovery.

Causes

Although there are many things that may cause Ceph to experience slow performance, here are some of the most likely causes.

Increased client workload

Sometimes, slow performance may not be due to an underlying fault; it may just be that the number and type of client requests may have exceeded the capability of the hardware. Whether this is due to a number of separate workloads all running at the same time, or just a slow general increase over a period of time, if you are capturing the number of client requests across your cluster, this should be easy to trend. If the increased workload looks like it's permanent, the only solution is to add some additional hardware.

Down OSDs

If a significant number of OSDs are marked as down in a cluster, perhaps due to a whole OSD node going offline – although recovery will not start until the OSDs are marked out – the performance will be affected, as the number of IOPs available to service the client IO will now be lower. Your monitoring solution should alert you if this is happening and allow you to take action.

Recovery and backfilling

When an OSD is marked out, the affected PGs will re-peer with new OSDs and start the process of recovering and backfilling data across the cluster. This process can put a strain on the disks in a Ceph cluster and lead to higher latencies for client requests. There are several tuning options that can reduce the impact of backfilling by reducing the rate and priority. These should be evaluated against the impact of slower recovery from failed disks, which may reduce the durability of the cluster.

Scrubbing

When Ceph performs deep scrubbing to check your data for any inconsistencies, it has to read all the objects from the OSD; this can be a very IO-intensive task, and on large drives, the process can take a long time. Scrubbing is vital to protect against data loss and therefore should not be disabled. Various tuning options were discussed in Chapter 9, *Tuning Ceph*, regarding setting windows for scrubbing and its priority. By tweaking these settings, a lot of the performance impact on client workloads from scrubbing can be avoided.

Snaptrimming

When you remove a snapshot, Ceph has to delete all the objects that have been created due to the copy-on-write nature of the snapshot process. From Ceph 10.2.8 onward, there is an improved OSD setting called `osd_snap_trim_sleep`, which makes Ceph wait for the specified number of settings between the trimming of each snapshot object. This ensures that the backing object store does not become overloaded.

 Although this setting was available in previous jewel releases, its behavior was not the same and should not be used.

Hardware or driver issues

If you have recently introduced new hardware into your Ceph cluster and, after backfilling has rebalanced your data, you start experiencing slow performance, check for firmware or driver updates relating to your hardware, as newer drivers may require a newer kernel. If you have only introduced a small amount of hardware, you can temporarily mark the OSDs out on it without going below your pool's `min_size`; this can be a good way to rule out hardware issues.

Monitoring

This is where the monitoring you configured in `Chapter 8`, *Tiering with Ceph*, can really come in handy, as it will allow you to compare long-term trends with current metric readings and see whether there are any clear anomalies.

It is recommended you first look at the disk performance as, in most cases of poor performance, the underlying disks are normally the components that become the bottleneck.

If you do not have monitoring configured or wish to manually drill deeper into the performance metrics, there are a number of tools you can use to accomplish this.

iostat

iostat can be used to get a running overview of the performance and latency of all the disks running in your OSD nodes. Run iostat with the following command:

```
iostat -d 1 -x
```

You will get a display similar to this, which will refresh once a second:

Device:	rrqm/s	wrqm/s	r/s	w/s	rkB/s	wkB/s	avgrq-sz	avgqu-sz	await	r_await	w_await	svctm	%util
sda	0.00	4.00	2.00	24.00	68.00	9396.00	728.00	0.34	12.92	12.00	13.00	8.77	22.80
sdc	0.00	9.00	17.00	42.00	548.00	20468.00	712.41	1.11	18.71	27.76	15.05	10.17	60.00
sdd	0.00	8.00	9.00	51.00	36.00	20888.00	697.47	1.61	26.93	27.56	26.82	8.53	51.20
sdb	0.00	2.00	10.00	18.00	416.00	8108.00	608.86	0.43	15.29	16.00	14.89	5.57	15.60
nvme0n1	0.00	0.00	0.00	1254.00	0.00	126556.00	201.84	1.66	1.32	0.00	1.32	0.06	8.00
sde	0.00	2.00	10.00	9.00	416.00	3304.00	391.58	0.26	12.84	12.40	13.33	12.42	23.60
sdf	1.00	1.00	78.00	9.00	20492.00	3820.00	558.90	1.05	12.09	9.03	38.67	4.87	42.40
sdg	0.00	18.00	117.00	108.00	29600.00	47020.00	681.07	14.59	55.38	8.17	106.52	3.70	83.20
sdh	0.00	3.00	2.00	35.00	384.00	15816.00	875.68	0.38	10.38	10.00	10.40	5.41	20.00
sdi	0.00	1.00	83.00	15.00	20508.00	7024.00	561.88	1.56	15.96	7.57	62.40	3.59	35.20
sdj	0.00	5.00	87.00	52.00	14740.00	18760.00	482.01	2.78	25.84	11.77	49.38	7.19	100.00
sdk	0.00	0.00	3.00	160.00	12.00	5748.00	70.67	11.08	350.06	17.33	356.30	1.84	30.00
sdl	0.00	0.00	6.00	0.00	24.00	0.00	8.00	0.07	11.33	11.33	0.00	9.33	5.60

As a rule of thumb, if a large number of your disks are showing a high % util over a period of time, it is likely that your disks are being saturated. It may also be worth looking at the r_await time to see whether read requests are taking longer than what is expected for the type of disk in your OSD nodes. As mentioned earlier, if you find that high disk utilization is the cause of slow performance and the triggering factor is unlikely to dissipate soon, extra disks are the only solution.

htop

Like the standard top utility, htop provides a live view of the CPU and the memory consumption of the host. However, it also produces a more intuitive display that may make judging overall system-resource use easier, especially with the rapidly-changing resource usage of Ceph:

```
  1  [||||||                        8.9%]   5  [||||||                       9.5%]
  2  [||||||||||||                 25.6%]   6  [||||                         8.0%]
  3  [|||||||||                    20.0%]   7  [|||||||||                   14.9%]
  4  [||||||||||                   16.7%]   8  [||                           4.4%]
Mem[|||||||||||||||||||| ||||||||||||||23.8G/62.7G]   Tasks: 49, 7845 thr; 1 running
Swp[|                           88.2M/9.31G]   Load average: 6.46 6.33 6.09
                                              Uptime: 7 days, 08:32:23

  PID USER      PRI  NI  VIRT   RES   SHR S CPU% MEM%   TIME+  Command
 7308 ceph       20   0 2662M 1045M  6788 S 11.9  1.6 13h51:18 /usr/bin/ceph-osd -f --cluster ceph
 3945 ceph       20   0 2778M 1059M  7996 S 11.9  1.7 14h12:58 /usr/bin/ceph-osd -f --cluster ceph
```

atop

atop is another useful tool. It captures performance metrics for CPU, RAM, disk, network, and can present this all in one view; this makes it very easy to get a complete overview of the system resource usage.

Diagnostics

There are a number of internal Ceph tools that can be used to help diagnose slow performance. The most useful command for investigating slow performance is dumping current inflight operations, which can be done with the following command:

```
sudo ceph daemon osd.x dump_ops_in_flight
```

This will dump all current operations for the specified OSD and break down all the various timings for each step of the operation. Here is an example of an inflight IO:

```
        "description": "osd_op(client.29342781.1:262455793 17.768b3a6 rb.0.4d983.238e1
f29.000000001988 [set-alloc-hint object_size 4194304 write_size 4194304,write 1318912~1228
8] snapc 0=[] ondisk+write e98614)",
        "initiated_at": "2017-04-21 22:23:11.401997",
        "age": 0.000626,
        "duration": 0.000704,
        "type_data": [
            "waiting for sub ops",
            {
                "client": "client.29342781",
                "tid": 262455793
            },
            [
                {
                    "time": "2017-04-21 22:23:11.401997",
                    "event": "initiated"
                },
                {
                    "time": "2017-04-21 22:23:11.402107",
                    "event": "queued_for_pg"
                },
                {
                    "time": "2017-04-21 22:23:11.402122",
                    "event": "reached_pg"
                },
                {
                    "time": "2017-04-21 22:23:11.402146",
                    "event": "started"
                },
                {
                    "time": "2017-04-21 22:23:11.402177",
                    "event": "waiting for subops from 14,37"
                },
                {
                    "time": "2017-04-21 22:23:11.402368",
                    "event": "commit_queued_for_journal_write"
                },
                {
                    "time": "2017-04-21 22:23:11.402379",
                    "event": "write_thread_in_journal_buffer"
                },
                {
                    "time": "2017-04-21 22:23:11.402585",
                    "event": "journaled_completion_queued"
                },
                {
                    "time": "2017-04-21 22:23:11.402598",
                    "event": "op_commit"
                }
```

From the previous example IO, we can see all the stages that are logged for each operation; it is clear that this operation is running without any performance problems. However, in the event of slow performance, you may see a large delay between two steps, and directing your investigation into this area may lead you to the root cause.

Extremely slow performance or no IO

If your cluster is performing really slowly, to the point that it is barely servicing IO requests, there is probably an underlying fault or configuration issue. These slow requests will likely be highlighted on the Ceph status display with a counter for how long the request has been blocked. There are a number of things to check in this case.

Flapping OSDs

Check `ceph.log` on the monitors, and see whether it looks like any OSDs are flapping up and down. When an OSD joins a cluster, its PGs begin peering. During this peering process, IO is temporarily halted, so in the event of a number of OSDs flapping, the client IO can be severely impacted. If there is evidence of flapping OSDs, the next step is to go through the logs for the OSDs that are flapping, and see whether there are any clues as to what is causing them to flap. Flapping OSDs can be tough to track down as there can be several different causes, and the problem can be widespread.

Jumbo frames

Check that a network change hasn't caused problems with jumbo frames if in use. If jumbo frames are not working correctly, smaller packets will most likely be successfully getting through to other OSDs and MONs, but larger packets will be dropped. This will result in OSDs that appear to be half-functioning, and it can be very difficult to find an obvious cause. If something odd seems to be happening, always check that jumbo frames are being allowed across your network using ping.

Failing disks

As Ceph stripes data across all disks in the cluster, a single disk, which is in the process of failing but has not yet completely failed, may start to cause slow or blocked IO across the cluster. Often, this will be caused by a disk that is suffering from a large number of read errors, but it is not severe enough for the disk to completely fail. Normally, a disk will only reallocate sectors when a bad sector is written to. Monitoring the SMART stats from the disks will normally pick up conditions such as these and allow you to take action.

Slow OSDs

Sometimes an OSD may start performing very poorly for no apparent reason. If there is nothing obvious being revealed by your monitoring tools, consult `ceph.log` and the Ceph health detail output. You can also run Ceph `osd perf`, which will list all the commit and apply latencies of all your OSDs and may also help you identify a problematic OSD.
If there is a common pattern of OSDs referenced in the slow requests, there is a good chance that the mentioned OSD is the cause of the problems. It is probably worth restarting the OSD in case that resolves the issue; if the OSD is still problematic, it would be advisable to mark it out and then replace the OSD.

Out of capacity

If your Ceph cluster fills up past 95%, the OSDs will stop accepting IO. The only way to recover from this situation is to delete some data to reduce the utilization on each OSD. If an OSD will not start or you are unable to delete data, you can adjust the full threshold with the `mon_osd_full_ratio` variable. This will hopefully buy you enough time to remove some data and get the cluster into a usable state.

Investigating PGs in a down state

A PG in a down state will not service any client operations, and any object contained within the PG will be unavailable. This will cause slow requests to build up across the cluster as clients try to access these objects. The most common reason for a PG to be in a down state is when a number of OSDs are offline, which means that there are no valid copies of the PGs on any active OSDs. However, to find out why a PG is down, you can run the following command:

```
ceph pg x.y query
```

This will produce a large amount of output; the section we are interested in shows the peering status. The example here was taken from a PG whose pool was set to min_size 1 and had data written to it when only OSD 0 was up and running. OSD 0 was then stopped and OSDs 1 and 2 were started:

```
"probing_osds": [
    "1",
    "2"
],
"blocked": "peering is blocked due to down osds",
"down_osds_we_would_probe": [
    0
],
"peering_blocked_by": [
    {
        "osd": 0,
        "current_lost_at": 0,
        "comment": "starting or marking this osd lost may let us proceed"
    }
]
},
```

We can see that the peering process is being blocked, as Ceph knows that the PG has newer data written to OSD 0. It has probed OSDs 1 and 2 for the data, which means that it didn't find anything it needed. It wants to try to poll OSD 0, but it can't because the OSD is down, hence the starting or marking this osd lost may let us proceed message appeared.

Large monitor databases

Ceph monitors use leveldb to store all of the required monitor data for your cluster. This includes things such as the monitor map, OSD map, and PG map, which OSDs and clients pull from the monitors to be able to locate objects in the RADOS cluster. One particular feature that you should be aware of is that during a period where the health of the cluster doesn't equal HEALTH_OK, the monitors do not discard any of the older cluster maps from its database. If the cluster is in a degraded state for an extended period of time and/or the cluster has a large number of OSDs, the monitor database can grow very large.

In normal operating conditions, the monitors are very lightweight on resource consumption; because of this, it's quite common for smaller disk sizes to be used for the monitors. In the scenario where a degraded condition continues for an extended period, it's possible for the disk holding the monitor database to fill up, which, if it occurs across all your monitor nodes, will take down the entire cluster.

To guard against this behavior, it may be worth deploying your monitor nodes using LVM so that, if the disks need to be expanded, it can be done a lot more easily. When you get into this situation, adding disk space is the only solution, until you can get the rest of your cluster into a HEALTH_OK state.

If your cluster is in a HEALTH_OK state, but the monitor database is still large, you can compact it by running the following command:

```
sudo ceph tell mon.{id} compact
```

However, this will only work if your cluster is in a HEALTH_OK state; the cluster will not discard old cluster maps, which can be compacted, until it's in a HEALTH_OK state.

Summary

In this chapter, you learned how to deal with problems that Ceph is not able to solve by itself. You now understand the necessary steps to troubleshoot a variety of issues that, if left unhandled, could become bigger problems. Furthermore, you have a good idea of the key areas to look at when your Ceph cluster is not performing as expected. You should feel confident that you are in a good place to handle Ceph-related issues whenever they appear.

In the next chapter, we will continue to look into troubleshooting processes and will explore the situations where data loss has already happened.

Questions

1. What is the command to repair an inconsistent PG?
2. What command can you use to change the logging level on the fly?
3. Why might the monitor databases grow large over time?
4. What is the command to query a PG?
5. Why might scrubbing have a performance impact on a Ceph cluster?

12
Disaster Recovery

In the previous chapter, you learned how to troubleshoot common Ceph problems, which, although they may be affecting the operation of the cluster, weren't likely to cause a total outage or data loss. This chapter will cover more serious scenarios, where the Ceph cluster is down or unresponsive. It will also cover various techniques to recover from data loss. It is to be understood that these techniques are more than capable of causing severe data loss themselves and should only be attempted as a last resort. If you have a support contract with your Ceph vendor or have a relationship with Red Hat, it is highly advisable to consult them first before carrying out any of the recovery techniques listed in this chapter.

In this chapter, we will cover the following topics:

- Avoiding data loss
- Using RBD mirroring to provide highly available block storage
- Investigating asserts
- Rebuilding monitor databases from OSDs
- Extracting PGs from a dead OSD
- Examining data from an offline Bluestore OSD
- Recovering from lost objects or inactive PGs
- Recovering from a failed CephFS filesystem
- Rebuilding an RBD from dead OSDs

What is a disaster?

To be able to recover from a disaster, you first have to understand and be able to recognize one. For the purpose of this chapter, we will assume that anything that leads to a sustained period of downtime is classed as a disaster. This will not cover scenarios where a failure happens that Ceph is actively working to recover from, or where it is believed that the cause is likely to be short-lived. The other type of disaster is one that leads to a permanent loss of data unless recovery of the Ceph cluster is possible. Data loss is probably the most serious issue, as the data may be irreplaceable or can cause serious harm to the future of the business.

Avoiding data loss

Before starting to cover some recovery techniques, it is important to cover some points discussed in Chapter 1, *Planning for Ceph*. Disaster-recovery should be seen as a last resort; the recovery guides in this chapter should not be relied upon as a replacement for adhering to best practices.

First, make sure you have working and tested backups of your data; in the event of an outage, you will feel a million times more relaxed if you know that in the worst cases, you can fall back to backups. While an outage may cause discomfort for your users or customers, informing them that their data, which they had entrusted you with, is now gone is far worse. Also, just because you have a backup system in place, does not mean you should blindly put your trust in it. Regular test restores will mean that you will be able to rely on them when needed.

Make sure you follow some design principles also mentioned in Chapter 1, *Planning for Ceph*. Don't use configuration options, such as nobarrier, and strongly consider the replication level you use with in Ceph to protect your data. The chances of data loss are strongly linked to the redundancy level configured in Ceph, so careful planning is advised here.

What can cause an outage or data loss?

The majority of outages and cases of data loss will be directly caused by the loss of a number of OSDs that exceed the replication level in a short period of time. If these OSDs do not come back online, either due to a software or hardware failure, and Ceph was not able to recover objects between OSD failures, these objects are now lost.

If an OSD has failed due to a failed disk, it is unlikely that recovery will be possible unless costly disk-recovery services are utilized, and there is no guarantee that any recovered data will be in a consistent state. This chapter will not cover recovering from physical disk failures and will simply suggest that the default replication level of 3 should be used to protect you against multiple disk failures.

If an OSD has failed due to a software bug, the outcome is possibly a lot more positive, but the process is complex and time-consuming. Usually an OSD, which, although the physical disk is in a good condition is unable to start, is normally linked to either a software bug or some form of corruption. A software bug may be triggered by an uncaught exception that leaves the OSD in a state that it cannot recover from. Corruption may occur after an unexpected loss of power, where the hardware or software was not correctly configured to maintain data consistency. In both cases, the outlook for the OSD itself is probably terminal, and if the cluster has managed to recover from the lost OSDs, it's best just to erase and reintroduce the OSD as an empty disk.

If the number of offline OSDs has meant that all copies of an object are offline, recovery procedures should be attempted to extract the objects from the failed OSDs, and insert them back into the cluster.

RBD mirroring

As mentioned, working backups are a key strategy in ensuring that a failure does not result in the loss of data. Starting with the Jewel release, Ceph introduced RBD mirroring, which allows you to asynchronously mirror an RBD from one cluster to another. Note the difference between Ceph's native replication, which is synchronous, and RBD mirroring. With synchronous replication, low latency between peers is essential, and asynchronous replication allows the two Ceph clusters to be geographically remote, as latency is no longer a factor.

By having a replicated copy of your RBD images on a separate cluster, you can dramatically reduce both your **Recovery Time Objective (RTO)** and **Recovery Point Objective (RPO)**. The RTO is a measure of how long it takes from initiating recovery to when the data is usable. It is the worst-case measurement of time between each data point and describes the expected data loss. A daily backup would have an RPO of 24 hours; for example, potentially, any data written up to 24 hours since the last backup would be lost if you had to restore from a backup.

With RBD mirroring, data is asynchronously replicated to the target RBD, and so, in most cases, the RPO should be under a minute. As the target RBD is also a replica and not a backup that would need to be first restored, the RTO is also likely going to be extremely low. Additionally, as the target RBD is stored on a separate Ceph cluster, it offers additional protection for snapshots, which could also be impacted if the Ceph cluster itself experiences issues. At first glance, this makes RBD mirroring seem like the perfect tool to protect against data loss, and in most cases, it is a very useful tool. RBD mirroring is not a replacement for a proper backup routine though. In cases where data loss is caused by actions internal to the RBD, such as filesystem corruption or user error, these changes will be replicated to the target RBD. A separate isolated copy of your data is vital.

With that said, let's take a closer look at how RBD mirroring works.

The journal

One of the key components in RBD mirroring is the journal. The RBD mirroring journal stores all writes to the RBD and notifies the client once they have been written. These writes are then written to the primary RBD image. The journal itself is stored as an RADOS object, prefixed similarly to how RBD images are. Separately, the remote `rbd-mirror` daemon polls the configured RBD mirrors and pulls the newly-written journal objects across to the target cluster and replays them in the target RBD.

The rbd-mirror daemon

The `rbd-mirror` daemon is responsible for replaying the contents of the journal to a target RBD in another Ceph cluster. The `rbd-mirror` daemon only needs to run on the target cluster, unless you wish to replicate both ways, in which case, it will need to run on both clusters.

Configuring RBD mirroring

In order to use the RBD mirroring functionality, we will require two Ceph clusters. We could deploy two identical clusters we have been using previously, but the number of VMs involved may exceed the capabilities of what most people's personal machines can run. Therefore, we will modify our vagrant and ansible configuration files to deploy two separate Ceph clusters, each with a single monitor and an OSD node.

The required `Vagrantfile` is very similar to the one used in `Chapter 2`, *Deploying Ceph with Containers*, to deploy your initial test cluster; the hosts part at the top should now look like this:

```
nodes = [
  { :hostname => 'ansible', :ip => '192.168.0.40', :box => 'xenial64' },
    { :hostname => 'site1-mon1', :ip => '192.168.0.41', :box => 'xenial64' },
    { :hostname => 'site2-mon1', :ip => '192.168.0.42', :box => 'xenial64' },
    { :hostname => 'site1-osd1',  :ip => '192.168.0.51', :box => 'xenial64',
:ram => 1024, :osd => 'yes' },
    { :hostname => 'site2-osd1',  :ip => '192.168.0.52', :box => 'xenial64',
:ram => 1024, :osd => 'yes' }
]
```

For the Anisble configuration, we will maintain two separate Ansible configuration instances so that each cluster can be deployed separately. We will then maintain separate hosts files per instance, which we will specify when we run the playbook. To do this, we will not copy the `ceph-ansible` files into `/etc/ansible`, but keep them in the home directory by using the following command:

git clone https://github.com/ceph/ceph-ansible.git

cp -a ceph-ansible ~/ceph-ansible2

Create the same two files, called `all` and `Ceph`, in the `group_vars` directory as we did in `Chapter 2`, *Deploying Ceph with Containers*. This needs to be done in both copies of `ceph-ansible`:

1. Create a hosts file in each `ansible` directory, and place the two hosts in each:

```
vagrant@ansible:~/ceph-ansible$ cat hosts
[mons]
site1-mon1

[osds]
site1-osd1

[ceph:children]
mons
osds
```

The preceding screenshot is for the first host and the following screenshot is for the second host:

```
vagrant@ansible:~/ceph-ansible2$ cat hosts
[mons]
site2-mon1

[osds]
site2-osd1

[ceph:children]
mons
osds
```

2. Run the `site.yml` playbook under each `ceph-ansible` instance to deploy our two Ceph clusters:

```
ansible-playbook -K -i hosts site.yml
```

3. Adjust the replication level of the default pools to 1, as our clusters only have 1 OSD. Run these commands on both clusters:

```
vagrant@site1-mon1:~$ sudo ceph osd pool set rbd size 1
set pool 0 size to 1
vagrant@site1-mon1:~$ sudo ceph osd pool set rbd min_size 1
set pool 0 min_size to 1
```

4. Install the RBD mirroring daemon on both clusters:

```
sudo apt-get install rbd-mirror
```

The following screenshot is the output for the preceding command:

```
vagrant@mon1:~$ sudo apt-get install rbd-mirror
Reading package lists... Done
Building dependency tree
Reading state information... Done
The following NEW packages will be installed:
  rbd-mirror
0 upgraded, 1 newly installed, 0 to remove and 121 not upgraded.
Need to get 1,726 kB of archives.
After this operation, 7,240 kB of additional disk space will be used.
Get:1 http://download.ceph.com/debian-kraken xenial/main amd64 rbd-mirror amd64 11.2.0-1xenial [1,726 kB]
Fetched 1,726 kB in 1s (1,289 kB/s)
Selecting previously unselected package rbd-mirror.
(Reading database ... 54945 files and directories currently installed.)
Preparing to unpack .../rbd-mirror_11.2.0-1xenial_amd64.deb ...
Unpacking rbd-mirror (11.2.0-1xenial) ...
Processing triggers for ureadahead (0.100.0-19) ...
Processing triggers for man-db (2.7.5-1) ...
Setting up rbd-mirror (11.2.0-1xenial) ...
ceph-rbd-mirror.target is a disabled or a static unit, not starting it.
Processing triggers for ureadahead (0.100.0-19) ...
```

5. Copy `ceph.conf` and `keyring` from both clusters to each other.

6. Copy `ceph.conf` from `site1-mon1` to `site2-mon1` and call it `remote.conf`.

7. Copy `ceph.client.admin.keyring` from `site1-mon1` to `site2-mon1` and call it `remote.client.admin.keyring`.

8. Repeat the preceding two steps but this time copy the files from `site2-mon1` to `site1-mon1`.

9. Make sure the instances of `keyring` are owned by `ceph:ceph`:

```
sudo chown ceph:ceph /etc/ceph/remote.client.admin.keyring
```

10. Tell Ceph that the pool called `rbd` should have the mirroring function enabled:

```
sudo rbd --cluster ceph mirror pool enable rbd image
```

11. Repeat this for the target cluster:

```
sudo rbd --cluster remote mirror pool enable rbd image
```

12. Add the target cluster as a peer of the pool mirroring configuration:

```
sudo rbd --cluster ceph mirror pool peer add rbd
client.admin@remote
```

13. Run the same command locally on the second Ceph cluster:

```
sudo rbd --cluster ceph mirror pool peer add rbd
client.admin@remote
```

14. Back on the first cluster, let's create a test RBD to use with our mirroring lab:

```
sudo rbd create mirror_test --size=1G
```

15. Enable the journaling feature on the RBD image:

```
sudo rbd feature enable rbd/mirror_test journaling
```

16. Enable mirroring for the RBD:

```
sudo rbd mirror image enable rbd/mirror_test
```

```
vagrant@site1-mon1:~$ sudo rbd mirror image enable rbd/mirror_test
Mirroring enabled
```

It's important to note that RBD mirroring works via a pull system. The `rbd-mirror` daemon needs to run on the cluster that you wish to mirror the RBDs to; it then connects to the source cluster and pulls the RBDs across. If you were intending to implement a two-way replication where each Ceph cluster replicates with each other, you would run the `rbd-mirror` daemon on both clusters. With this in mind, let's enable and start the `systemd` service for `rbd-mirror` on your target host:

```
sudo systemctl enable ceph-rbd-mirror@admin
sudo systemctl start ceph-rbd-mirror@admin
```

The `rbd-mirror` daemon will now start processing all the RBD images configured for mirroring on your primary cluster.

We can confirm that everything is working as expected by running the following command on the target cluster:

```
sudo rbd --cluster remote mirror pool status rbd –verbose
```

The following screenshot is the output for the preceding command:

```
vagrant@site1-mon1:~$ sudo rbd --cluster remote mirror pool status rbd --verbose
health: OK
images: 1 total
    1 replaying

mirror_test:
  global_id:   a90b307a-98ec-4835-9ea8-fc2f91b4ae37
  state:       up+replaying
  description: replaying, master_position=[object_number=3, tag_tid=1, entry_tid=2607], mirror_position=
[object_number=3, tag_tid=1, entry_tid=2607], entries_behind_master=0
  last_update: 2017-04-17 14:37:09
```

In the previous screenshot, we can see that our `mirror_test` RBD is in a up+replaying state; this means that mirroring is in progress, and we can see via `entries_behind_master` that it is currently up to date.

Note the difference in the output of the RBD `info` commands on either of the clusters. On the source cluster, the primary status is `true`, which allows you to determine which cluster the RBD is the master state and can be used by clients. This also confirms that although we only created the RBD on the primary cluster, it has been replicated to the secondary one.

The source cluster is shown here:

```
rbd image 'mirror_test':
        size 1024 MB in 256 objects
        order 22 (4096 kB objects)
        block_name_prefix: rbd_data.374b74b0dc51
        format: 2
        features: layering, exclusive-lock, object-map, fast-diff, deep-flatten, journaling
        flags:
        journal: 374b74b0dc51
        mirroring state: enabled
        mirroring global id: a90b307a-98ec-4835-9ea8-fc2f91b4ae37
        mirroring primary: true
```

The target cluster is shown here:

```
rbd image 'mirror_test':
        size 1024 MB in 256 objects
        order 22 (4096 kB objects)
        block_name_prefix: rbd_data.377d2eb141f2
        format: 2
        features: layering, exclusive-lock, object-map, fast-diff, deep-flatten, journaling
        flags:
        journal: 377d2eb141f2
        mirroring state: enabled
        mirroring global id: a90b307a-98ec-4835-9ea8-fc2f91b4ae37
        mirroring primary: false
```

Performing RBD failover

Before we failover the RBD to the secondary cluster, let's map it, create a filesystem, and place a file on it, so we can confirm that the mirroring is working correctly. As of Linux kernel 4.11, the kernel RBD driver does not support the RBD journaling feature required for RBD mirroring; this means you cannot map the RBD using the kernel RBD client. As such, we will need to use the `rbd-nbd` utility, which uses the `librbd` driver in combination with Linux `nbd` devices to map RBDs via user space. Although there are many things that may cause Ceph to experience slow performance, here are some of the most likely causes:

```
sudo rbd-nbd map mirror_test
```

```
vagrant@site1-mon1:~$ sudo rbd-nbd map mirror_test
/dev/nbd0
```

```
sudo mkfs.ext4 /dev/nbd0
```

```
vagrant@site1-mon1:~$ sudo mkfs.ext4 /dev/nbd0
mke2fs 1.42.13 (17-May-2015)
Discarding device blocks: done
Creating filesystem with 262144 4k blocks and 65536 inodes
Filesystem UUID: d4ff2036-a10b-4003-8a0a-144b0863b55a
Superblock backups stored on blocks:
        32768, 98304, 163840, 229376

Allocating group tables: done
Writing inode tables: done
Creating journal (8192 blocks): done
Writing superblocks and filesystem accounting information: done
```

```
sudo mount /dev/nbd0 /mnt
echo This is a test | sudo tee /mnt/test.txt
sudo umount /mnt
sudo rbd-nbd unmap /dev/nbd0
Now lets demote the RBD on the primary cluster and promote it on the
secondary
sudo rbd --cluster ceph mirror image demote rbd/mirror_test
sudo rbd --cluster remote mirror image promote rbd/mirror_test
```

Now, map and mount the RBD on the secondary cluster, and you should be able to read the test text file that you created on the primary cluster:

```
vagrant@site2-mon1:~$ sudo rbd-nbd map mirror_test
/dev/nbd0
vagrant@site2-mon1:~$ sudo mount /dev/nbd0 /mnt
vagrant@site2-mon1:~$ cat /mnt/test.txt
This is a test
```

We can clearly see that the RBD has successfully been mirrored to the secondary cluster, and the filesystem content is just as we left it on the primary cluster.

 If you try to map and mount the RBD on the cluster where the RBD is not in the primary state, the operation will just hang; this is because Ceph will not permit I/O to an RBD image in a non-master state.

RBD recovery

In the event that a number of OSDs have failed, and you are unable to recover them via the `ceph-object-store` tool, your cluster will most likely be in a state where most, if not all, RBD images are inaccessible. However, there is still a chance that you may be able to recover RBD data from the disks in your Ceph cluster. There are tools that can search through the OSD data structure, find the object files relating to RBDs, and then assemble these objects back into a disk image, resembling the original RBD image.

In this section, we will focus on a tool by Lennart Bader to recover a test RBD image from our test Ceph cluster. The tool allows the recovery of RBD images from the contents of Ceph OSDs, without any requirement that the OSD is in a running or usable state. It should be noted that if the OSD has been corrupted due to an underlying filesystem corruption, the contents of the RBD image may still be corrupt. The RBD recovery tool can be found in the following GitHub repository: `https://gitlab.lbader.de/kryptur/ceph-recovery`.

Before we start, make sure you have a small test RBD with a valid filesystem created on your Ceph cluster. Due to the size of the disks in the test environment that we created in `Chapter 2`, *Deploying Ceph with Containers*, it is recommended that the RBD is only a gigabyte in size.

We will perform the recovery on one of the monitor nodes, but in practice, this recovery procedure can be done from any node that can access the Ceph OSD disks. To access the disks, we need to make sure that the recovery server has sufficient space to recover the data.

In this example, we will mount the remote OSDs contents via `sshfs`, which allows you to mount remote directories over `ssh`. However in real life, there is nothing to stop you from physically inserting disks into another server or whatever method is required. The tool only requires to see the OSDs data directories:

1. Clone the Ceph recovery tool from the Git repository:

   `git clone https://gitlab.lbader.de/kryptur/ceph-recovery.git`

   The following screenshot is the output for the preceding command:

```
vagrant@mon1:~$ git clone https://gitlab.lbader.de/kryptur/ceph-recovery.git
Cloning into 'ceph-recovery'...
remote: Counting objects: 18, done.
remote: Compressing objects: 100% (18/18), done.
remote: Total 18 (delta 6), reused 0 (delta 0)
Unpacking objects: 100% (18/18), done.
Checking connectivity... done.
```

2. Make sure you have `sshfs` installed:

```
sudo apt-get install sshfs
```

The following screenshot is the output for the preceding command:

```
vagrant@mon1:~$ sudo apt-get install sshfs
Reading package lists... Done
Building dependency tree
Reading state information... Done
The following packages were automatically installed and are no longer required:
  libboost-iostreams1.58.0 libboost-program-options1.58.0 libboost-random1.58.0 libboost-regex1.58.0 libboost-system1.58.0
  libboost-thread1.58.0 libcephfs1 libfcgi0ldbl
Use 'sudo apt autoremove' to remove them.
The following NEW packages will be installed:
  sshfs
0 upgraded, 1 newly installed, 0 to remove and 103 not upgraded.
Need to get 41.7 kB of archives.
After this operation, 138 kB of additional disk space will be used.
Get:1 http://us.archive.ubuntu.com/ubuntu xenial/universe amd64 sshfs amd64 2.5-1ubuntu1 [41.7 kB]
Fetched 41.7 kB in 0s (109 kB/s)
Selecting previously unselected package sshfs.
(Reading database ... 40714 files and directories currently installed.)
Preparing to unpack .../sshfs_2.5-1ubuntu1_amd64.deb ...
Unpacking sshfs (2.5-1ubuntu1) ...
Processing triggers for man-db (2.7.5-1) ...
Setting up sshfs (2.5-1ubuntu1) ...
```

3. Change into the cloned tool directory, and create the empty directories for each of the OSDs:

```
cd ceph-recovery
sudo mkdir osds
sudo mkdir osds/ceph-0
sudo mkdir osds/ceph-1
sudo mkdir osds/ceph-2
```

Filestore

For filestore, we can simply mount each remote OSD to the directories that we have just created. Note that you need to make sure your OSD directories match your actual test cluster:

```
sudo sshfs vagrant@osd1:/var/lib/ceph/osd/ceph-0 osds/ceph-0
sudo sshfs vagrant@osd2:/var/lib/ceph/osd/ceph-2 osds/ceph-2
sudo sshfs vagrant@osd3:/var/lib/ceph/osd/ceph-1 osds/ceph-1
```

BlueStore

As Bluestore does not store the objects in a native Linux filesystem, we can't just mount the filesystems. However, the `ceph-object-store` tool allows you to mount the contents of a BlueStore OSD as a `fuse` filesystem.

On each OSD node, create a directory under the `/mnt` folder to mount each OSD on that node:

```
mkdir /mnt/osd-0
```

Now mount the BlueStore OSD to this new directory:

```
ceph-objectstore-tool --op fuse --data-path /var/lib/ceph/osd/ceph-0 --mountpoint /mnt/osd-0
```

The following screenshot is the output for the preceding command:

```
root@osd1:~# ceph-objectstore-tool --op fuse --data-path /var/lib/ceph/osd/ceph-0 --mountpoint /mnt/osd-0
mounting fuse at /mnt/osd-0 ...
```

The BlueStore OSD is now mounted as a `fuse` filesystem to the `/mnt/osd-0` directory. However, it will only remain mounted while the `ceph-object-store` command is running. So if you wish to mount multiple OSDs or manually browse through the directory tree, open additional SSH sessions to the Ceph node. The following is a screenshot showing the contents of the `/mnt/osd-0` directory from a new SSH session:

```
root@osd1:~# ls /mnt
1.0_head   1.20_head  1.31_head  1.42_head  1.53_head  1.64_head  1.75_head  1.e_head  4.0_head  6.2_head  8.4_head
1.10_head  1.21_head  1.32_head  1.43_head  1.54_head  1.65_head  1.76_head  1.f_head  4.1_head  6.3_head  8.5_head
1.11_head  1.22_head  1.33_head  1.44_head  1.55_head  1.66_head  1.77_head  2.0_head  4.2_head  6.4_head  8.6_head
1.12_head  1.23_head  1.34_head  1.45_head  1.56_head  1.67_head  1.78_head  2.1_head  4.3_head  6.5_head  8.7_head
1.13_head  1.24_head  1.35_head  1.46_head  1.57_head  1.68_head  1.79_head  2.2_head  4.4_head  6.6_head  9.0_head
1.14_head  1.25_head  1.36_head  1.47_head  1.58_head  1.69_head  1.7a_head  2.3_head  4.5_head  6.7_head  9.1_head
1.15_head  1.26_head  1.37_head  1.48_head  1.59_head  1.6a_head  1.7b_head  2.4_head  4.6_head  7.0_head  9.2_head
1.16_head  1.27_head  1.38_head  1.49_head  1.5a_head  1.6b_head  1.7c_head  2.5_head  4.7_head  7.1_head  9.3_head
1.17_head  1.28_head  1.39_head  1.4a_head  1.5b_head  1.6c_head  1.7d_head  2.6_head  5.0_head  7.2_head  9.4_head
1.18_head  1.29_head  1.3a_head  1.4b_head  1.5c_head  1.6d_head  1.7e_head  2.7_head  5.1_head  7.3_head  9.5_head
1.19_head  1.2a_head  1.3b_head  1.4c_head  1.5d_head  1.6e_head  1.7f_head  3.0_head  5.2_head  7.4_head  9.6_head
1.1a_head  1.2b_head  1.3c_head  1.4d_head  1.5e_head  1.6f_head  1.7_head   3.1_head  5.3_head  7.5_head  9.7_head
1.1b_head  1.2c_head  1.3d_head  1.4e_head  1.5f_head  1.6_head   1.8_head   3.2_head  5.4_head  7.6_head  meta
1.1c_head  1.2d_head  1.3e_head  1.4f_head  1.5_head   1.70_head  1.9_head   3.3_head  5.5_head  7.7_head  type
1.1d_head  1.2e_head  1.3f_head  1.4_head   1.60_head  1.71_head  1.a_head   3.4_head  5.6_head  8.0_head
1.1e_head  1.2f_head  1.3_head   1.50_head  1.61_head  1.72_head  1.b_head   3.5_head  5.7_head  8.1_head
1.1f_head  1.2_head   1.40_head  1.51_head  1.62_head  1.73_head  1.c_head   3.6_head  6.0_head  8.2_head
1.1_head   1.30_head  1.41_head  1.52_head  1.63_head  1.74_head  1.d_head   3.7_head  6.1_head  8.3_head
```

When you have finished with the OSD, simply use *Ctrl + C* on the SSH session running the `ceph-objectstore-tool` command to unmount.

Now we can mount the fuse-mounted OSDs to our management server like we did with filestore:

```
sudo sshfs vagrant@osd1:/mnt/osd-0 osds/ceph-0
sudo sshfs vagrant@osd2:/mnt/osd-1 osds/ceph-1
sudo sshfs vagrant@osd3:/mnt/osd-2 osds/ceph-2
```

RBD assembly – filestore

Now we can use the tool to scan the OSD directories and compile a list of the RBDs that are available. The only parameter needed for this command is the location where the OSDs are mounted. In this case, it is in a directory called `osds`. The results will be listed in the VM directory:

```
sudo ./collect_files.sh osds
```

The following screenshot is the output for the preceding command:

```
vagrant@mon1:~/ceph-recovery$ sudo ./collect_files.sh osds
Scanning ceph-0
Scanning ceph-1
Scanning ceph-2
Preparing UDATA files
UDATA files ready
Extracting VM IDs
VM IDs extracted
```

If we look inside the VM directory, we can see that the tool has found our test RBD image. Now that we have located the image, the next step is to assemble various objects located on the OSDs. The three parameters for this command are the name of the RBD image found in the previous step, the size of the image, and the destination for the recovered image file. The size of the image is specified in bytes, and it is important that it is at least as big as the original image; it can be bigger, but the RBD will not recover if the size is smaller:

```
sudo ./assemble.sh vms/test.id 1073741824 .
```

The following screenshot is the output for the preceding command:

```
vagrant@mon1:~/ceph-recovery$ sudo ./assemble.sh vms/test.id 1073741824 .
1e502238e1f29
test
file_lists/1e502238e1f29.files
-------------------------------
CEPH RECOVERY
Assemble test with ID 1e502238e1f29
-------------------------------
Searching file list
file_lists/1e502238e1f29.files found
-------------------------------
Output Image will be ./test.raw
-------------------------------
There are 15 blocks found
The output file will be created as a file of size 1073741824 Bytes
The blocksize is 512
-------------------------------
Creating Image file...
Starting reassembly...
100% [########################################################################################## ]
Image written to ./test.raw  _
```

The RBD will now be recovered from the mounted OSD contents to the specified image file. Depending on the size of the image, it may take a while, and a progress bar will show you its progress.

RBD assembly – BlueStore

The RBD assembly script will not work with BlueStore OSDs as BlueStore stores the RBD objects with a slightly different naming convention. An updated script is provided in the following steps to aid with RBD recovery.

Download the script to assist with the recovery of RBDs from BlueStore OSDs:

```
wget
https://raw.githubusercontent.com/fiskn/assemble_bluestore_rbd/master/assem
ble_bluestore.sh
chmod +x ./assemble_bluestore.sh
```

Run the recovery script with three parameters, where first is the RBD image hash name, the second is the RBD size in bytes, and the third is the output filename.

The following example is from a 10 GB test RBD:

```
./assemble_bluestore.sh 7d8ad6b8b4567 1073741824 text.img
```

The following screenshot is the output for the preceding command:

```
root@osd1:~# ./assemble_bluestore.sh 7d8ad6b8b4567 1073741824 text.img
The output file will be created as a file of size 1073741824 Bytes
The blocksize is 512

Creating Image file...
Starting reassembly...
100% [#########################################################################################################_____]
Image written to text.img
```

The RBD image should now be recovered.

Confirmation of recovery

Once completed, we can run a file system called `fsck` on the image to make sure that it has been recovered correctly. In this case, the RBD was formatted with `ext4`, so we can use the `e2fsck` tool to check the image:

```
sudo e2fsck test.raw
```

The following screenshot is the output for the preceding command:

```
vagrant@mon1:~/ceph-recovery$ sudo e2fsck test.raw
e2fsck 1.42.13 (17-May-2015)
test.raw: clean, 11/65536 files, 12635/262144 blocks
```

Excellent, the image file is clean, which means that there is now a very high chance that all our data has been recovered successfully.

Now we can finally mount the image as a loopback device to access our data. If the command returns no output, we have successfully mounted it:

```
sudo mount -o loop test.raw /mnt
```

You can see that the image is successfully mounted as a loop device:

```
vagrant@mon1:~/ceph-recovery$ df -h
Filesystem                     Size  Used Avail Use% Mounted on
udev                           225M     0  225M   0% /dev
tmpfs                           49M  5.7M   44M  12% /run
/dev/mapper/vagrant--vg-root    38G  2.6G   34G   8% /
tmpfs                          245M     0  245M   0% /dev/shm
tmpfs                          5.0M     0  5.0M   0% /run/lock
tmpfs                          245M     0  245M   0% /sys/fs/cgroup
/dev/sda1                      472M   57M  391M  13% /boot
vagrant                        238G   95G  144G  40% /vagrant
tmpfs                           49M     0   49M   0% /run/user/1000
/dev/loop0                     976M  1.3M  908M   1% /mnt
```

RGW Multisite

Ceph also supports the ability to run two or more RADOS Gateway Zones to provide high availability of the S3 and swift-compatible storage across multiple sites. Each zone is backed by a completely separate Ceph cluster, meaning that it is extremely unlikely that any hardware of software failure can take the service completely offline. When using RGW in a multisite configuration, it's important to note that data is eventually consistent, so that data is not guaranteed to be in the same state in every zone immediately after it has been written.

For more information on RGW multi-site configurations, please consult the official Ceph documentation.

CephFS recovery

Unlike RBDs, which are simply a concatenation of objects, CephFS requires consistent data in both the data and metadata pools. It also requires a healthy CephFS journal; if any of these data sources have issues, CephFS will go offline and may not recover. This section of the chapter will look at recovering CephFS to an active state and then further recovery steps in the scenario that the metadata pool is corrupt or incomplete.

There are a number of conditions where CephFS may go offline but will not result in any permanent data loss; these are often caused by transient events in the Ceph cluster but shouldn't result in any long-term data loss, and in most cases CephFS should automatically recover.

As CephFS sits on RADOS, barring any software bugs in CephFS, any data loss or corruption should only occur in the instance where there has been a data loss occurrence in the RADOS layer, perhaps due to multiple OSD failures leading to the loss of a PG.

The loss of objects or PGs from the data pool will not take the CephFS filesystem offline, but will result in access requests to the affected files to return zeroes. This will likely cause any applications higher up the stack to fail and, due to the semi-random nature of files or parts of files, which map to PGs, the result would likely mean that the CephFS filesystem is largely usable. The best case in this scenario would be to try to recover the RADOS pool PGs as seen later in this chapter.

The loss of objects or PGs from the metadata pool will take the CephFS filesystem offline and it will not recover without manual intervention. It is important to point out that the actual data contents are unaffected by metadata loss, but the objects storing this data would be largely meaningless without the metadata. Ceph has a number of tools that can be used to recover and rebuild metadata, which may enable you to recover from metadata loss. However, as has been mentioned several times throughout this book, prevention is better than cure and as such, these tools should not been seen as a standard recovery mechanism, but only to be used as a last resort when recovery from regular backups have failed.

Creating the disaster

To create the scenario where a CephFS filesystem has lost or corrupted its metadata pool, we will simply delete all objects in the metadata pool. This example will use the filesystem deployed in Chapter 5, *RADOS Pools and Client Access*, but the procedure should be identical to any other deployed CephFS filesystem.

First, let's switch to the root account and mount the CephFS filesystem:

```
sudo -i
mount -t ceph 192.168.0.41:/ /mnt/cephfs -o
name=admin,secret=AQC4Q85btsqTCRAAgzaNDpnLeo4q/c/q/0fEpw==
```

Place a few test files on the CephFS filesystem that we will later attempt to recover:

```
echo "doh" > /mnt/cephfs/doh
echo "ray" > /mnt/cephfs/ray
echo "me" > /mnt/cephfs/me
```

Now that we have the test files in place, let's delete all the objects in the metadata pool to simulate a loss of the metadata pool:

```
rados purge cephfs_metadata --yes-i-really-really-mean-it
```

The following screenshot is the output for the preceding command:

```
root@mon1:~# rados purge cephfs_metadata --yes-i-really-really-mean-it
Warning: using slow linear search
Removed 22 objects
successfully purged pool cephfs_metadata
```

Let's restart the mds daemon; trigger the failure:

```
systemctl restart ceph-mds@*
```

If we now check the CephFS status with the ceph -s command, we can see that mds has detected metadata damage and taken the filesystem offline:

```
root@mon2:~# ceph -s
  cluster:
    id:     66fd555c-7a6c-40e9-b775-9d712b4256e1
    health: HEALTH_ERR
            1 filesystem is degraded
            1 filesystem has a failed mds daemon
            1 filesystem is offline
            application not enabled on 1 pool(s)

  services:
    mon: 3 daemons, quorum mon1,mon2,mon3
    mgr: mon1(active)
    mds: cephfs-0/1/1 up , 1 failed
    osd: 3 osds: 3 up, 3 in
    rgw: 1 daemon active
```

To get more information on the damage, we can run the following command. Check the CephFS journal:

```
cephfs-journal-tool journal inspect
```

The following screenshot is the output for the preceding command:

```
root@mon2:~# cephfs-journal-tool journal inspect
Overall journal integrity: DAMAGED
Corrupt regions:
  0x400000-ffffffffffffffff
```

Yep, that's severely damaged, as expected.

CephFS metadata recovery

Normally it would be suggested to export the journal for safe-keeping to minimize data loss, but in this case as we know we can safely just reset it straight away:

```
cephfs-journal-tool journal reset
```

The following screenshot is the output for the preceding command:

```
root@mon2:~# cephfs-journal-tool journal reset
old journal was 4194304~51377
new journal start will be 8388608 (4142927 bytes past old end)
writing journal head
writing EResetJournal entry
done
```

The next command resets the RADOS state of the filesystem to allow the recovery process to rebuild from a consistent state:

```
ceph fs reset cephfs --yes-i-really-mean-it
```

Next, the MDS tables are reset to enable them to be generated from scratch. These tables are stored as objects in the metadata pool. The following commands create new objects:

```
cephfs-table-tool all reset session
cephfs-table-tool all reset snap
cephfs-table-tool all reset inode
```

The following screenshot is the output for the preceding command:

```
root@mon2:~# cephfs-table-tool all reset session
{
    "0": {
        "data": {},
        "result": 0
    }
}

root@mon2:~# cephfs-table-tool all reset snap
{
    "result": 0
}

root@mon2:~# cephfs-table-tool all reset inode
{
    "0": {
        "data": {},
        "result": 0
    }
}
```

Reset the CephFS journal:

```
cephfs-journal-tool --rank=0 journal reset
```

Finally, create the root inodes and prepare for data-object discovery:

```
cephfs-data-scan init
```

Now that the state of CephFS has been fully reset, scans of the data pool can be undertaken to rebuild the metadata from the available data objects. This is a three-stage process using the following three commands. The first command scans through the data pool, finds all the extents that make up each file, and stores this as temporary data. Information, such as creation time and file size is also calculated and stored. The second stage then searches through this temporary data and rebuilds inodes into the metadata pool. Finally the linking of the inodes occurs:

```
cephfs-data-scan scan_extents cephfs_data
cephfs-data-scan scan_inodes cephfs_data
cephfs-data-scan scan_links
```

The scan inodes and extents commands can take an extremely long time to run on large filesystems. The operations can be run in parallel to speed the process up; check out the official Ceph documentation for more information.

Once the process is complete, check that the CephFS filesystem is now in a healthy state:

```
root@mon2:~# ceph -s
  cluster:
    id:     66fd555c-7a6c-40e9-b775-9d712b4256e1
    health: HEALTH_WARN
            application not enabled on 1 pool(s)
            clock skew detected on mon.mon2, mon.mon3

  services:
    mon: 3 daemons, quorum mon1,mon2,mon3
    mgr: mon1(active)
    mds: cephfs-1/1/1 up  {0=mon2=up:active}
    osd: 3 osds: 3 up, 3 in
    rgw: 1 daemon active
```

We should also now be able to browse the filesystem from the mount point where we mounted it at the start of this section:

```
root@mon1:~# ls /mnt/cephfs
lost+found
root@mon1:~# ls /mnt/cephfs/lost+found/
10000000000  10000000001  10000000002  10000000003
root@mon1:~# cat /mnt/cephfs/lost+found/*
After Snap
doh
ray
me
```

Note that although the recovery tools have managed to locate the files and rebuild some of their metadata, information such as their name has been lost and hence placed inside the lost+found directory. By examining the contents of the files, we could identify which file is which and rename it to the original filename.

In practice, although we have restored the CephFS filesystem, the fact that we are missing the files' original names and directory location likely means recovery is only partially successful. It should also be noted that the recovered filesystem may not be stable and it is highly recommended that any salvaged files be recovered before the filesystem is trashed and rebuilt. This is a disaster-recovery process that should only be used after ruling out restoring from backups.

Lost objects and inactive PGs

This section of the chapter will cover the scenario where a number of OSDs have gone offline in a short period of time, leaving some objects with no valid replica copies. It's important to note that there is a difference between an object that has no remaining copies and an object that has a remaining copy, but it is known that another copy has had more recent writes. The latter is normally seen when running the cluster with min_size set to 1.

To demonstrate how to recover an object that has an out-of-date copy of data, let's perform a series of steps to break the cluster:

1. Set min_size to 1; hopefully by the end of this example, you will see why you don't ever want to do this in real life:

   ```
   sudo ceph osd pool set rbd min_size 1
   ```

The following screenshot is the output for the preceding command:

```
vagrant@mon1:~/ceph-recovery$ sudo ceph osd pool set rbd min_size 1
set pool 0 min_size to 1
```

2. Create a test object that we will make later make Ceph believe is lost:

```
sudo rados -p rbd put lost_object logo.png
sudo ceph osd set norecover
sudo ceph osd set nobackfill
```

These two flags make sure that when the OSDs come back online after making the write to a single OSD, the changes are not recovered. Since we are only testing with a single option, we need these flags to simulate the condition in real life, where it's likely that not all objects can be recovered in sufficient time before the OSD, when the only copy goes offline for whatever reason.

3. Shut down two of the OSD nodes, so only one OSD is remaining. Since we have set min_size to 1, we will still be able to write data to the cluster. You can see that the Ceph status shows that the two OSDs are now down:

```
  cluster d9f58afd-3e62-4493-ba80-0356290b3d9f
   health HEALTH_WARN
          64 pgs degraded
          26 pgs stuck unclean
          64 pgs undersized
          recovery 46/69 objects degraded (66.667%)
          too few PGs per OSD (21 < min 30)
          2/3 in osds are down
          nobackfill,norecover flag(s) set
          all OSDs are running kraken or later but the 'require_kraken_osds' osdmap flag is not set
   monmap e2: 3 mons at {mon1=192.168.0.41:6789/0,mon2=192.168.0.42:6789/0,mon3=192.168.0.43:6789/0}
          election epoch 258, quorum 0,1,2 mon1,mon2,mon3
      mgr active: mon1 standbys: mon2, mon3
   osdmap e398: 3 osds: 1 up, 3 in; 64 remapped pgs
          flags nobackfill,norecover,sortbitwise,require_jewel_osds
    pgmap v5286: 64 pgs, 1 pools, 37579 kB data, 23 objects
          226 MB used, 26668 MB / 26994 MB avail
          46/69 objects degraded (66.667%)
                64 active+undersized+degraded
```

4. Write to the object again, the write will go to the remaining OSD:

```
sudo rados -p rbd put lost_object logo.png
```

5. Shut down the remaining OSDs; once it has gone offline, power back the remaining two OSDs:

```
cluster d9f58afd-3e62-4493-ba80-0356290b3d9f
 health HEALTH_WARN
        64 pgs degraded
        1 pgs recovering
        64 pgs stuck unclean
        64 pgs undersized
        recovery 25/69 objects degraded (36.232%)
        recovery 1/23 unfound (4.348%)
        1/3 in osds are down
        all OSDs are running kraken or later but the 'require_kraken_osds' osdmap flag is not set
 monmap e2: 3 mons at {mon1=192.168.0.41:6789/0,mon2=192.168.0.42:6789/0,mon3=192.168.0.43:6789/0}
        election epoch 258, quorum 0,1,2 mon1,mon2,mon3
    mgr active: mon1 standbys: mon2, mon3
 osdmap e409: 3 osds: 2 up, 3 in; 64 remapped pgs
        flags sortbitwise,require_jewel_osds
  pgmap v5319: 64 pgs, 1 pools, 37579 kB data, 23 objects
        220 MB used, 26674 MB / 26894 MB avail
        25/69 objects degraded (36.232%)
        1/23 unfound (4.348%)
              63 active+undersized+degraded
               1 active+recovering+undersized+degraded
```

You can see that Ceph knows that it already has an unfound object even before the recovery process has started. This is because during the peering phase, the PG containing the modified object knows that the only valid copy is on osd.0, which is now offline.

6. Remove the `nobackfill` and `norecover` flags, and let the cluster try to perform recovery. You will see that even after the recovery has progressed, there will be one PG in a degraded state, and the unfound object warning will still be present. This is a good thing, as Ceph is protecting your data from corruption. Imagine what would happen if a 4 MB chunk of an RBD that contained a database suddenly went back in time.

If you try to read or write to our test object, you will notice the request will just hang; this is Ceph protecting your data. There are three ways to fix this problem. The first solution and the most ideal one is to get a valid copy of this object back online; this could either be done by bringing osd.0 online, or by using the objectstore tool to export and import this object into a healthy OSD. For the purpose of this section, let's assume that neither of those options is possible. Before we cover the remaining two options, let's investigate further to uncover what is going on under the hood.

Run the Ceph health detail to find out which PG is having the problem:

```
vagrant@mon1:~$ sudo ceph health detail
HEALTH_WARN 1 pgs degraded; 1 pgs stuck unclean; recovery 2/46 objects degraded (4.348%); recovery 1
 are running kraken or later but the 'require_kraken_osds' osdmap flag is not set
pg 0.31 is stuck unclean for 1370.786568, current state active+degraded, last acting [2,1]
pg 0.31 is active+degraded, acting [2,1], 1 unfound
recovery 2/46 objects degraded (4.348%)
recovery 1/23 unfound (4.348%)
```

In this case, it's pg 0.31, which is in a degraded state, because it has an unfound object. Let's query the pg:

```
ceph pg 0.31 query
```

The following screenshot is the output for the preceding command:

```
"recovery_state": [
    {
        "name": "Started\/Primary\/Active",
        "enter_time": "2017-03-28 21:17:56.412097",
        "might_have_unfound": [
            {
                "osd": "0",
                "status": "osd is down"
            },
            {
                "osd": "1",
                "status": "already probed"
            }
```

Look for the recovery section; we can see that Ceph has tried to probe "osd": "0" for the object, but it is down. It has tried to probe "osd": "1" for the object, but for whatever reason it was of no use, we know the reason is that it is an out-of-date copy.

Now, let's look into some more detail on the missing object:

```
sudo ceph pg 0.31 list_missing
```

The following screenshot is the output for the preceding command:

```
vagrant@mon1:~$ sudo ceph pg 0.31 list_missing
{
    "offset": {
        "oid": "",
        "key": "",
        "snapid": 0,
        "hash": 0,
        "max": 0,
        "pool": -9223372036854775808,
        "namespace": ""
    },
    "num_missing": 1,
    "num_unfound": 1,
    "objects": [
        {
            "oid": {
                "oid": "lost_object",
                "key": "",
                "snapid": -2,
                "hash": 1434772465,
                "max": 0,
                "pool": 0,
                "namespace": ""
            },
            "need": "398'6",
            "have": "383'5",
            "locations": []
        }
    ],
    "more": false
```

The need and have lines reveal the reason. We have epoch 383'5, but the valid copy of the object exists in 398'6; this is why min_size=1 is bad. You might be in a situation where you only have a single valid copy of an object. If this was caused by a disk failure, you would have bigger problems.

To recover from this, we have two options: we can either choose to use the older copy of the object or simply delete it. It should be noted that if this object is new and an older copy does not exist on the remaining OSDs, it will also delete the object.

To delete the object, run this:

```
ceph pg 0.31 mark_unfound_lost delete
```

To revert it, run this:

```
ceph pg 0.31 mark_unfound_lost revert
```

Recovering from a complete monitor failure

In the unlikely event that you lose all of your monitors, all is not lost. You can rebuild the monitor database from the contents of the OSDs with the use of `ceph-objectstore-tool`.

To set the scenario, we will assume that an event has occurred and has corrupted all three monitors, effectively leaving the Ceph cluster inaccessible. To recover the cluster, we will shut down two of the monitors and leave a single failed monitor running. We will then rebuild the monitor database, overwrite the corrupted copy, and restart the monitor to bring the Ceph cluster back online.

The `objectstore` tool needs to be able to access every OSD in the cluster to rebuild the monitor database; in this example, we will use a script, which will connect via `ssh` to access the OSD data. As the OSD data is not accessible by every user, we will use the root user to log into the OSD hosts. By default, most Linux distributions will not allow remote, password-based root logins, so ensure you have copied your public `ssh` key to the root users on some remote OSD nodes.

The following script will connect to each of the OSD nodes specified in the hosts variable, and it will extract the data required to build the monitor database:

```bash
#!/bin/bash
hosts="osd1 osd2 osd3"
ms=/tmp/mon-store/
mkdir $ms
# collect the cluster map from OSDs
for host in $hosts; do
 echo $host
 rsync -avz $ms root@$host:$ms
 rm -rf $ms
 ssh root@$host <<EOF
 for osd in /var/lib/ceph/osd/ceph-*; do
 ceph-objectstore-tool --data-path \$osd --op update-mon-db --mon-store-
path $ms
 done
EOF
 rsync -avz root@$host:$ms $ms
done
```

This will generate the following contents in the `/tmp/mon-store` directory:

```
vagrant@mon1:~$ ls /tmp/mon-store/
kv_backend  store.db
```

We also need to assign new permissions via the `keyring`:

```
sudo ceph-authtool /etc/ceph/ceph.client.admin.keyring --create-keyring --
gen-key -n client.admin --cap mon 'allow *' --cap osd 'allow *' --cap mds
'allow *'
```

The following screenshot is the output for the preceding command:

```
vagrant@mon1:~$ sudo ceph-authtool /etc/ceph/ceph.client.admin.keyring --create-keyring --gen-key -n client.admin --cap mon 'allow *' --cap
osd 'allow *' --cap mds 'allow *'
creating /etc/ceph/ceph.client.admin.keyring
```

```
sudo ceph-authtool /etc/ceph/ceph.client.admin.keyring --gen-key -n mon. --
cap mon 'allow *'
sudo cat /etc/ceph/ceph.client.admin.keyring
```

```
vagrant@mon1:~$ sudo cat /etc/ceph/ceph.client.admin.keyring
[mon.]
        key = AQBODeBYfJFeIRAALrl1DmvSO16983LxfCsDpA==
        caps mon = "allow *"
[client.admin]
        key = AQAzDeBYbuP+IRAA4mi1ZnbZW41v4F8taiRPHg==
        caps mds = "allow *"
        caps mon = "allow *"
        caps osd = "allow *"
```

Now that the monitor database is rebuilt, we can copy it to the monitor directory, but before we do so, let's take a backup of the existing database:

```
sudo mv /var/lib/ceph/mon/ceph-mon1/store.db /var/lib/ceph/mon/ceph-
mon1/store.bak
```

Now, copy the rebuilt version:

```
sudo mv /tmp/mon-store/store.db /var/lib/ceph/mon/ceph-mon1/store.db
sudo chown -R ceph:ceph /var/lib/ceph/mon/ceph-mon1
```

If you try to start the monitor now, it will get stuck in a probing state, as it tries to probe for other monitors. This is Ceph trying to avoid a split-brain scenario; however, in this case, we want to force it to form a quorum and go fully online. To do this, we need to edit `monmap`, remove the other monitors, and then inject it back into the monitors database:

```
sudo ceph-mon -i mon1 --extract-monmap /tmp/monmap
```

Check the contents of monmap:

```
sudo monmaptool /tmp/monmap -print
```

The following screenshot is the output for the preceding command:

```
vagrant@mon1:~$ sudo monmaptool /tmp/monmap --print
monmaptool: monmap file /tmp/monmap
epoch 0
fsid d9f58afd-3e62-4493-ba80-0356290b3d9f
last_changed 2017-03-29 21:14:32.762117
created 2017-03-29 21:14:32.762117
0: 192.168.0.41:6789/0 mon.noname-a
1: 192.168.0.42:6789/0 mon.noname-b
2: 192.168.0.43:6789/0 mon.noname-c
```

You will see that there are three mons present, so let's remove two of them:

```
sudo monmaptool /tmp/monmap --rm noname-b
sudo monmaptool /tmp/monmap --rm noname-c
```

Now, check again to make sure they are completely gone:

```
sudo monmaptool /tmp/monmap -print
```

The following screenshot is the output for the preceding command:

```
vagrant@mon1:~$ sudo monmaptool /tmp/monmap --print
monmaptool: monmap file /tmp/monmap
epoch 0
fsid d9f58afd-3e62-4493-ba80-0356290b3d9f
last_changed 2017-03-29 21:14:32.762117
created 2017-03-29 21:14:32.762117
0: 192.168.0.41:6789/0 mon.noname-a
```

```
sudo ceph-mon -i mon1 --inject-monmap /tmp/monmap
```

Restart all your OSDs, so they rejoin the cluster; then you will be able to successfully query the cluster status and see that your data is still there:

```
vagrant@mon1:~$ sudo ceph -s
    cluster d9f58afd-3e62-4493-ba80-0356290b3d9f
     health HEALTH_WARN
            all OSDs are running kraken or later but the 'require_kraken_osds' osdmap flag is not set
     monmap e2: 1 mons at {mon1=192.168.0.41:6789/0}
            election epoch 3, quorum 0 mon1
        mgr no daemons active
     osdmap e460: 3 osds: 3 up, 3 in
            flags sortbitwise,require_jewel_osds
      pgmap v90: 64 pgs, 1 pools, 37579 kB data, 23 objects
            174 MB used, 26720 MB / 26894 MB avail
                 64 active+clean
recovery io 199 kB/s, 0 objects/s
vagrant@mon1:~$ sudo rbd ls
test
```

Using the Ceph object-store tool

Hopefully, if you have followed best practices, your cluster is running with three replicas and is not configured with any dangerous configuration options. Ceph, in most cases, should be able to recover from any failure.

However, in the scenario where a number of OSDs go offline, a number of PGs and/or objects may become unavailable. If you are unable to reintroduce these OSDs back into the cluster to allow Ceph to recover them gracefully, the data in those PGs is effectively lost. However, there is a possibility that the OSD is still readable to use the objectstore tool to recover the PGs contents. The process involves exporting the PGs from the failed OSDs and then importing the PGs back into the cluster. The objectstore tool requires that the OSDs' internal metadata is still in a consistent state, so full recovery is not guaranteed.

In order to demonstrate the use of the objectstore tool, we will shut down two of our three test cluster OSDs, and then recover the missing PGs back into the cluster. In real life, it's unlikely you would be facing a situation where every single PG from the failed OSDs is missing, but for demonstration purposes, the required steps are the same:

1. Set the pool size to 2, so we can make sure that we lose all the copies of some PGs when we stop the OSD service:

```
vagrant@mon1:~$ sudo ceph osd pool set rbd size 2
set pool 0 size to 2
```

2. Shut down two of the OSD services, and you will see from the Ceph status screen that the number of PGs will go offline:

```
vagrant@mon1:~$ sudo ceph -s
    cluster d9f58afd-3e62-4493-ba80-0356290b3d9f
     health HEALTH_ERR
            27 pgs are stuck inactive for more than 300 seconds
            64 pgs degraded
            23 pgs stale
            27 pgs stuck inactive
            27 pgs stuck unclean
            64 pgs undersized
            recovery 18/36 objects degraded (50.000%)
            too few PGs per OSD (21 < min 30)
            2/3 in osds are down
     monmap e2: 3 mons at {mon1=192.168.0.41:6789/0,mon2=192.168.0.42:6789/0,mon3=192.168.0.43:6789/0}
            election epoch 10, quorum 0,1,2 mon1,mon2,mon3
        mgr active: mon2 standbys: mon3, mon1
     osdmap e22: 3 osds: 1 up, 3 in; 41 remapped pgs
            flags sortbitwise,require_jewel_osds,require_kraken_osds
      pgmap v105: 64 pgs, 1 pools, 37572 kB data, 18 objects
            233 MB used, 26661 MB / 26894 MB avail
            18/36 objects degraded (50.000%)
                  41 undersized+degraded+peered
                  23 stale+undersized+degraded+peered
```

3. Running a Ceph health detail will also show which PGs are in a degraded state:

```
pg 0.21 is stale+undersized+degraded+peered, acting [2]
pg 0.22 is stale+undersized+degraded+peered, acting [2]
pg 0.23 is stale+undersized+degraded+peered, acting [2]
pg 0.24 is undersized+degraded+peered, acting [0]
pg 0.25 is undersized+degraded+peered, acting [0]
pg 0.26 is undersized+degraded+peered, acting [0]
pg 0.27 is undersized+degraded+peered, acting [0]
pg 0.28 is undersized+degraded+peered, acting [0]
pg 0.29 is undersized+degraded+peered, acting [0]
pg 0.2a is stale+undersized+degraded+peered, acting [2]
pg 0.2b is stale+undersized+degraded+peered, acting [2]
pg 0.2c is undersized+degraded+peered, acting [0]
pg 0.2d is stale+undersized+degraded+peered, acting [2]
```

The stale PGs are the ones that no longer have a surviving copy, and it can be seen that the acting OSD is the one that was shut down.

If we use `grep` to filter out just the stale PGs, we can use the resulting list to work out what PGs we need to recover. If the OSDs have actually been removed from the cluster, the PGs will be listed as incomplete rather than stale.

4. Check the OSD to make sure the PG exists in it:

```
ceph-objectstore-tool --op list-pgs --data-path
/var/lib/ceph/osd/ceph-0
```

The following screenshot is the output for the preceding command:

```
root@osd1:~# ceph-objectstore-tool --op list-pgs --data-path /var/lib/ceph/osd/ceph-0
9.7
9.3
9.0
8.7
8.5
8.3
8.1
8.0
7.6
```

5. Use the `objectstore` tool to export the `pg` to a file. As the amount of data in our test cluster is small, we can just export the data to the OS disk. In real life, you probably want to consider connecting additional storage to the server. USB disks are ideal for this, as they can easily be moved between servers as part of the recovery process:

```
sudo ceph-objectstore-tool --op export --pgid 0.2a --data-path
/var/lib/ceph/osd/ceph-2 --file 0.2a_export
```

The following screenshot is the output for the preceding command:

```
vagrant@osd3:~$ sudo ceph-objectstore-tool --op export --pgid 0.2a --data-path /var/lib/ceph/osd/ceph-2 --file 0.2a_export
Exporting 0.2a
Read #0:54d415a2:::rbd_data.fa68238e1f29.0000000000000060:head#
Export successful
```

If you experience an assert while running the tool, you can try running it with the `--skip-journal-replay` flag, which will skip replaying the journal into the OSD. If there was any outstanding data in the journal, it will be lost. But this may allow you to recover the bulk of the missing PGs that would have otherwise been impossible. And repeat this until you have exported all the missing PGs.

6. Import the missing PGs back into an operating OSD. While we could import the PGs into an existing OSD, it is much safer to perform the import on a new OSD, so we don't risk further data loss. For this, create a directory-based OSD on the disk used by the failed OSD. It's highly recommended in a real disaster scenario that the data would be inserted into an OSD running on a separate disk, rather than using an existing OSD. This is done so that there is no further risk to any data in the Ceph cluster.

Also, it doesn't matter that the PGs that are being imported are all inserted into the same temporary OSD. As soon as Ceph discovers the objects, it will recover them to the correct location in the cluster.

7. Create a new empty folder for the OSD:

```
sudo mkdir /var/lib/ceph/osd/ceph-2/tmposd/
```

8. Use `ceph-disk` or `ceph-volume` to prepare the directory for Ceph:

```
sudo ceph-disk prepare  /var/lib/ceph/osd/ceph-2/tmposd/
```

9. Change the ownership of the folder to the `ceph` user and the group:

```
sudo chown -R ceph:ceph /var/lib/ceph/osd/ceph-2/tmposd/
```

10. Activate the OSD to bring it online:

```
sudo ceph-disk activate  /var/lib/ceph/osd/ceph-2/tmposd/
```

11. Set the weight of the OSD to stop any objects from being backfilled into it:

```
sudo ceph osd crush reweight osd.3 0
```

12. Proceed with the PG import, specifying the temporary OSD location and the PG files that we exported earlier:

```
sudo ceph-objectstore-tool --op import --data-path
/var/lib/ceph/osd/ceph-3 --file 0.2a_export
```

The following screenshot is the output for the preceding command:

```
vagrant@osd3:~$ sudo ceph-objectstore-tool --op import --data-path /var/lib/ceph/osd/ceph-3 --file 0.2a_export
Importing pgid 0.2a
Write #0:54d415a2:::rbd_data.fa68238e1f29.0000000000000060:head#
Import successful
```

13. Repeat this for every PG that you exported previously. Once complete, reset file ownership and restart the new temp OSD:

```
sudo chown -R ceph:ceph /var/lib/ceph/osd/ceph-2/tmposd/
sudo systemctl start ceph-osd@3
```

14. Check the Ceph status output, you will see that your PGs are now active, but in a degraded state. In the case of our test cluster, there are not sufficient OSDs to allow the objects to recover to the correct amount of copies. If there were more OSDs in the cluster, the objects would then be backfilled around the cluster and would recover to full health with the correct number of copies:

```
vagrant@mon1:~$ sudo ceph -s
    cluster d9f58afd-3e62-4493-ba80-0356290b3d9f
     health HEALTH_WARN
            clock skew detected on mon.mon2
            41 pgs degraded
            64 pgs stuck unclean
            41 pgs undersized
            recovery 13/36 objects degraded (36.111%)
            recovery 5/36 objects misplaced (13.889%)
            Monitor clock skew detected
     monmap e2: 3 mons at {mon1=192.168.0.41:6789/0,mon2=192.168.0.42:6789/0,mon3=192.168.0.43:6789/0}
            election epoch 10, quorum 0,1,2 mon1,mon2,mon3
        mgr active: mon2 standbys: mon3, mon1
     osdmap e48: 4 osds: 2 up, 2 in; 23 remapped pgs
            flags sortbitwise,require_jewel_osds,require_kraken_osds
      pgmap v182: 64 pgs, 1 pools, 37572 kB data, 18 objects
            1184 MB used, 16744 MB / 17929 MB avail
            13/36 objects degraded (36.111%)
            5/36 objects misplaced (13.889%)
                  41 active+undersized+degraded
                  23 active+remapped
```

Investigating asserts

Assertions are used in Ceph to ensure that, during the execution of the code, any assumptions that have been made about the operating environment remain true. These assertions are scattered throughout the Ceph code and are designed to catch any conditions that may go on to cause further problems if the code is not stopped.

If you trigger an assertion in Ceph, it's likely that some form of data has a value that is unexpected. This may be caused by some form or corruption or unhandled bug.

If an OSD causes an assert and refuses to restart, the usual recommended approach would be to destroy the OSD, recreate it, and then let Ceph backfill objects back to it. If you have a reproducible failure scenario, it is probably also worth filing a bug in the Ceph bug tracker.

As mentioned, OSDs can fail either due to hardware or software faults in either the stored data or OSD code. Software faults are much more likely to affect multiple OSDs at once; if your OSDs have become corrupted due to a power outage, it's highly likely more than one OSD will be affected. In the case where multiple OSDs are failing with asserts and they are causing one or more PGs in the cluster to be offline, simply recreating the OSDs is not an option. The OSDs that are offline contain all the three copies of the PG, so recreating the OSDs would make any form of recovery impossible and result in permanent data loss.

Before attempting the recovery techniques in this chapter, such as exporting and importing PGs, investigation into the asserts should be done. Depending on your technical ability and how much downtime you can tolerate before you need to start focusing on other recovery steps, investigating the asserts may not result in any success. By investigating the assert and looking through the Ceph source referenced by the assert, it may be possible to identify the cause of the assert. If this is possible, a fix can be implemented in the Ceph code to avoid the OSD asserting. Don't be afraid to reach out to the community for help on these matters.

In some cases, the OSD corruption may be so severe that even the `objectstore` tool itself may assert when trying to read from the OSD. This will limit the recovery steps outlined in this chapter, and trying to fix the reason behind the assert might be the only option. Although by this point, it is likely that the OSD has sustained heavy corruption, and recovery may not be possible.

Example assert

The following assert was taken from the Ceph user's mailing list:

```
2017-03-02 22:41:32.338290 7f8bfd6d7700 -1 osd/ReplicatedPG.cc: In function
'void ReplicatedPG::hit_set_trim(ReplicatedPG::RepGather*, unsigned int)'
thread 7f8bfd6d7700 time 2017-03-02 22:41:32.335020

osd/ReplicatedPG.cc: 10514: FAILED assert(obc)


ceph version 0.94.7 (d56bdf93ced6b80b07397d57e3fa68fe68304432)
 1: (ceph::__ceph_assert_fail(char const*, char const*, int, char
const*)+0x85) [0xbddac5]
 2: (ReplicatedPG::hit_set_trim(ReplicatedPG::RepGather*, unsigned
int)+0x75f) [0x87e48f]
 3: (ReplicatedPG::hit_set_persist()+0xedb) [0x87f4ab]
 4: (ReplicatedPG::do_op(std::tr1::shared_ptr<OpRequest>&)+0xe3a)
[0x8a0d1a]
 5: (ReplicatedPG::do_request(std::tr1::shared_ptr<OpRequest>&,
ThreadPool::TPHandle&)+0x68a) [0x83be4a]
 6: (OSD::dequeue_op(boost::intrusive_ptr<PG>,
```

```
std::tr1::shared_ptr<OpRequest>, ThreadPool::TPHandle&)+0x405) [0x69a5c5]
 7: (OSD::ShardedOpWQ::_process(unsigned int,
ceph::heartbeat_handle_d*)+0x333) [0x69ab33]
 8: (ShardedThreadPool::shardedthreadpool_worker(unsigned int)+0x86f)
[0xbcd1cf]
 9: (ShardedThreadPool::WorkThreadSharded::entry()+0x10) [0xbcf300]
10: (()+0x7dc5) [0x7f8c1c209dc5]
11: (clone()+0x6d) [0x7f8c1aceaced]
```

The top part of the assert shows the function from where the assert was triggered and also the line number and file where the assert can be found. In this example, the `hit_set_trim` function is apparently the cause of the assert. We can look into the `ReplicatedPG.cc` file around line 10,514 to try to understand what might have happened. Note the version of the Ceph release (0.94.7), as the line number in GitHub will only match if you are looking at the same version.

From looking at the code, it appears that the returned value from the `get_object_context` function call is directly passed to the `assert` function. If the value is zero – indicating the object containing the hit-set to be trimmed could not be found – the OSD will assert. From this information, there is a chance that investigation could be done to work out why the object is missing and recover it. Or the `assert` command could be commented out to see whether it allows the OSD to continue functioning. In this example, allowing the OSD to continue processing will likely not cause an issue, but in other cases, an assert may be the only thing stopping more serious corruption from occurring. If you don't 100% understand why something is causing an assert, and the impact of any potential change you might make, seek help before continuing.

Summary

In this chapter, you learned how to troubleshoot Ceph when all looks lost. If Ceph is unable to recover PGs itself, you now understand how to manually rebuild PGs from failed OSDs. You can also rebuild the monitor's database if you lose all of your monitor nodes but still have access to your OSDs. You explored the process of recreating RBDs from the raw data remaining on your OSDs. Finally, you configured two separate Ceph clusters and configured replication between them using RBD mirroring to provide a failover option, should you encounter a complete Ceph cluster failure.

Questions

1. What Ceph daemon allows RBDs to be replicated to another Ceph cluster?
2. True or false: RBDs by default are just a concatenated string of objects.
3. What tool can be used to export or import a PG from or to an OSD?
4. True or false: An unfound object status means that data has been lost forever.
5. What is the main disadvantage you are left with after rebuilding CephFS metadata?

Assessments

Chapter 1, Planning for Ceph

1. Reliable Autonomic Distributed Object Store
2. Controlled Replication Under Scalable Hashing
3. Power loss protection
4. Consistency
5. BlueStore
6. Sage Weil
7. RADOS Block Devices (RBD)
8. Object Storage Daemon (OSD)

Chapter 2, Deploying Ceph with Containers

1. Vagrant
2. No
3. Rook
4. Containerization technology
5. Playbook

Chapter 3, BlueStore

1. BlueStore
2. RocksDB
3. Compaction
4. Deferred writes
5. Using `ceph-objectstore-tool`
6. Snappy
7. x10

Chapter 4, Ceph and Non-Native Protocols

1. iSCSI, NFS, and SMB
2. iSCSI
3. SMB
4. Ganesha
5. Pacemaker corosync
6. Security

Chapter 5, RADOS Pools and Client Access

1. Reed Solomon, Cauchy
2. Read, modify, write
3. Erasure coding with two parity shards can be accelerated
4. Flatten
5. MDS
6. Shard performance across multiple MDSs
7. RadosGW
8. S3 and Swift

Chapter 6, Developing with Librados

1. Removed performance overhead of third-party protocols or to access Ceph's full feature set
2. Notifies watchers of an object when it is modified
3. C, C++, Python, PHP, and Java

Chapter 7, Distributed Computation with Ceph RADOS Classes

1. OSD
2. Lua and C++
3. Performance, the ability to use combined processing power of all Ceph node CPUs
4. Instability and unwanted data corruption

Chapter 8, Monitoring Ceph

1. 8443
2. ceph-mgr —The Ceph Manager
3. A scrub has detected an error when reading or comparing the object contents
4. A PG containing one or more objects is being recovered to a new OSD
5. As much as possible

Chapter 9, Tuning Ceph

1. False—PG distribution will not be even on a new cluster and may change over time depending on the workload
2. A full stripe write requires only a single write operation, whereas a partial write requires a much higher write penalty
3. High GHz
4. CPU Speed, disk latency, and network speed
5. Ceph balancer

Chapter 10, Tiering with Ceph

1. Increase performance or to allow use of a lower-cost capacity tier
2. bcache, dmcache
3. Hitsets stored in Bloom filters
4. `min_read_recency_for_promote`
5. Workloads that have a strong bias towards a small number of hot objects

Chapter 11, Troubleshooting

1. `ceph pg repair <pg id>`
2. `ceph tell osd.0 injectargs --debug-osd 0/5`
3. Ceph cluster not in `HEALTH_OK` for a large period of time
4. `ceph pg query`
5. Scrubbing is read intensive and may overwhelm the disk with I/O

Chapter 12, Disaster Recovery

1. `rbd-mirror`
2. True
3. `ceph-objectstore-tool`
4. False, it may exist on an OSD that is currently not participating in the cluster
5. Missing filenames

Other Books You May Enjoy

If you enjoyed this book, you may be interested in these other books by Packt:

Implementing Microsoft Azure Infrastructure Solutions: Exam Guide 70-533
Melony QIN

ISBN: 978-1-78913-795-8

- Explore cloud basics and gain an overview of Microsoft Azure
- Plan and implement virtual machines and containers for scalability and resilience
- Understand virtual networks' cross-premises connectivity
- Learn how to manage your Azure identities
- Plan and implement storage, security, and the BCDR strategy
- Automate and monitor cloud management operations in Azure
- Manage app services for resilience and availability
- Interacting with Azure Services by using ARM, the Azure CLI, and PowerShell

Practical DevOps - Second Edition
Joakim Verona

ISBN: 978-1-78839-257-0

- Understand how all deployment systems fit together to form a larger system
- Set up and familiarize yourself with all the tools you need to be efficient with DevOps
- Design an application suitable for continuous deployment systems with DevOps in mind
- Store and manage your code effectively using Git, Gerrit, Gitlab, and more
- Configure a job to build a sample CRUD application
- Test your code using automated regression testing with Jenkins Selenium
- Deploy your code using tools such as Puppet, Ansible, Palletops, Chef, and Vagrant

Leave a review - let other readers know what you think

Please share your thoughts on this book with others by leaving a review on the site that you bought it from. If you purchased the book from Amazon, please leave us an honest review on this book's Amazon page. This is vital so that other potential readers can see and use your unbiased opinion to make purchasing decisions, we can understand what our customers think about our products, and our authors can see your feedback on the title that they have worked with Packt to create. It will only take a few minutes of your time, but is valuable to other potential customers, our authors, and Packt. Thank you!

Index

Made in the USA
Coppell, TX
10 January 2021